walkermaths 1.9

TRANSFORMATION GEOMETRY

NCEA Level 1 Internal

Charlotte Walker and Victoria Walker

Walker Maths 1.9 Transformation Geometry
1st Edition
Charlotte Walker
Victoria Walker

Designer: Cheryl Smith, Macarn Design
Production controller: Siew Han Ong

Any URLs contained in this publication were checked for currency during the production process. Note, however, that the publisher cannot vouch for the ongoing currency of URLs.

Acknowledgements
Cover photo courtesy of Shutterstock.
We wish to thank the Boards of Trustees of Darfield and Riccarton High Schools for allowing us to use materials and ideas developed while teaching. Our thanks also go to all past and present colleagues, especially Kath Wilson, who have generously shared their experience and ideas.

For product information and technology assistance,
in Australia call **1300 790 853**;
in New Zealand call **0800 449 725**

For permission to use material from this text or product, please email **aust.permissions@cengage.com**

National Library of New Zealand Cataloguing-in-Publication Data
A catalogue record for this book is available from the National Library of New Zealand.

978 0 17 041601 6

Cengage Learning Australia
Level 7, 80 Dorcas Street
South Melbourne, Victoria Australia 3205

Cengage Learning New Zealand
Unit 4B Rosedale Office Park
331 Rosedale Road, Albany, North Shore 0632, NZ

For learning solutions, visit **cengage.co.nz**

Printed in China by 1010 Printing International Limited
3 4 5 6 7 26 25 24 23 22

CONTENTS

Glossary 4

Transformations in general 6

Translation 7
- Describing translations of points — vectors 8
- Describing translations of figures 12
- Drawing translations 14
- Challenges 16

Reflection 18
- Describing reflections — mirror lines 19
- Drawing single reflections 22
- Drawing multiple reflections 26
- Line symmetry 28
- Challenges 30
- Mixing it up 32

Rotation 34
- Describing rotations 35
  - 1 Finding the angle of rotation 35
    - 1 Rotations from an attached point 36
    - 2 Rotations from an unattached point 38
  - 2 Finding the centre of rotation 40
- Drawing rotations 43
    - 1 Rotations from an attached point 43
    - 2 Rotations from an unattached point 46
- Rotational symmetry 49
- Challenges 51
- Mixing it up 52

Enlargement 54
- Describing enlargements 55
  - 1 Finding the scale factor 55
  - 2 Finding the centre of enlargement 57
- Drawing enlargements 60
- Recognising enlargements 64
- Challenges 67
- Mixing it up 71

Invariant points 73

Inverse transformations 75

Mini tasks 79

Practice tasks 82

Answers 91

Glossary

Make your own glossary of key terms:

Term	Definition	Picture/Example
Transformation		
Translation		
Reflection		
Rotation		
Enlargement		
Image		
Mirror line		
Centre of rotation		
Angle of rotation		
Magnitude		

ISBN: 9780170416016

Term	Definition	Picture/Example
Direction		
Vector		
Symmetry		
Asymmetry		
Invariant point		
Inverse transformations		
Perpendicular bisector		
Line symmetry		
Rotational symmetry		

ISBN: 9780170416016

Transformations in general

- A transformation is the **changing of a figure** obtained by following certain rules.
- The transformed figure is called the **image**.
- A transformation may change the **size**, **shape**, **orientation** and **position** of the object.

In this standard, you will be expected to understand and use:

Translation

Reflection

Rotation

Enlargement

Terminology

Original figure —**Transformation**→ **Image**

Labelling equivalent points on the original figure and the image:

On the original figure, use **A, B, C, D, …** —**Transformation**→ On the image, use **A′, B′, C′, D′, …**

Example:

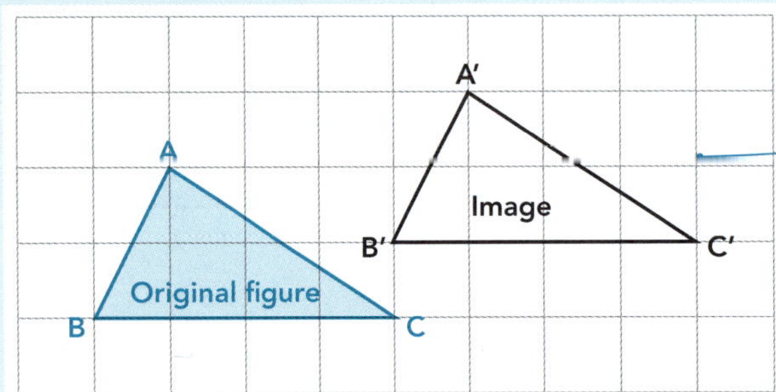

These colours will be used throughout this book:
teal shaded = original figure
black outline = image.

ISBN: 9780170416016

Translation

- Translation is the **sliding** of a figure from one position to another.
- The **size**, **shape** and **orientation** of the figure stay **the same**.
- The **position** of the figure **changes**.

Example:

Complete the table for translation:

	Stays the same	Changes
Size	✓	
Shape		
Orientation		
Position		

Describing translations of points — vectors

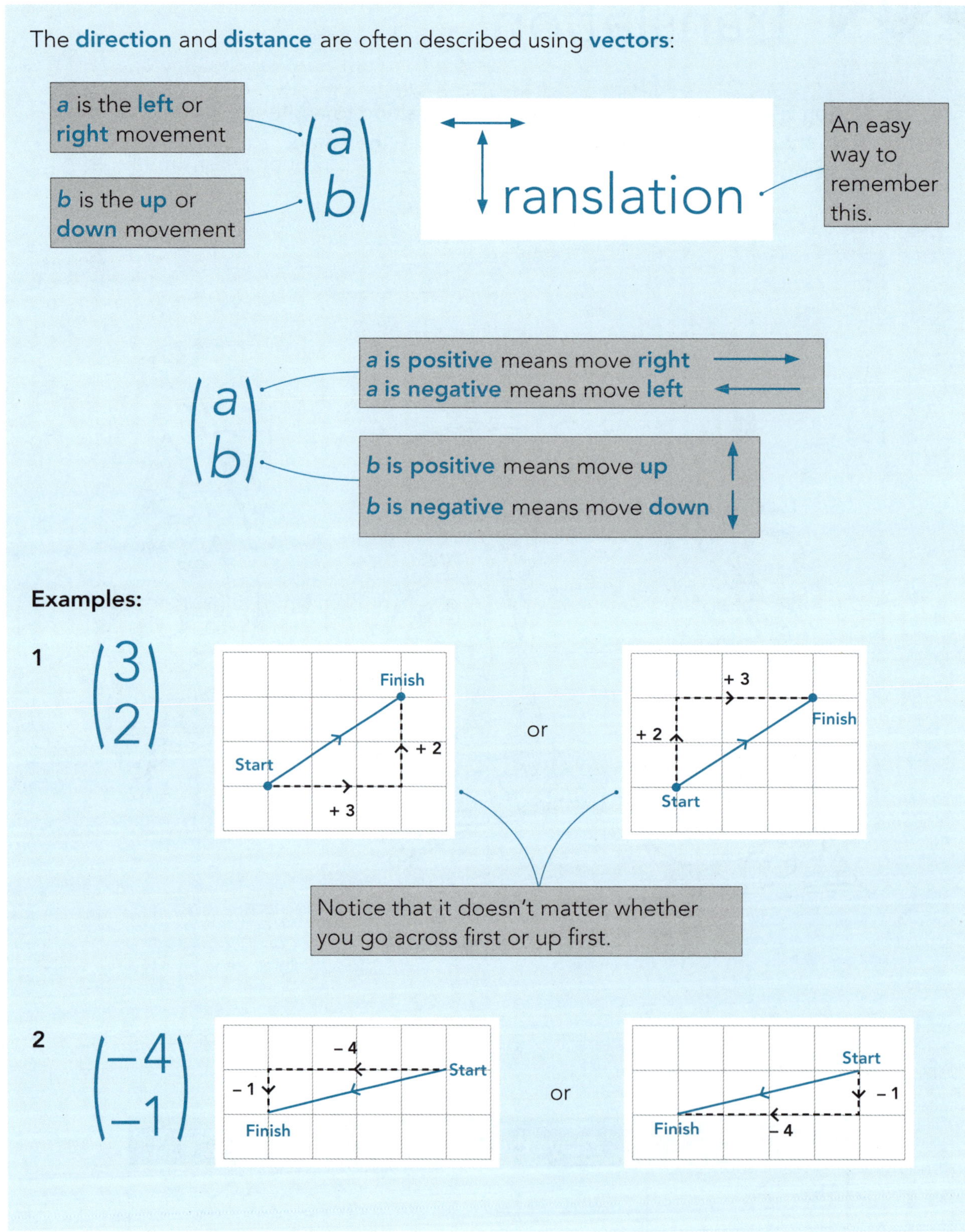

ISBN: 9780170416016

Write a vector for these descriptions.

1 Right three and up two $\begin{pmatrix} \\ \end{pmatrix}$

2 Right four and down two $\begin{pmatrix} \\ \end{pmatrix}$

3 Up one and left four $\begin{pmatrix} \\ \end{pmatrix}$

4 Down two and left three $\begin{pmatrix} \\ \end{pmatrix}$

5 Right nine and down four $\begin{pmatrix} \\ \end{pmatrix}$

6 Left seven and down two $\begin{pmatrix} \\ \end{pmatrix}$

7 Up two $\begin{pmatrix} \\ \end{pmatrix}$

8 Left six $\begin{pmatrix} \\ \end{pmatrix}$

Describe in words what these vectors mean.

9 $\begin{pmatrix} 1 \\ 3 \end{pmatrix}$ ______________________________

10 $\begin{pmatrix} 4 \\ 2 \end{pmatrix}$ ______________________________

11 $\begin{pmatrix} 0 \\ 3 \end{pmatrix}$ ______________________________

12 $\begin{pmatrix} -2 \\ 3 \end{pmatrix}$ ______________________________

13 $\begin{pmatrix} 2 \\ -1 \end{pmatrix}$ ______________________________

14 $\begin{pmatrix} -1 \\ -2 \end{pmatrix}$ ______________________________

15 $\begin{pmatrix} 2 \\ 0 \end{pmatrix}$ ______________________________

16 $\begin{pmatrix} 0 \\ -1 \end{pmatrix}$ ______________________________

ISBN: 9780170416016

17 Match these vectors to those on the grid.

$\begin{pmatrix}3\\1\end{pmatrix}$	$\begin{pmatrix}-4\\-2\end{pmatrix}$	$\begin{pmatrix}-3\\2\end{pmatrix}$	$\begin{pmatrix}-2\\0\end{pmatrix}$	$\begin{pmatrix}-3\\-1\end{pmatrix}$	$\begin{pmatrix}0\\3\end{pmatrix}$	$\begin{pmatrix}-2\\-2\end{pmatrix}$	$\begin{pmatrix}3\\-2\end{pmatrix}$	$\begin{pmatrix}3\\2\end{pmatrix}$	$\begin{pmatrix}2\\3\end{pmatrix}$

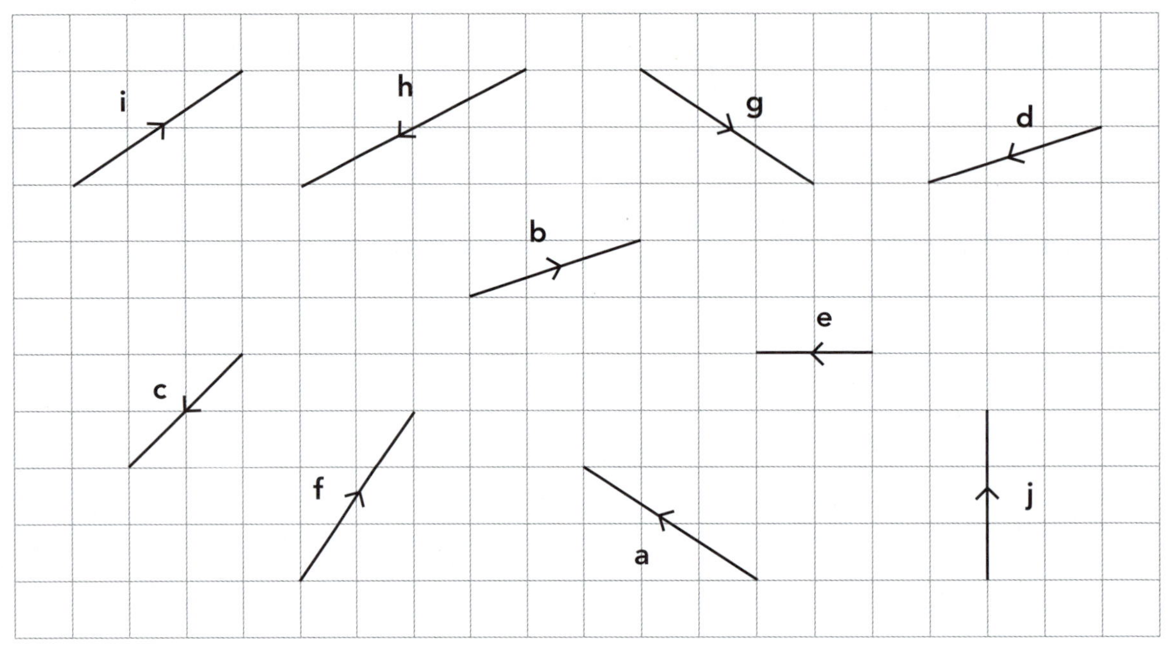

18 Write vectors for each of the those on the grid.

$\begin{pmatrix}\ \\ \ \end{pmatrix}$	$\begin{pmatrix}\ \\ \ \end{pmatrix}$	$\begin{pmatrix}\ \\ \ \end{pmatrix}$	$\begin{pmatrix}\ \\ \ \end{pmatrix}$	$\begin{pmatrix}\ \\ \ \end{pmatrix}$	$\begin{pmatrix}\ \\ \ \end{pmatrix}$	$\begin{pmatrix}\ \\ \ \end{pmatrix}$	$\begin{pmatrix}\ \\ \ \end{pmatrix}$	$\begin{pmatrix}\ \\ \ \end{pmatrix}$	$\begin{pmatrix}\ \\ \ \end{pmatrix}$
a	b	c	d	e	f	g	h	i	j

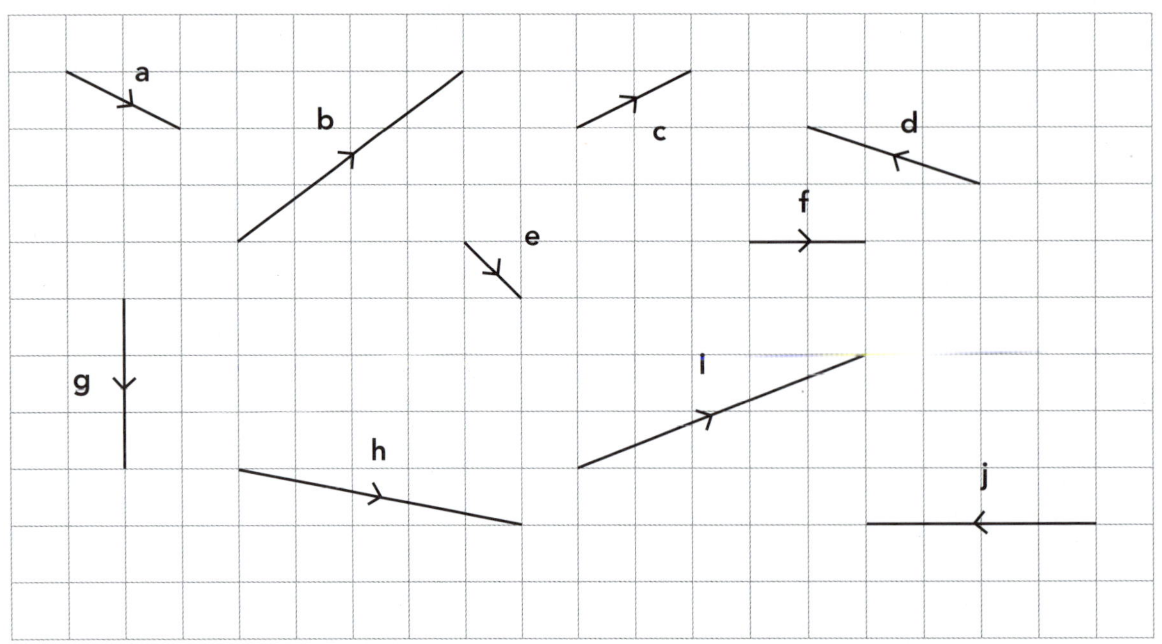

ISBN: 9780170416016

19 Draw and label these vectors on the grid below.

$\begin{pmatrix}3\\2\end{pmatrix}$	$\begin{pmatrix}1\\4\end{pmatrix}$	$\begin{pmatrix}4\\3\end{pmatrix}$	$\begin{pmatrix}3\\0\end{pmatrix}$	$\begin{pmatrix}1\\-4\end{pmatrix}$	$\begin{pmatrix}0\\8\end{pmatrix}$	$\begin{pmatrix}4\\4\end{pmatrix}$	$\begin{pmatrix}-4\\-2\end{pmatrix}$	$\begin{pmatrix}-3\\-4\end{pmatrix}$	$\begin{pmatrix}-1\\5\end{pmatrix}$
a	**b**	**c**	**d**	**e**	**f**	**g**	**h**	**i**	**j**

20 Rule and measure lines so that you can write values for each of the drawn vectors. Include units.

a

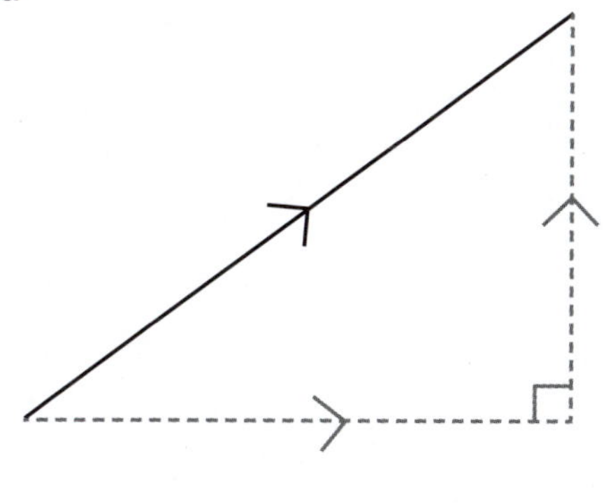

$\begin{pmatrix} \\ \\ \end{pmatrix}$

b

$\begin{pmatrix} \\ \\ \end{pmatrix}$

ISBN: 9780170416016

Describing translations of figures

Example:
The original figure (teal shaded) has been moved by the vector $\begin{pmatrix}4\\2\end{pmatrix}$ to a new position (black).

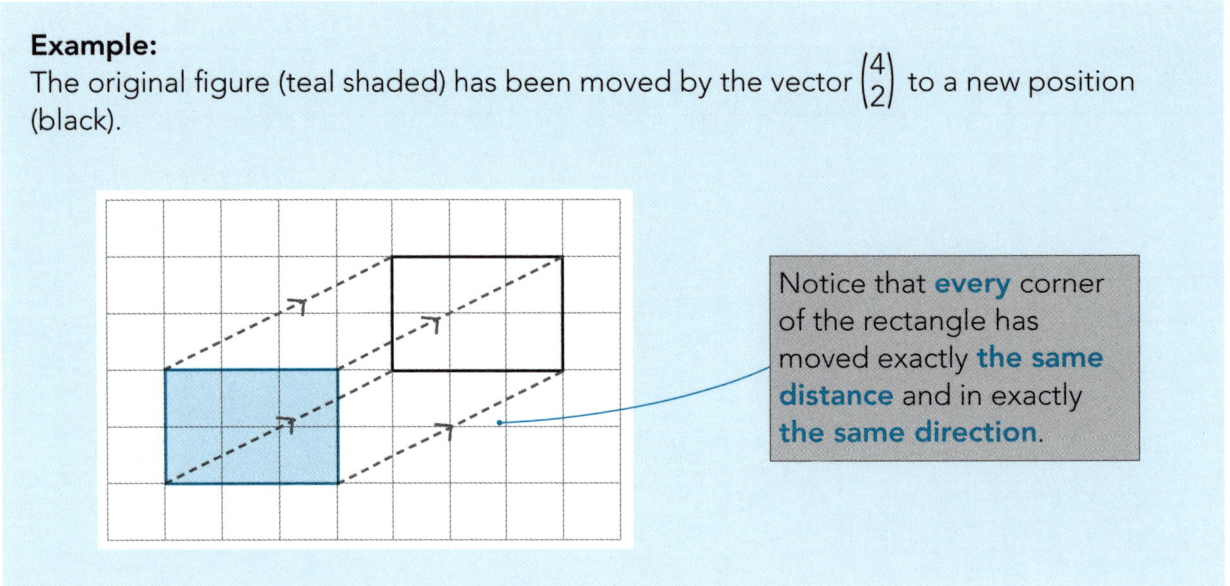

Write the vector for the translation of each figure (the teal-shaded figure is the original, the translated figure is black).

1

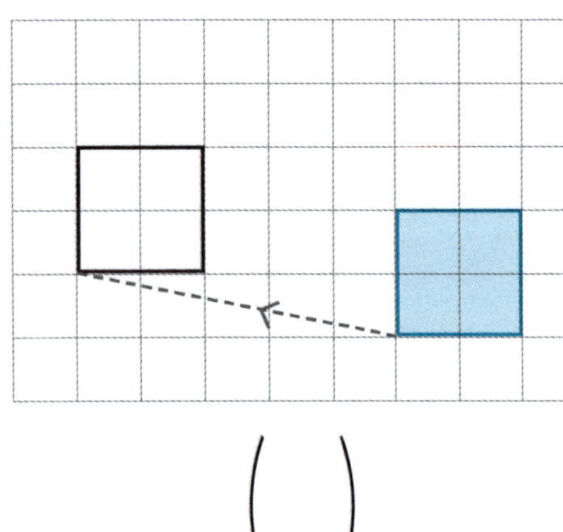

$\begin{pmatrix} \\ \end{pmatrix}$

2

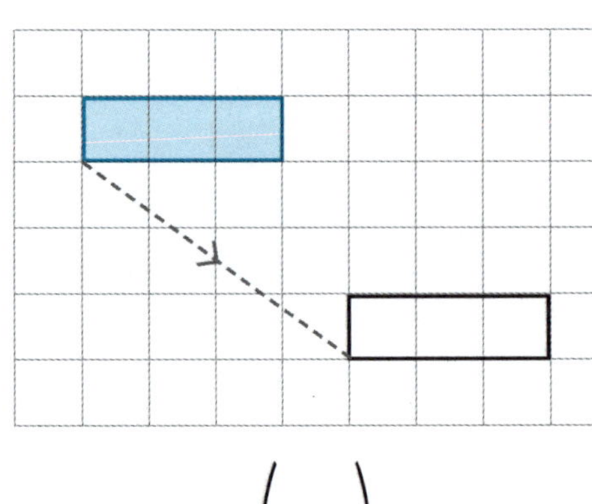

$\begin{pmatrix} \\ \end{pmatrix}$

3

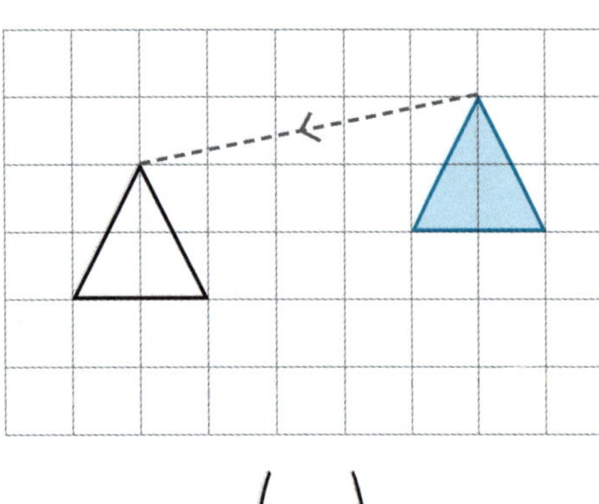

$\begin{pmatrix} \\ \end{pmatrix}$

4

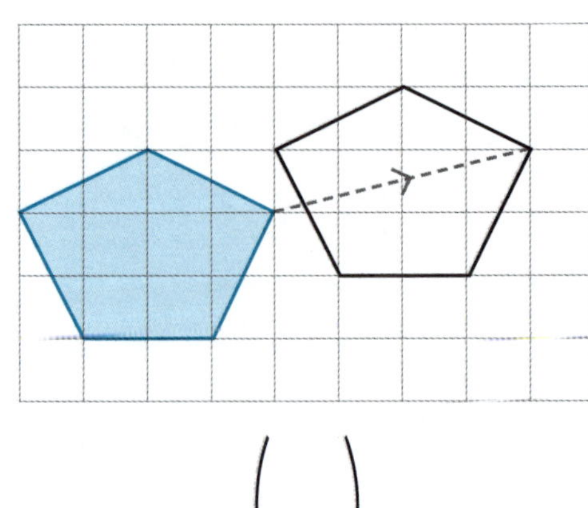

$\begin{pmatrix} \\ \end{pmatrix}$

ISBN: 9780170416016

5

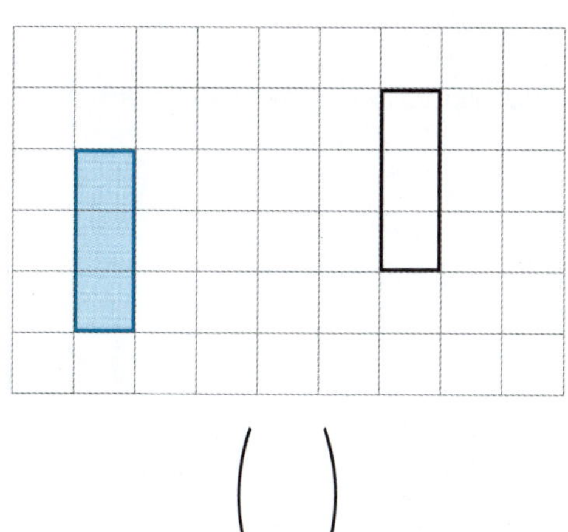

( )

6

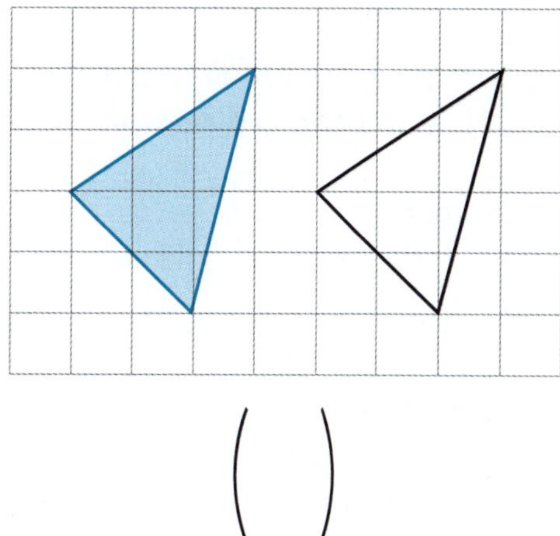

( )

7

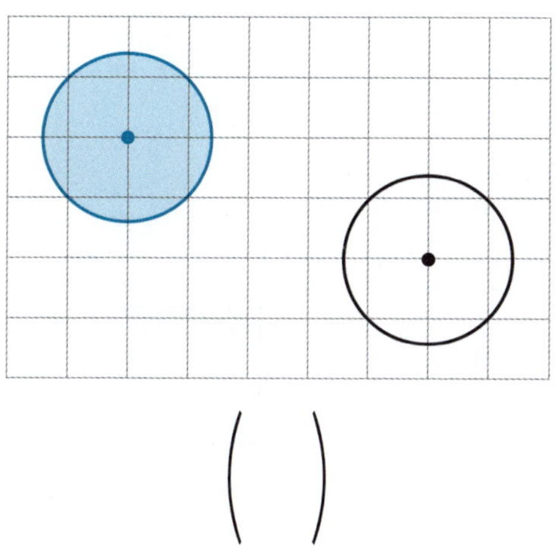

( )

8

( )

9

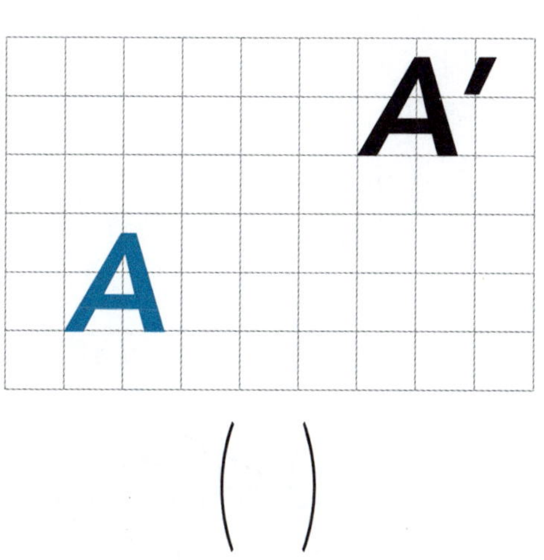

( )

10

( )

ISBN: 9780170416016

Drawing translations

- Remember that **every** corner of the figure moves exactly **the same distance** and in exactly **the same direction**.

Example:
Translate this shape by the vector $\begin{pmatrix}-5\\-2\end{pmatrix}$

Notice that the image is the same shape as the original figure.

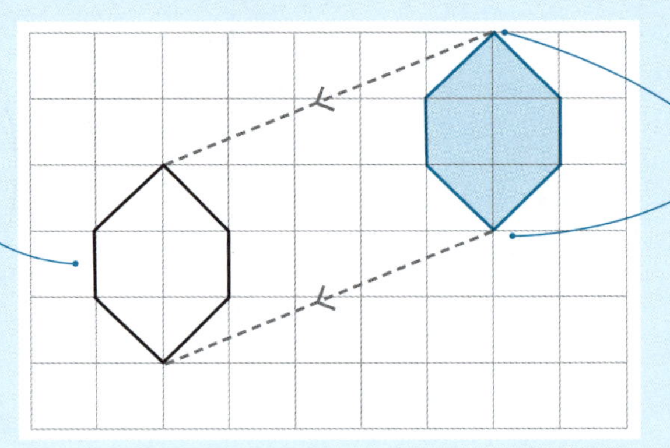

Often, you need to translate only a few critical points, and then copy the rest of the shape.

Draw a translated shape in the location given by the vector.

1 $\begin{pmatrix}1\\3\end{pmatrix}$

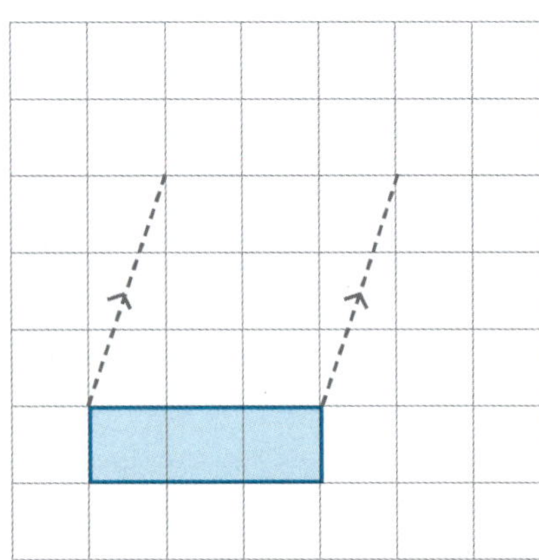

2 $\begin{pmatrix}2\\-3\end{pmatrix}$

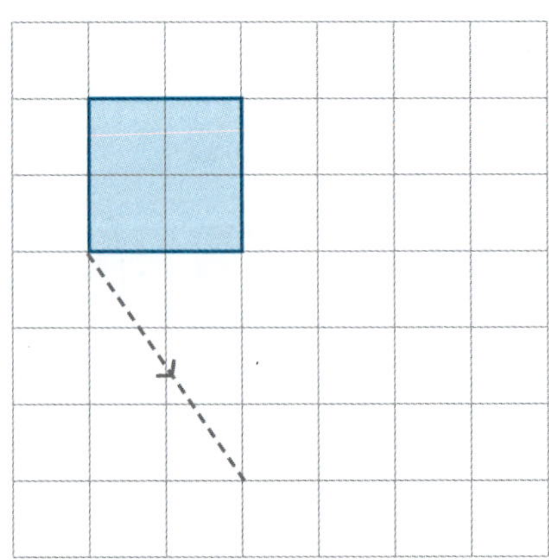

3 $\begin{pmatrix}1\\-3\end{pmatrix}$

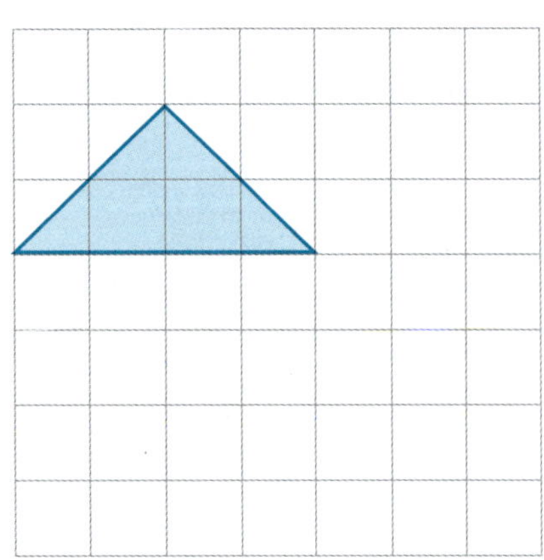

4 $\begin{pmatrix}0\\4\end{pmatrix}$

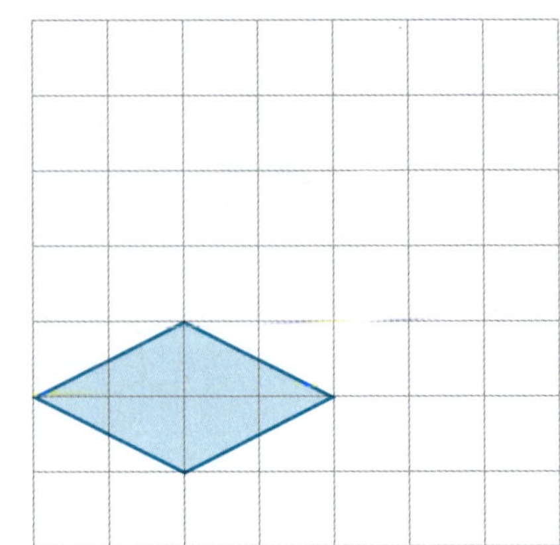

ISBN: 9780170416016

5 $\begin{pmatrix} 3 \\ 0 \end{pmatrix}$

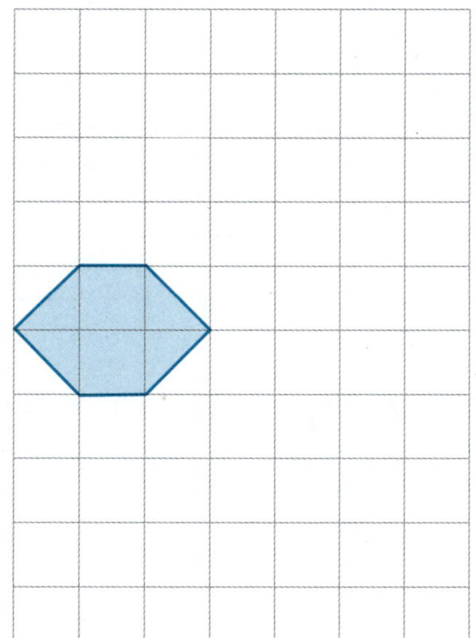

6 $\begin{pmatrix} -2 \\ -3 \end{pmatrix}$

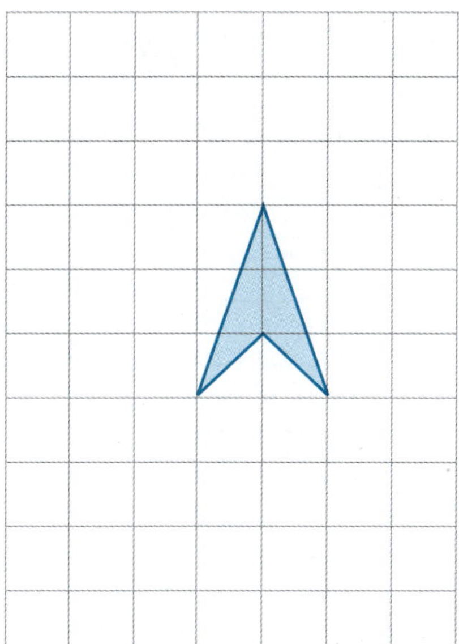

7 $\begin{pmatrix} 3 \\ -4 \end{pmatrix}$

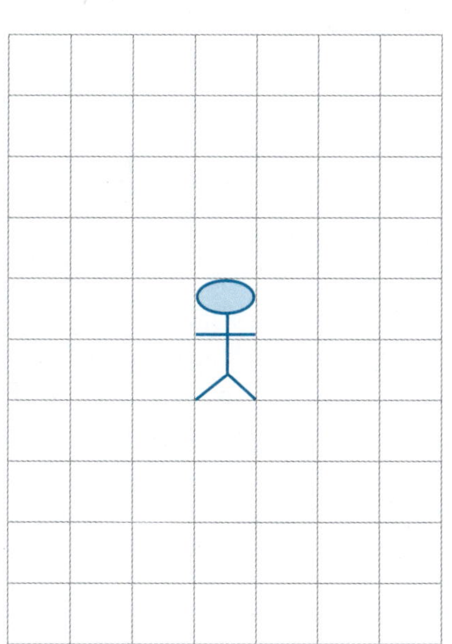

8 $\begin{pmatrix} -2 \\ -2 \end{pmatrix}$

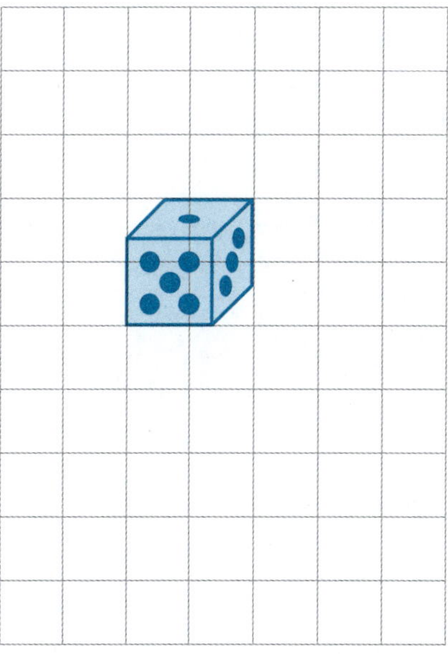

9 $\begin{pmatrix} 2 \\ -1 \end{pmatrix}$

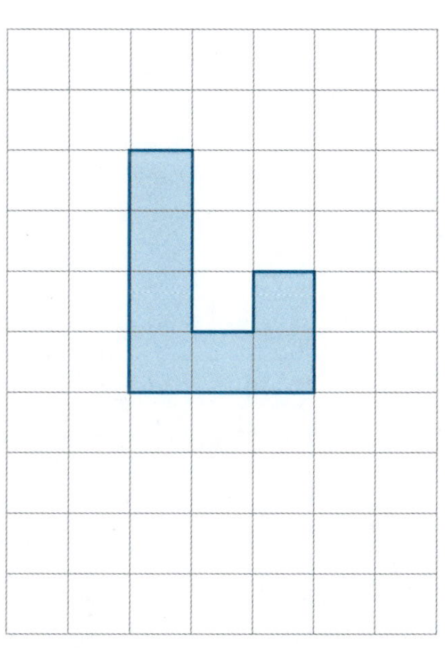

10 $\begin{pmatrix} -1 \\ 3 \end{pmatrix}$

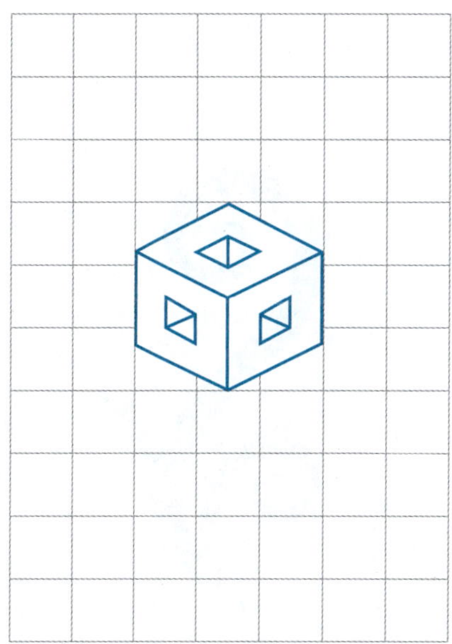

ISBN: 9780170416016

Challenges

1 Write down the translation required to move each figure to its new position.

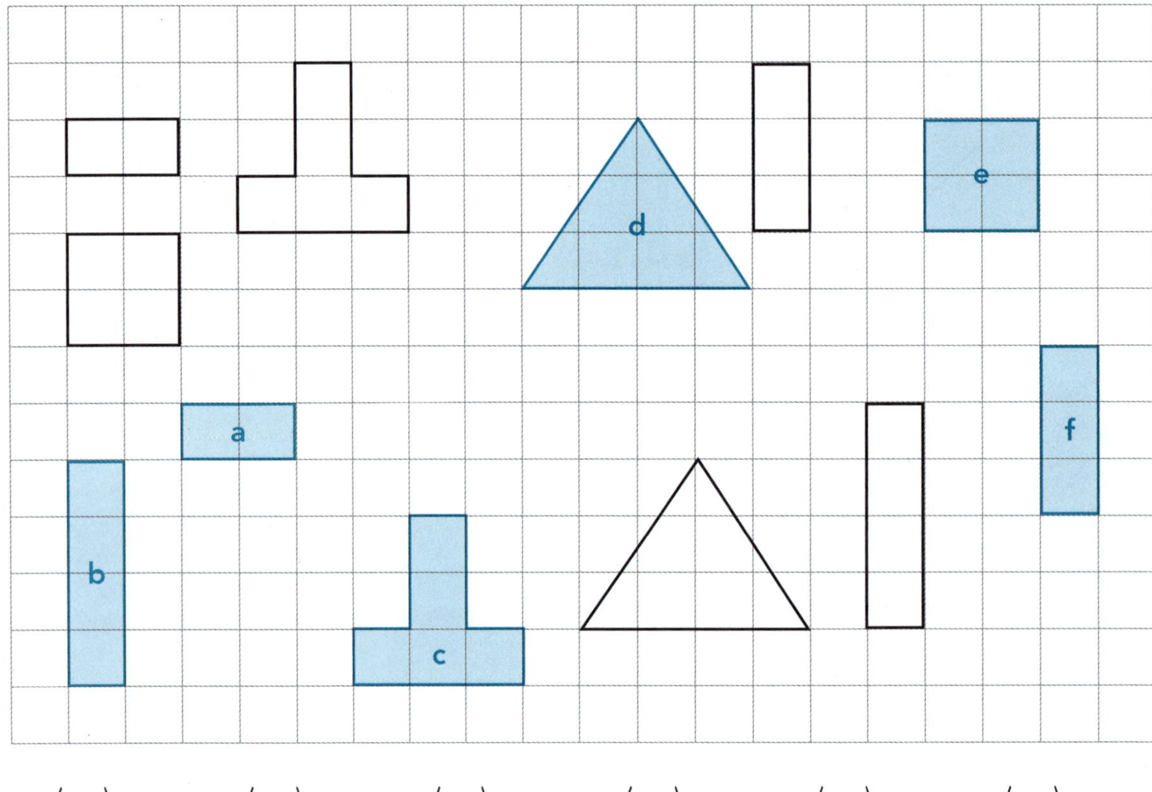

a ( ) b ( ) c ( ) d ( ) e ( ) f ( )

2 Use the grid to help you draw the translation of this image.

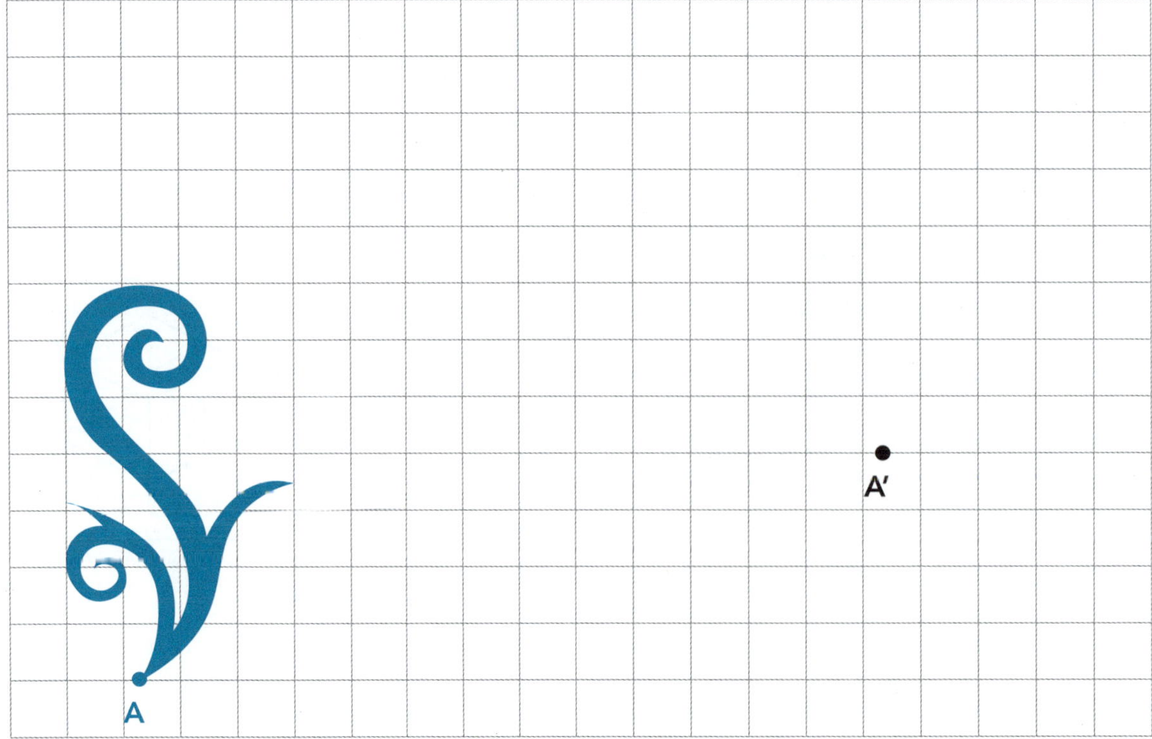

ISBN: 9780170416016

3 Challenge your classmates to see who can get around the racetrack using the smallest number of vectors.

Rules:

- All vectors must start and finish on an intersection of the gridlines.
- Vectors may not touch the outline of the track.
- You must start on one of the dots, and you must finish on the **same** dot.
- You must draw each vector used on the grid, **and** write a list of each.

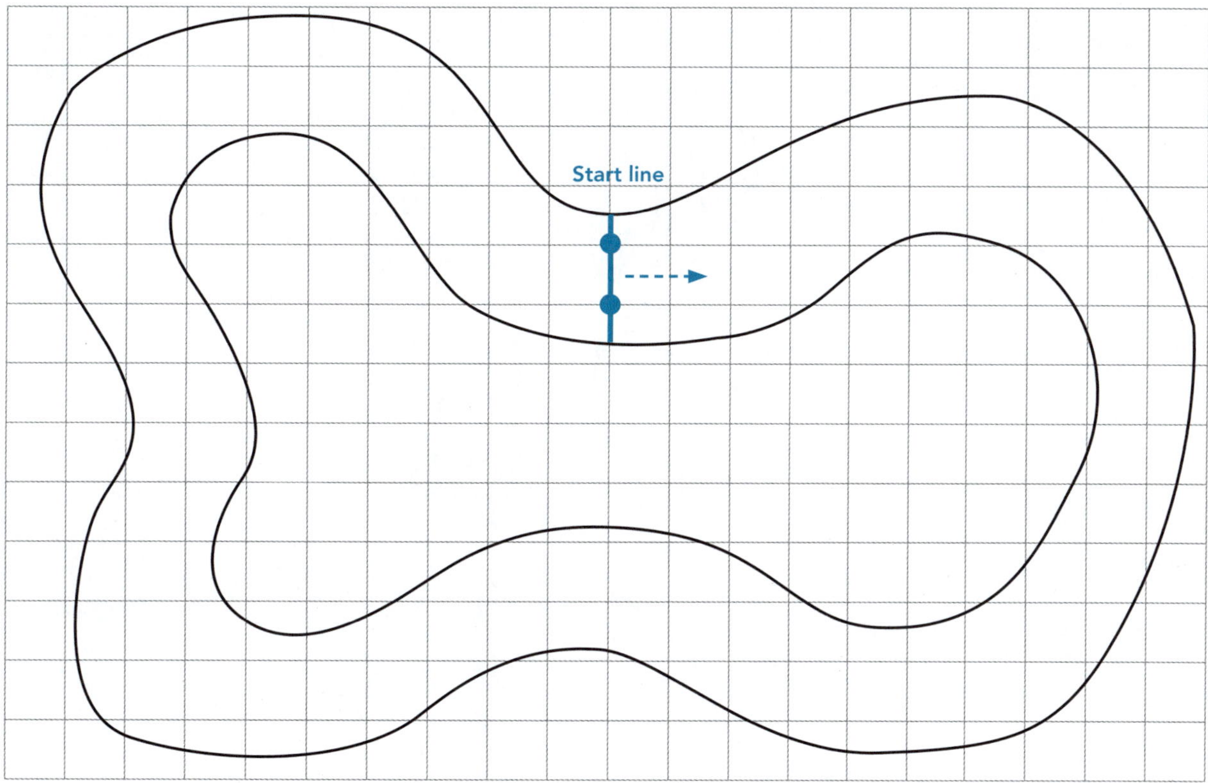

Vectors used:

( ) ( )

( ) ( )

( ) ( )

( ) ( )

( ) ( )

( ) ( )

ISBN: 9780170416016

Reflection

- A reflection is the image of a figure after it has been **reflected** in a **mirror line**.
- The **size** and **shape** of the figure stay **the same**.
- The **orientation** and **position** of the figure **change**.

Example:

Complete the table for reflection:

	Stays the same	Changes
Size	✓	
Shape		
Orientation		
Position		

 ISBN: 9780170416016

Describing reflections — mirror lines

- Every point on the original figure is the **same distance** from the mirror line as its image.

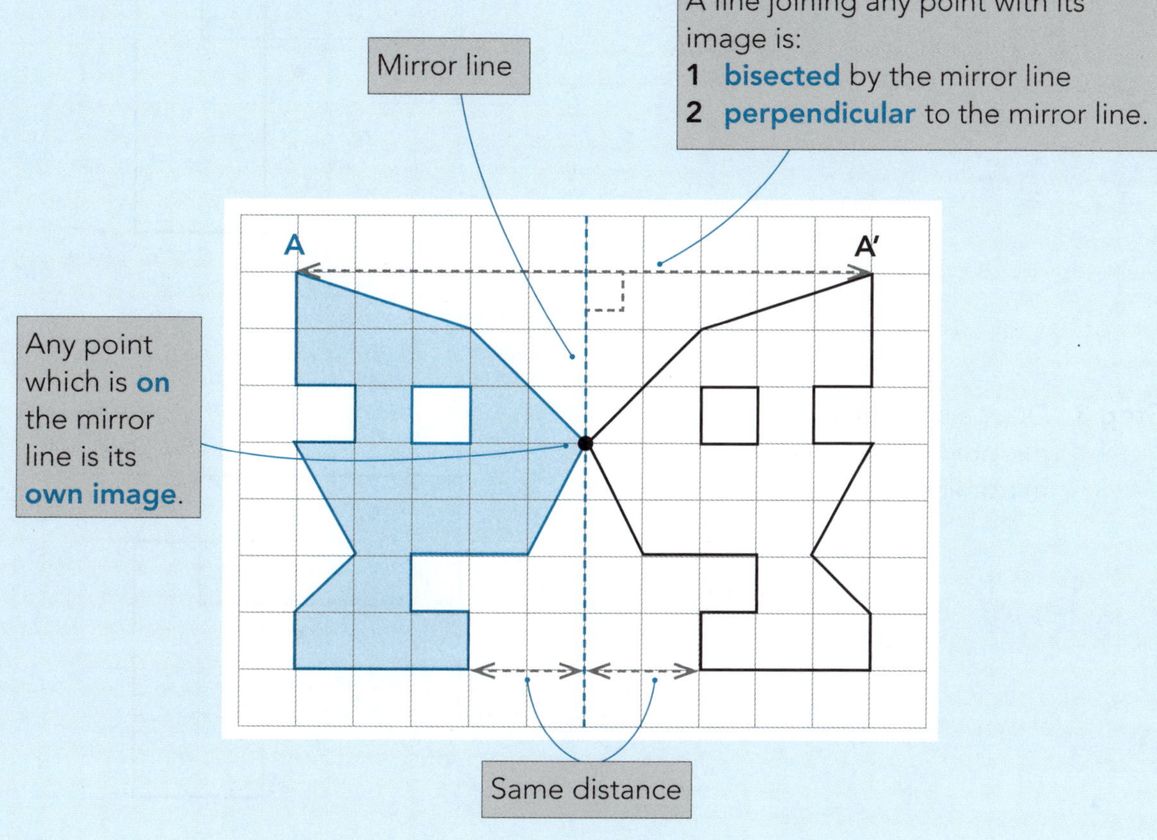

To find a mirror line:

Step 1 Rule a line from a point on the original figure to its image on the reflected figure.
Repeat for at least two more points.

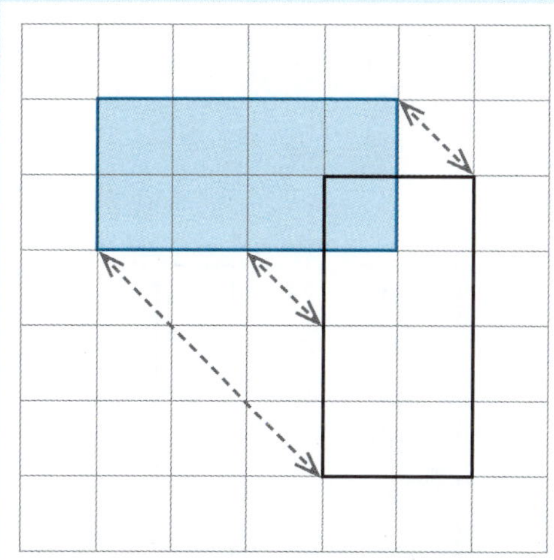

ISBN: 9780170416016

Step 2 Mark the midpoint of each line.

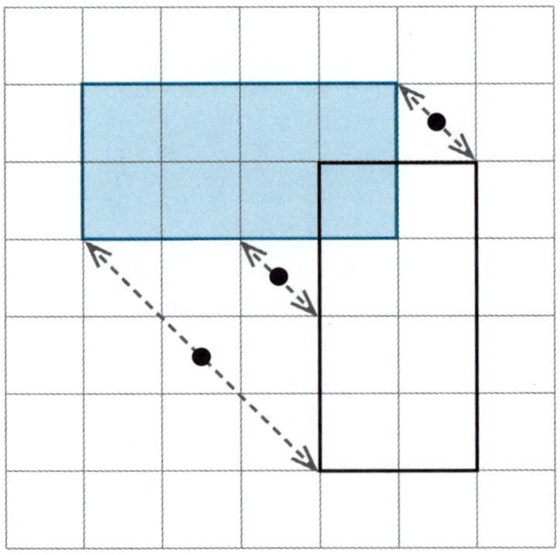

Step 3 Draw a line between the midpoints: this is the mirror line.

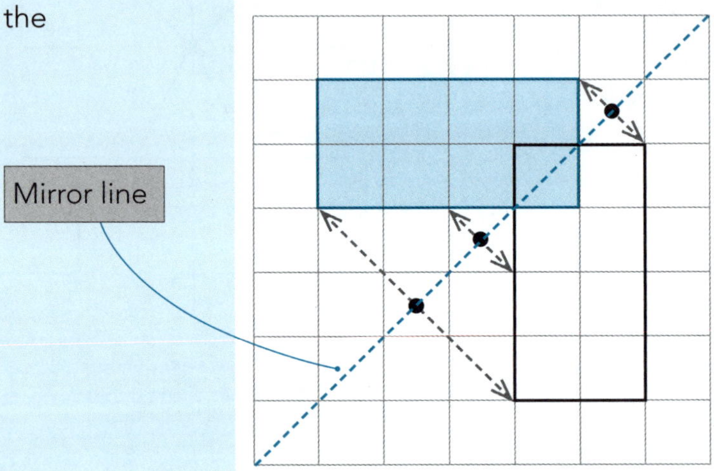

Mirror line

Draw mirror lines for the following reflections.

1

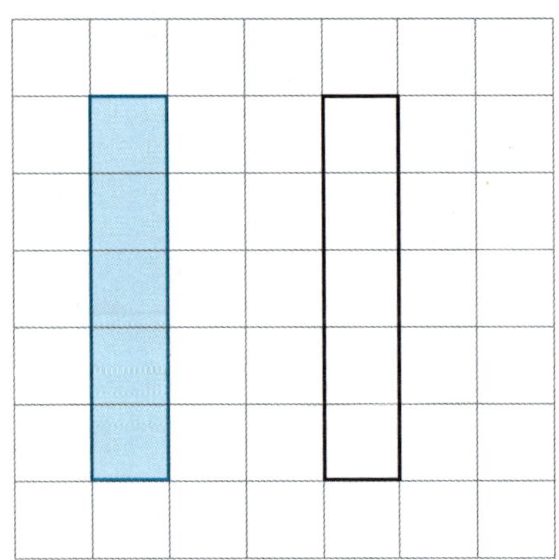

2

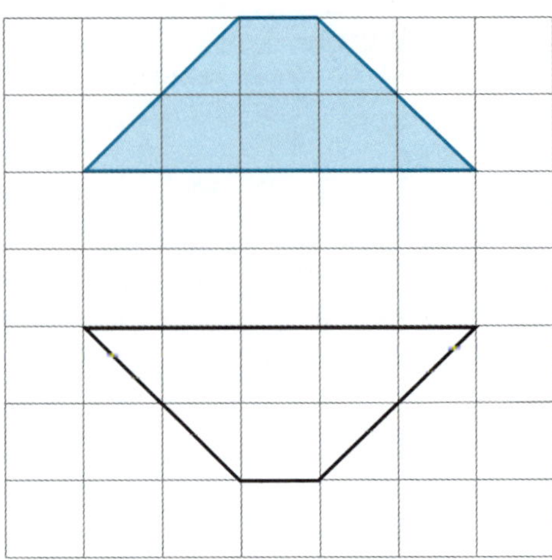

 ISBN: 9780170416016

3

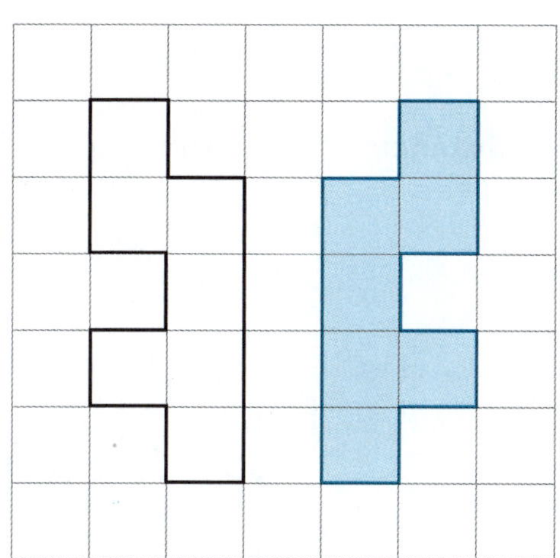

4

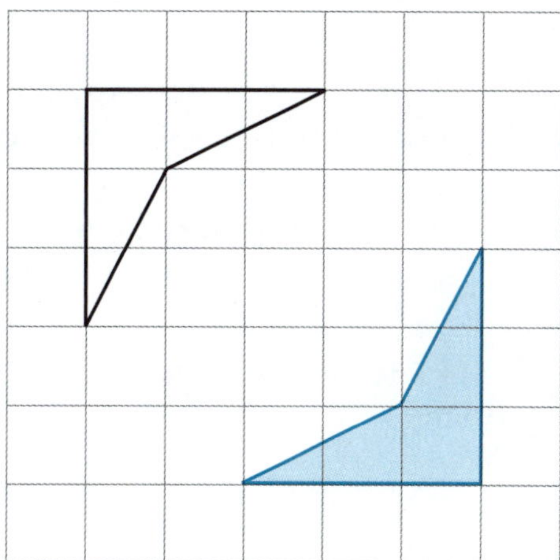

5

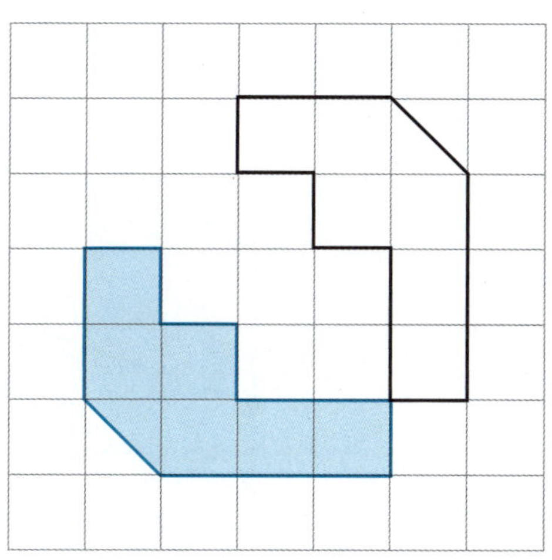

6

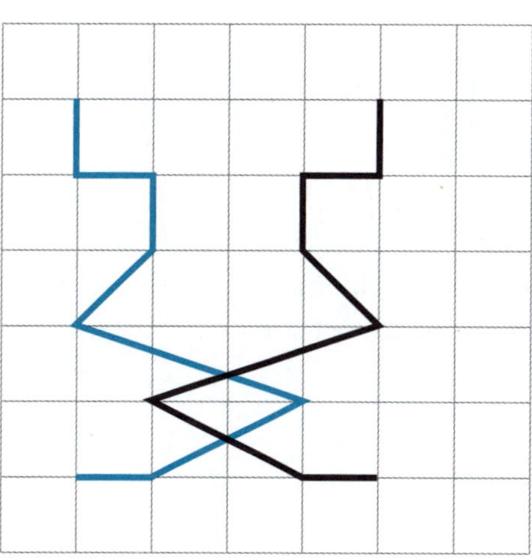

7

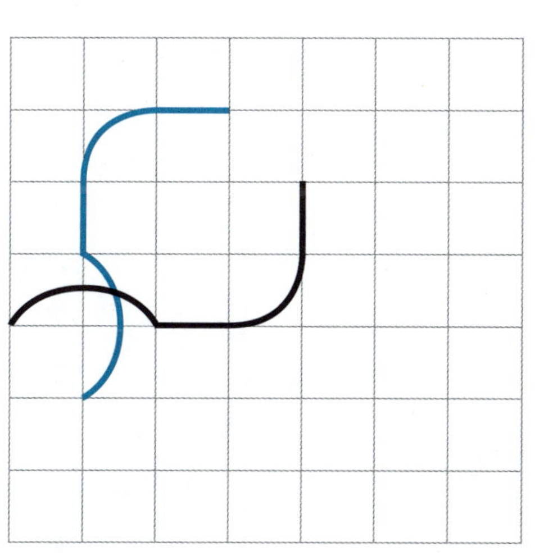

8

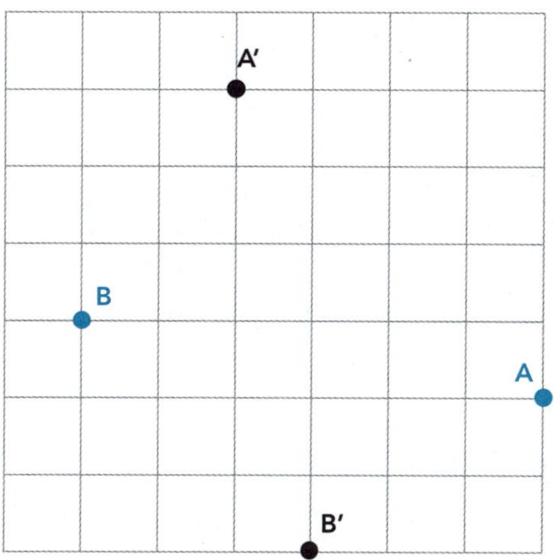

ISBN: 9780170416016

Drawing single reflections

- Points **on** the mirror line **stay** on the mirror line.
- Other points must be the **same perpendicular distance** from the mirror line.

With a horizontal or vertical mirror line:

Step 1
Mark any points that are on the mirror line.

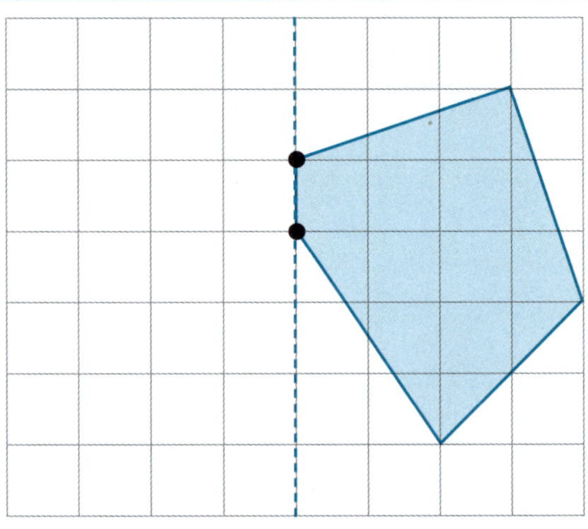

Step 2
Draw a line from each critical point perpendicular to the mirror line.

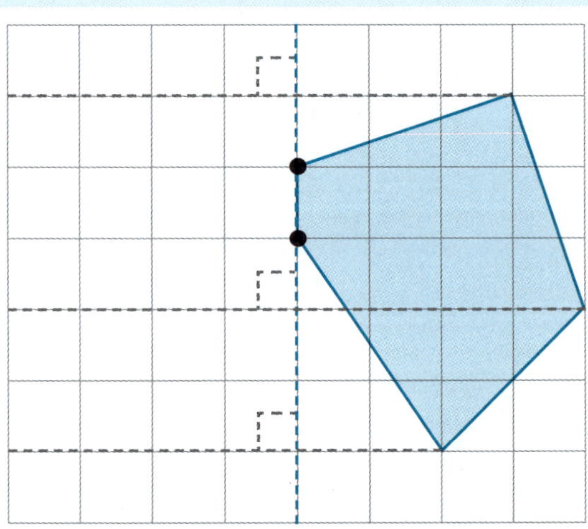

Step 3
Mark points on the opposite side of the mirror line the same distance from the mirror line as those on the original figure.

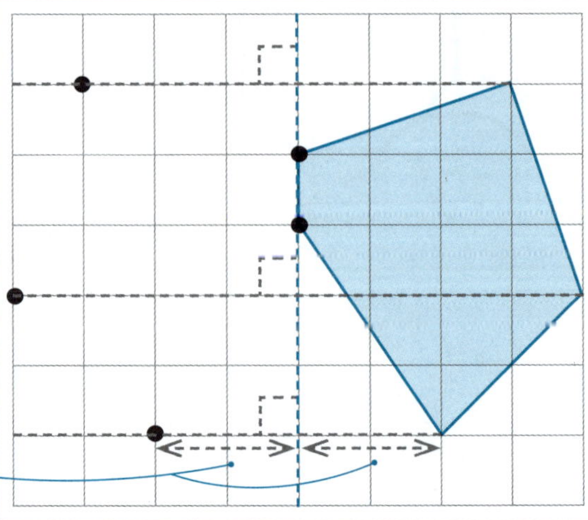

ISBN: 9780170416016

Step 4
Connect the points.

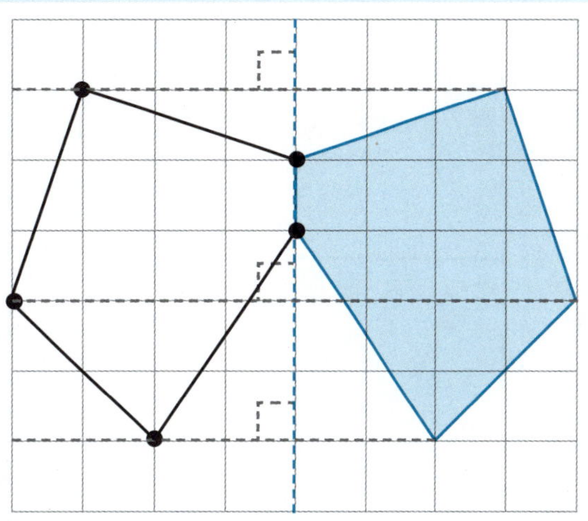

With a diagonal mirror line:

Step 1
Mark any points on the mirror line.

Step 2
Draw a line from each critical point perpendicular to the mirror line.

Hint: These will also be diagonal lines.

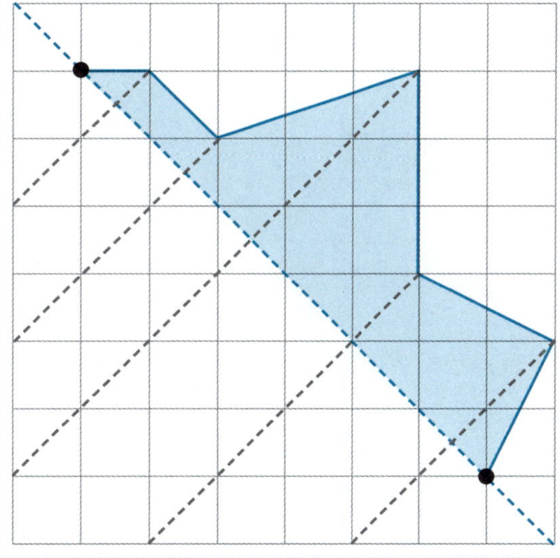

Step 3
Mark points on the opposite side of the mirror line the same distance from the mirror line as those on the original figure.

Step 4
Connect the points.

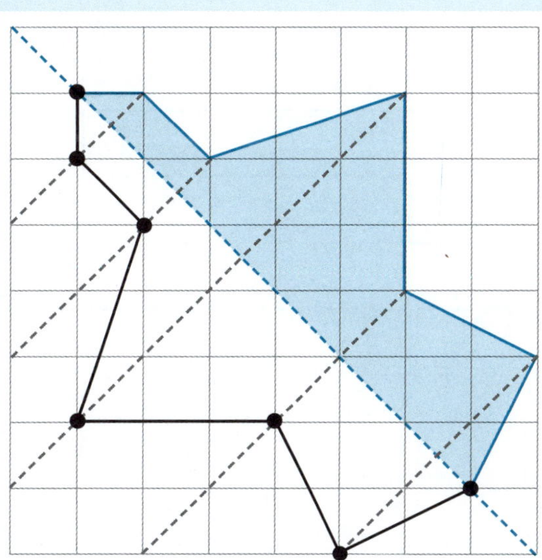

ISBN: 9780170416016

Draw reflections of the following figures.

1

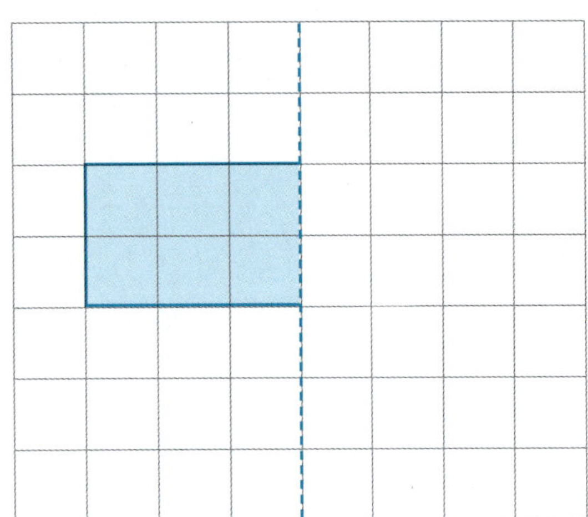

2

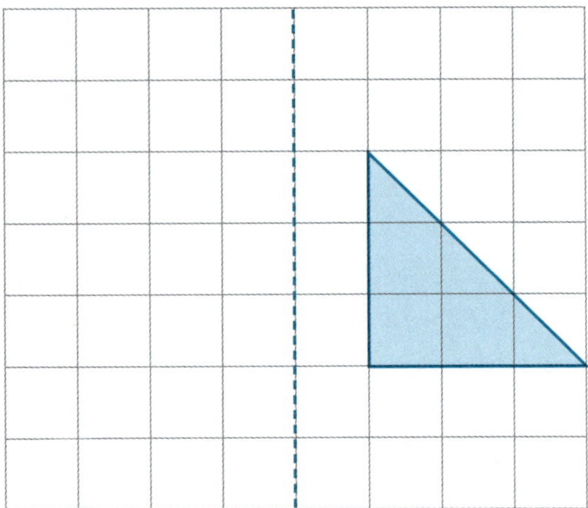

3

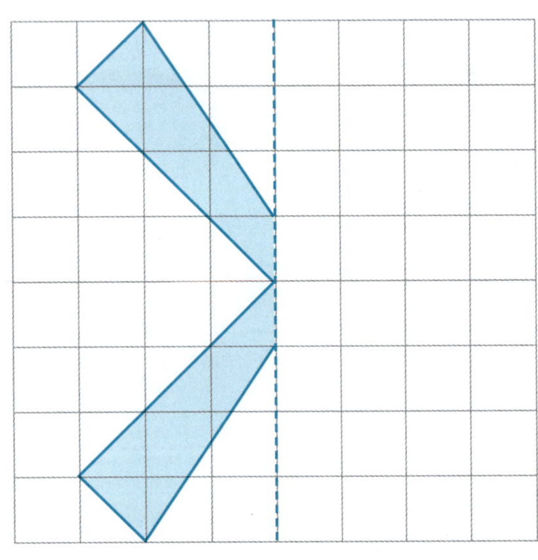

4

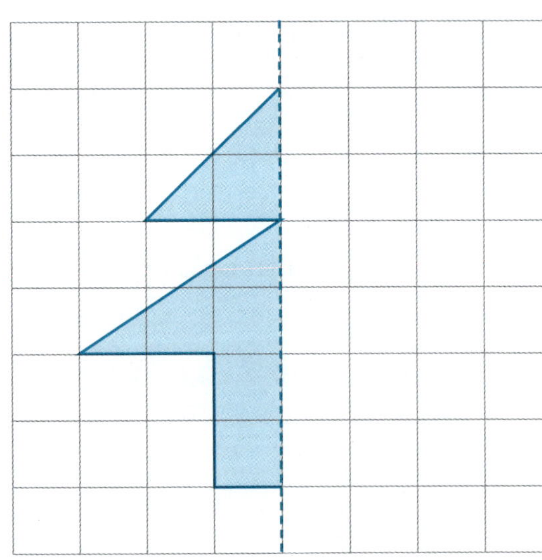

5

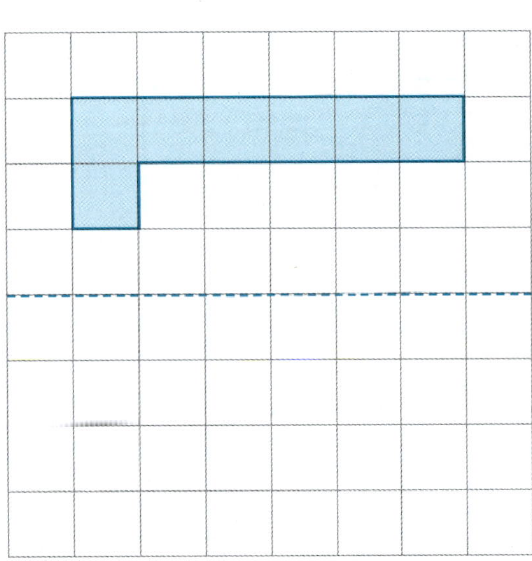

6

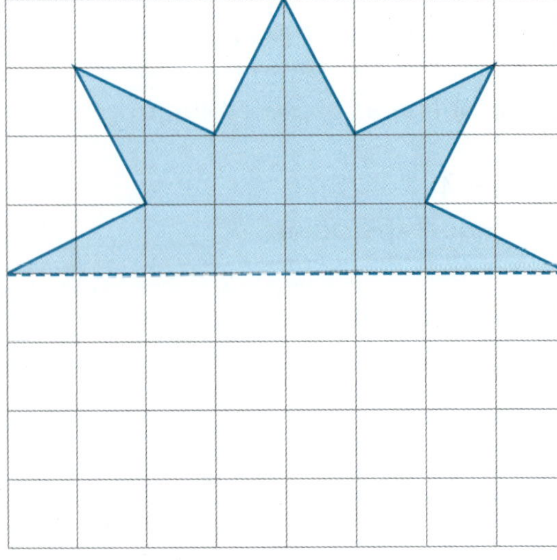

 ISBN: 9780170416016

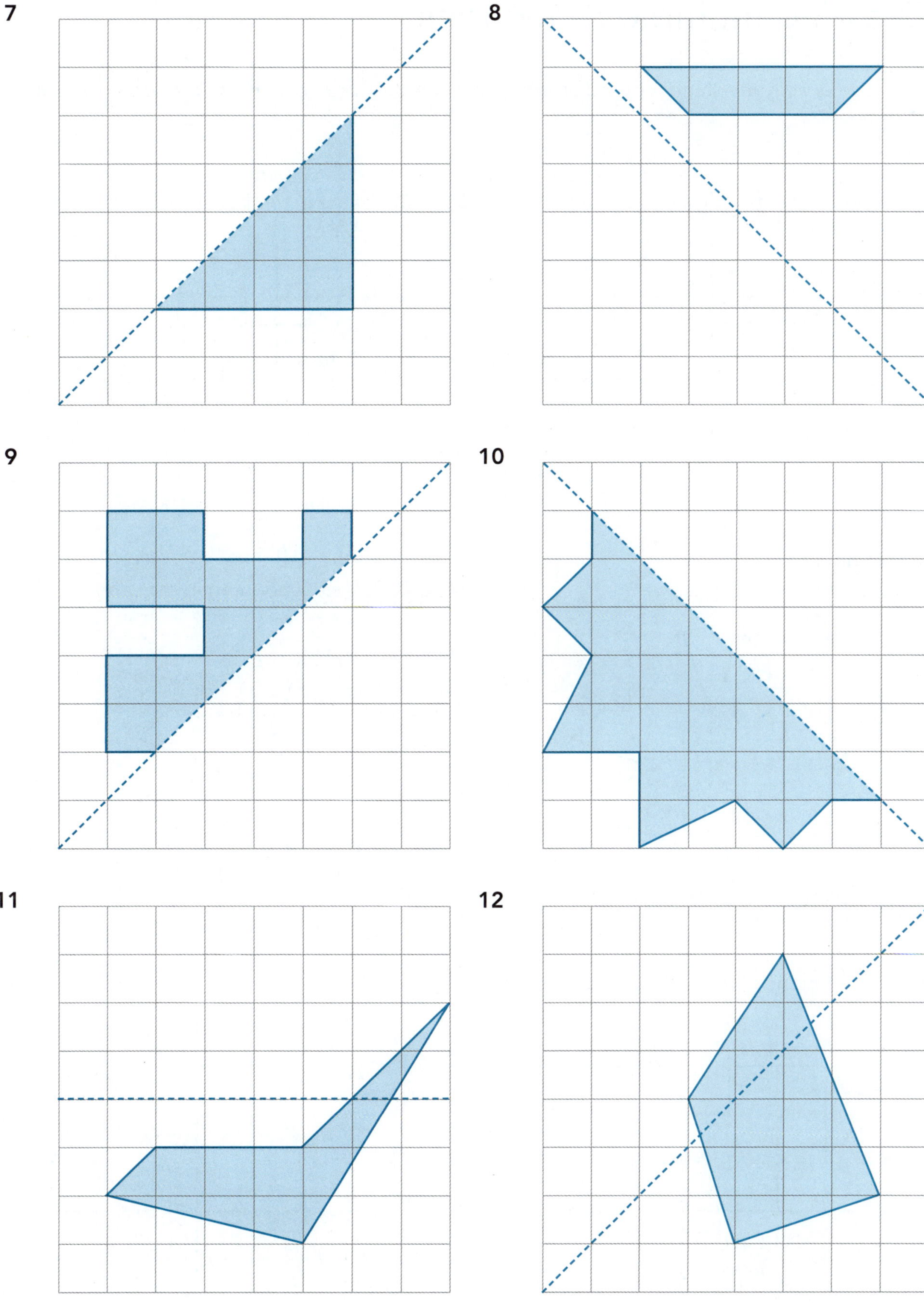

ISBN: 9780170416016

Drawing multiple reflections

- Use exactly the same method as in the last exercise, but you will need to do it several times.

Example 1:

Step 1: Reflect in the vertical axis.

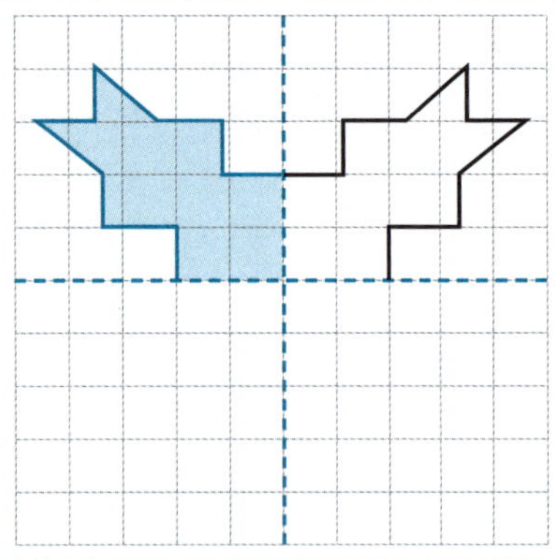

Step 2: Reflect in the horizontal axis.

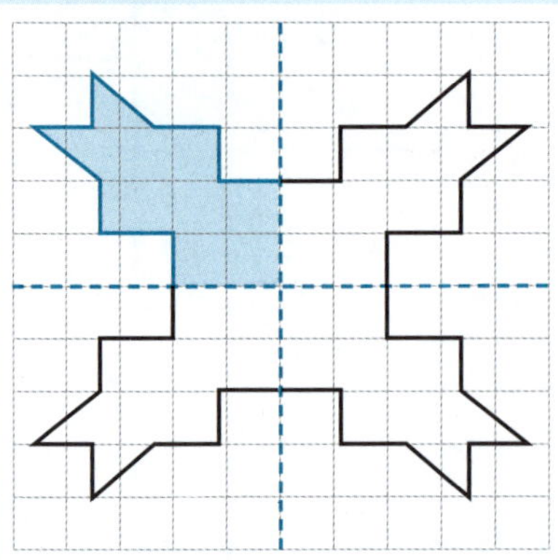

Example 2:

Step 1: Reflect in one axis.

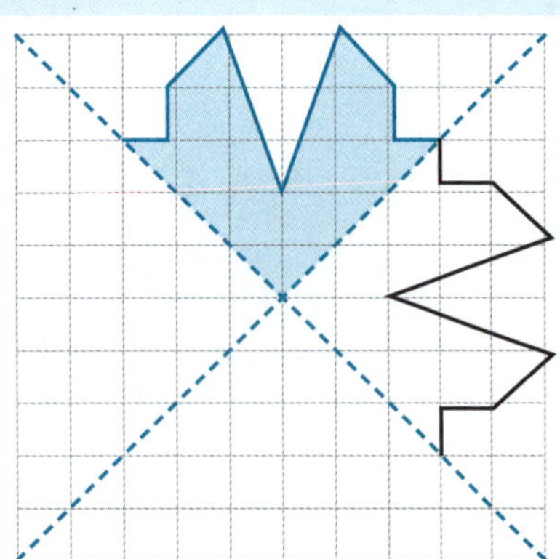

Step 2: Reflect everything in the other axis.

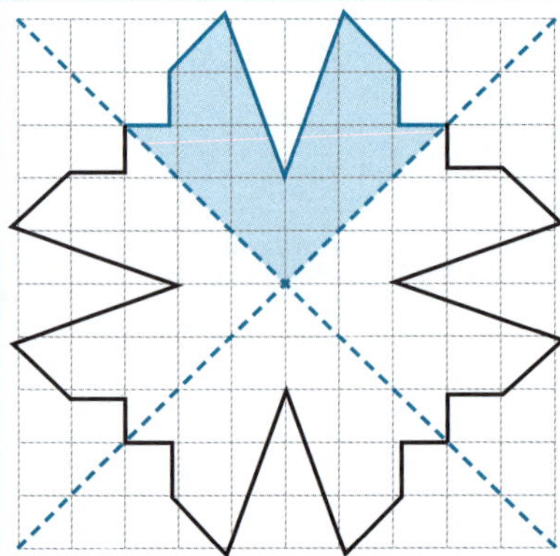

Draw reflections of the following figures.

1

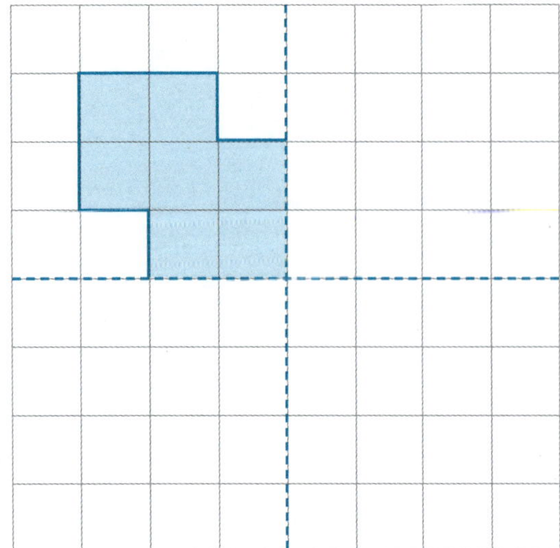

2

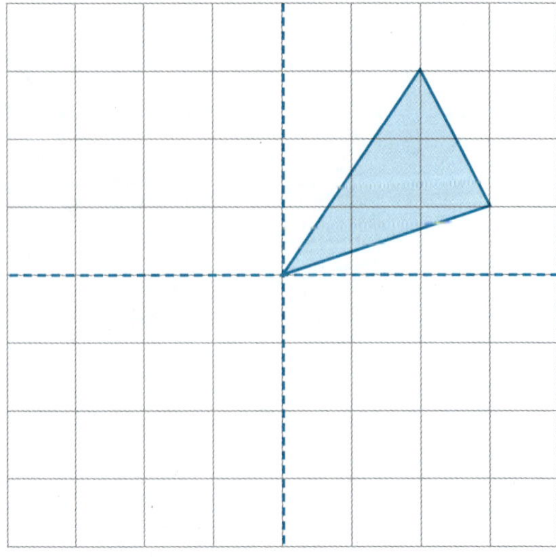

 ISBN: 9780170416016

3

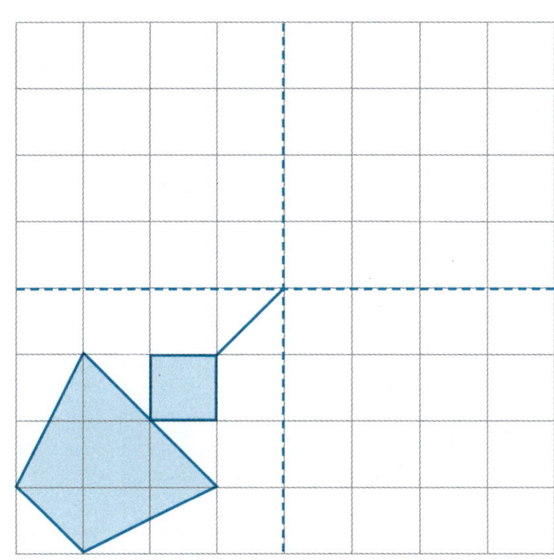

4

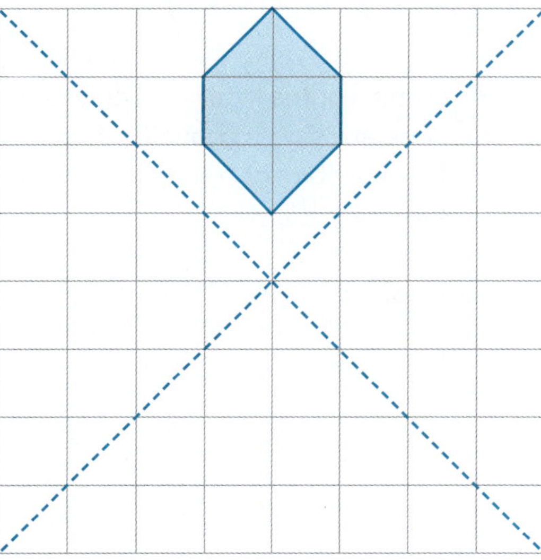

5

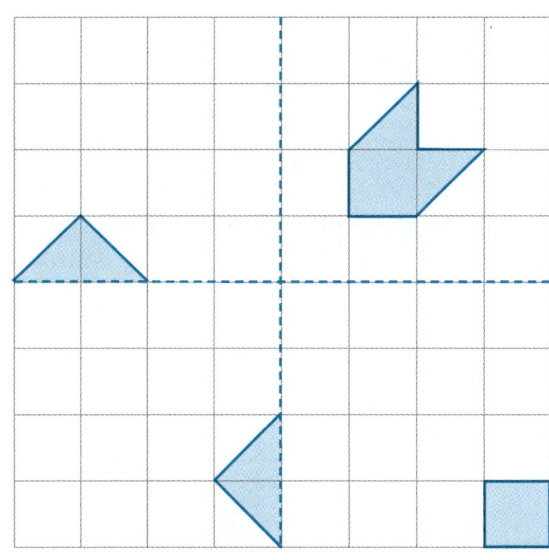

6

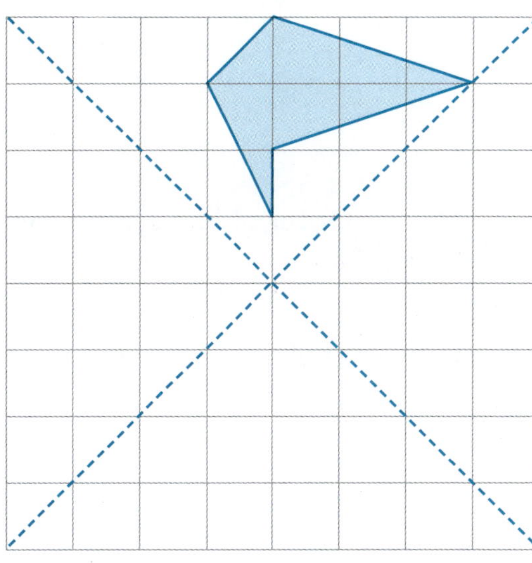

7

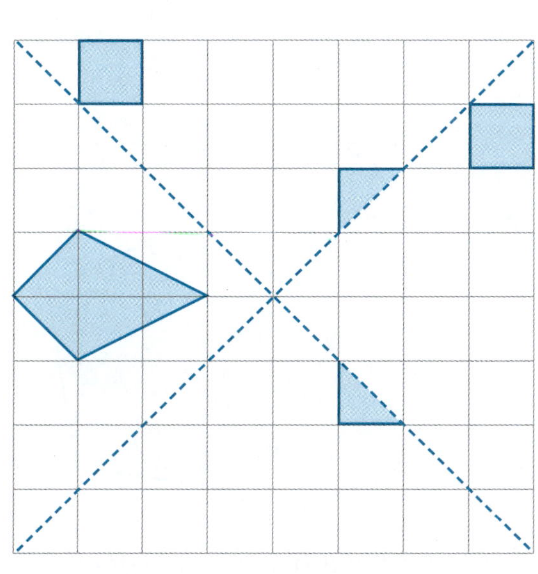

8

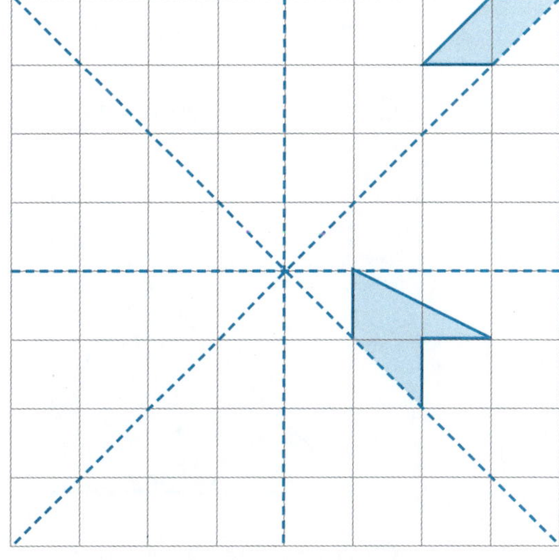

ISBN: 9780170416016

Line symmetry

- Some figures form reflections of themselves in a mirror line.
- They are said to have **line symmetry**.
- The **number** of mirror lines that can be drawn through a figure gives the **order of line symmetry**.

Examples:

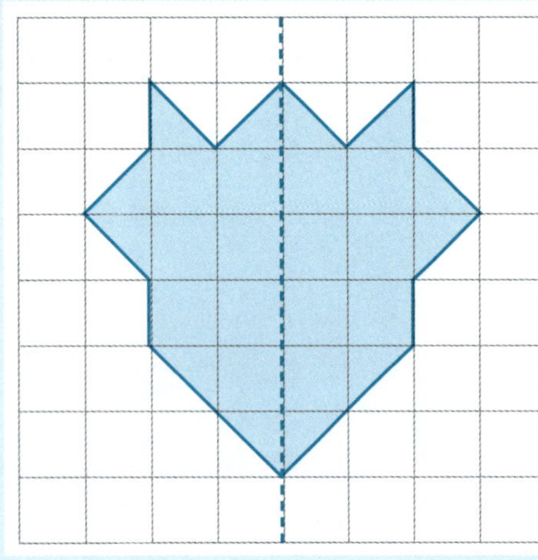

Order of line symmetry: 1

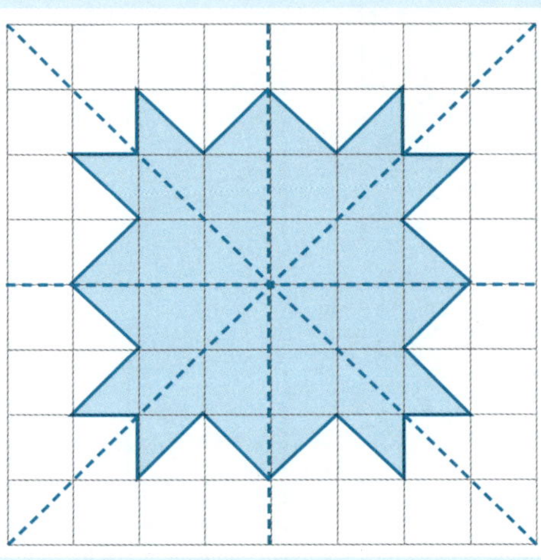

Order of line symmetry: 4

Draw any lines of symmetry on these figures, and state the order of line symmetry for each.

1

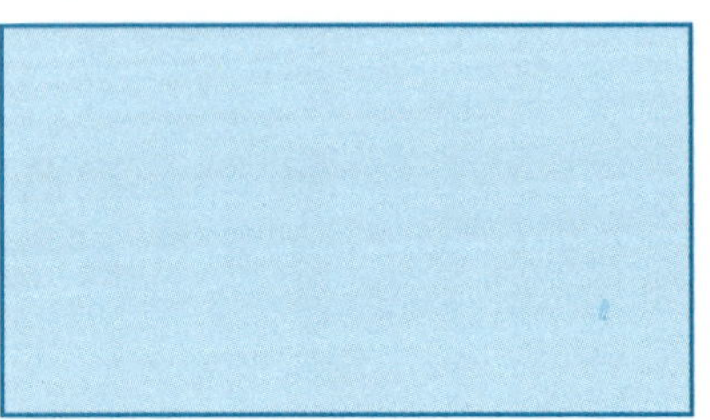

Order of line symmetry: ______

2

Order of line symmetry: ______

3

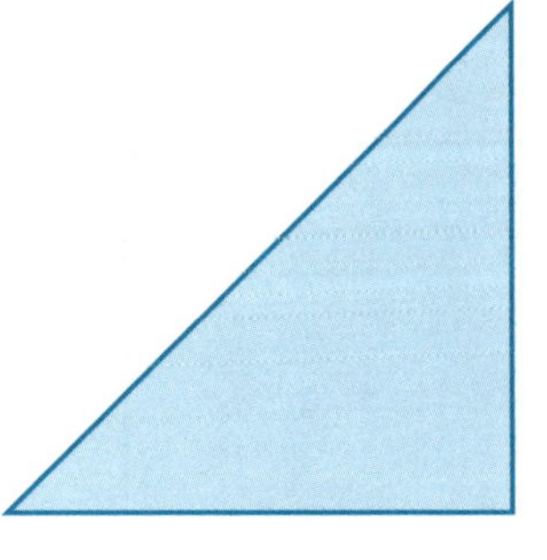

Order of line symmetry: ______

4

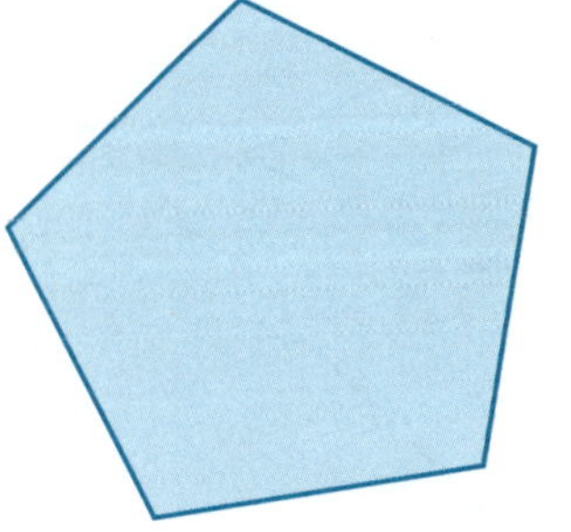

Order of line symmetry: ______

ISBN: 9780170416016

5

Order of line symmetry: ______

6

Order of line symmetry: ______

7

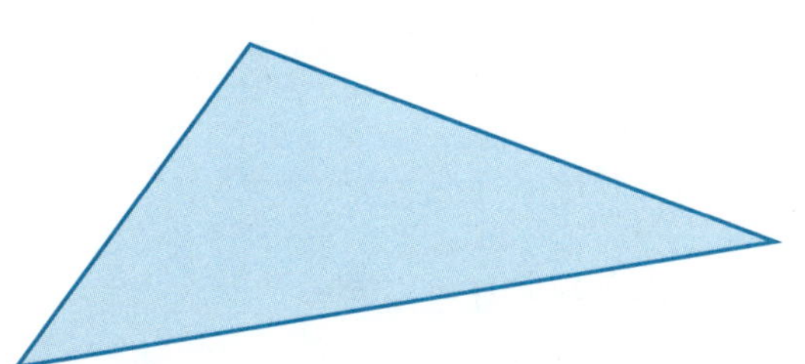

Order of line symmetry: ______

8

Order of line symmetry: ______

9

Order of line symmetry: ______

10

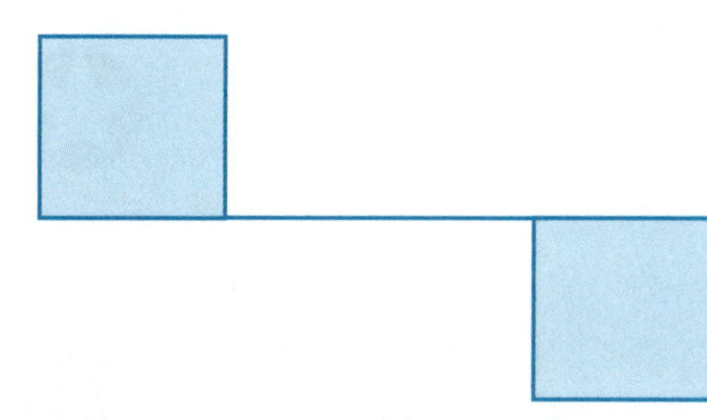

Order of line symmetry: ______

11

Order of line symmetry: ______

12

Order of line symmetry: ______

ISBN: 9780170416016

Challenges

1 Draw a figure with no lines of symmetry.

2 Draw a figure with three lines of symmetry.

3 Write the order of line symmetry for each of the following figures.

 ISBN: 9780170416016

4 Draw reflections of these figures.

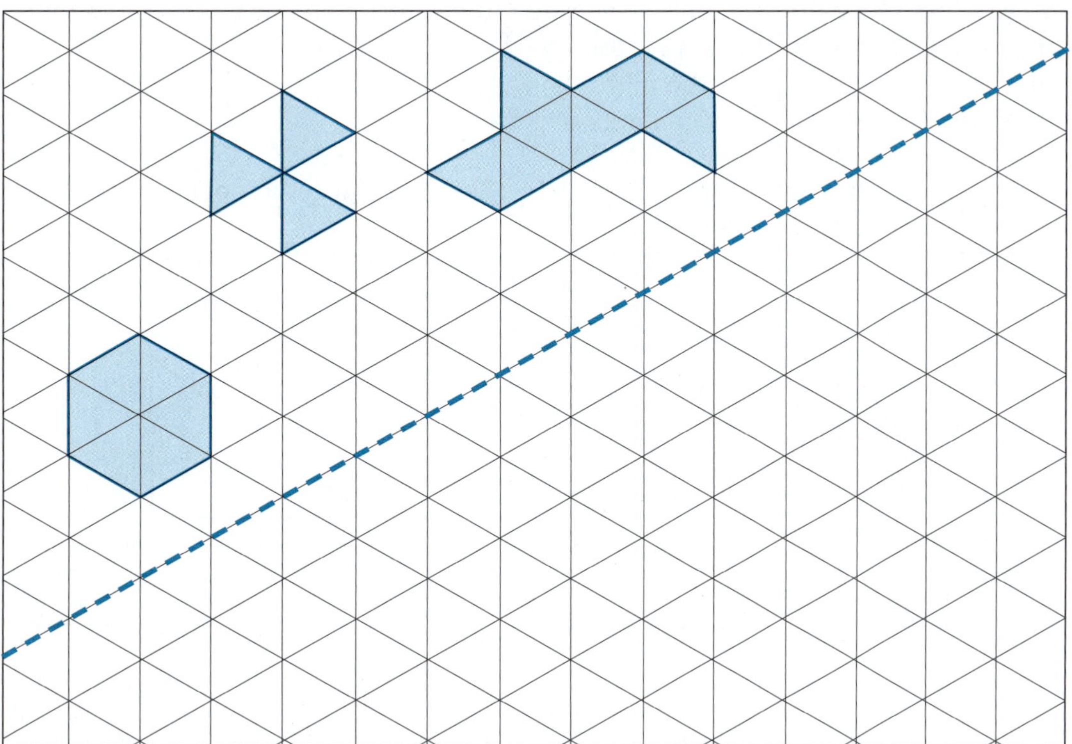

5 Draw the reflection of this figure.

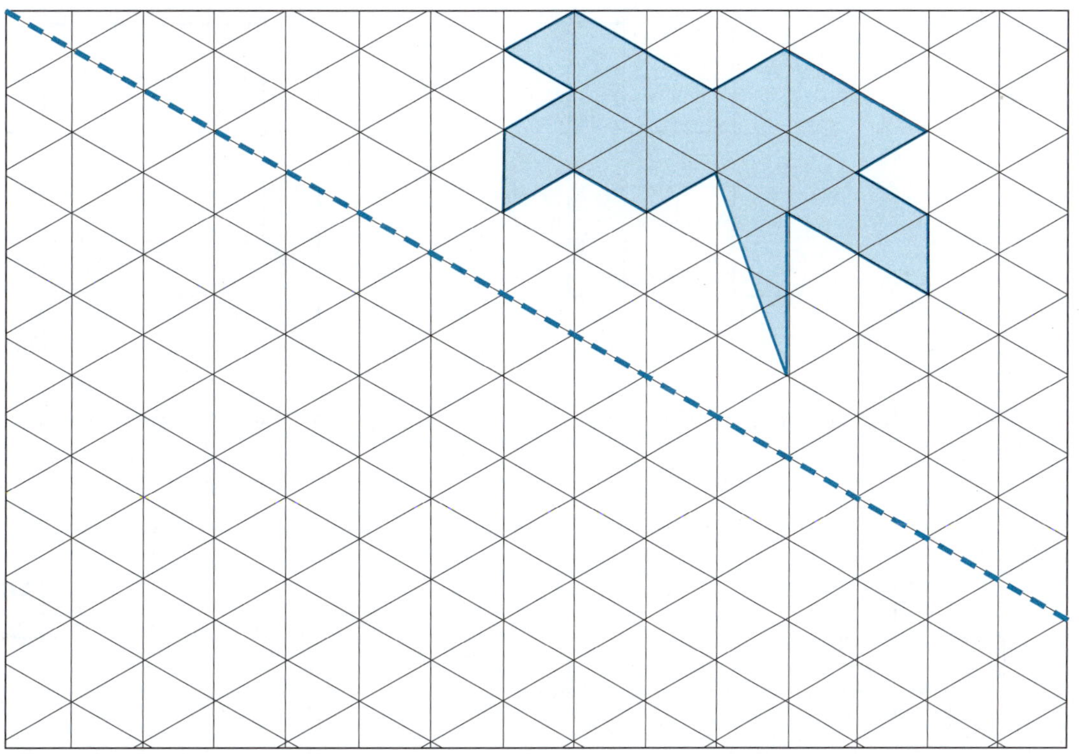

ISBN: 9780170416016

Mixing it up

Decide whether these figures could have been translated, reflected, both or neither.

- If they show translation, write a vector.
- If they show reflection, draw the mirror line(s).
- If they show both, do both of the above.

1 Translation/Reflection/Both/Neither

____

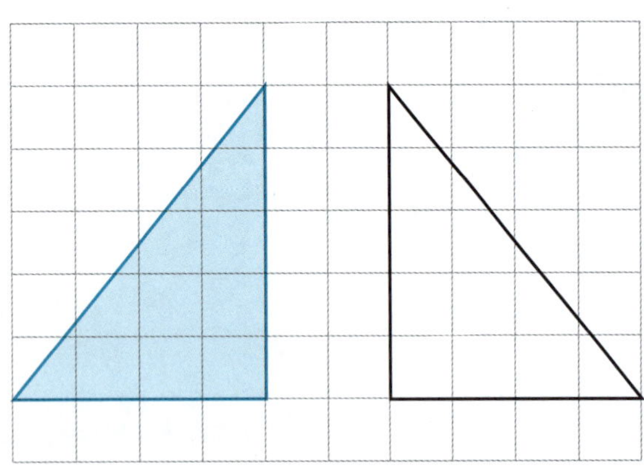

2 Translation/Reflection/Both/Neither

____

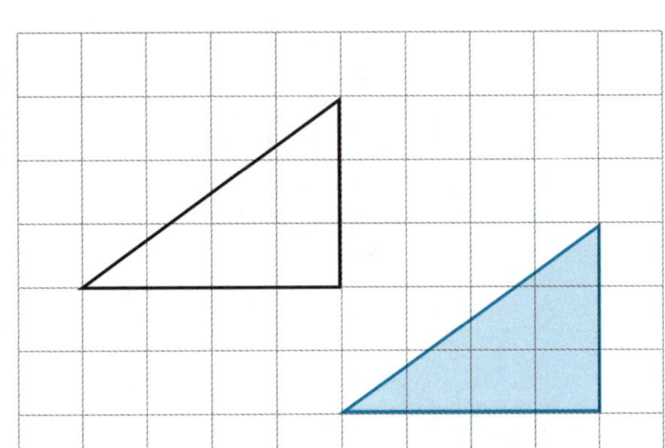

3 Translation/Reflection/Both/Neither

____

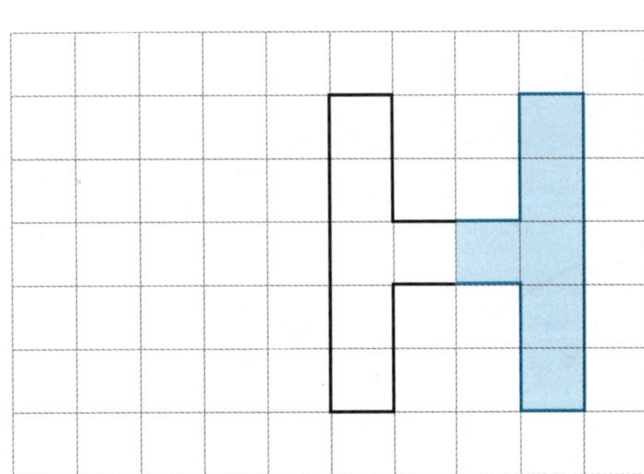

4 Translation/Reflection/Both/Neither

____

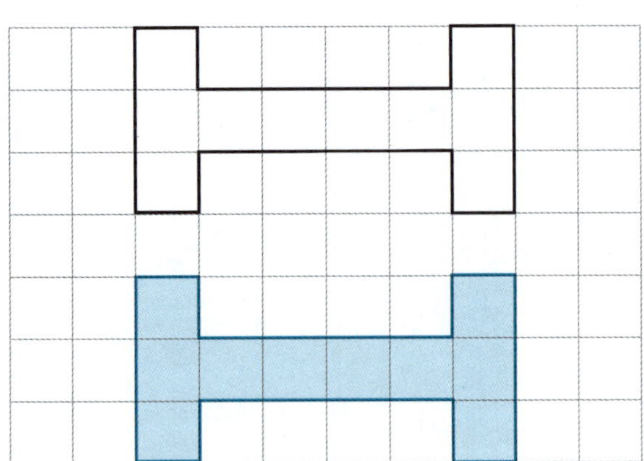

5 Translation/Reflection/Both/Neither

____

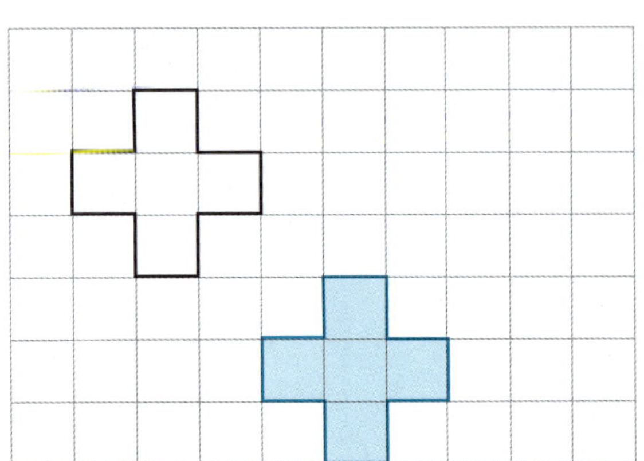

6 Translation/Reflection/Both/Neither

____

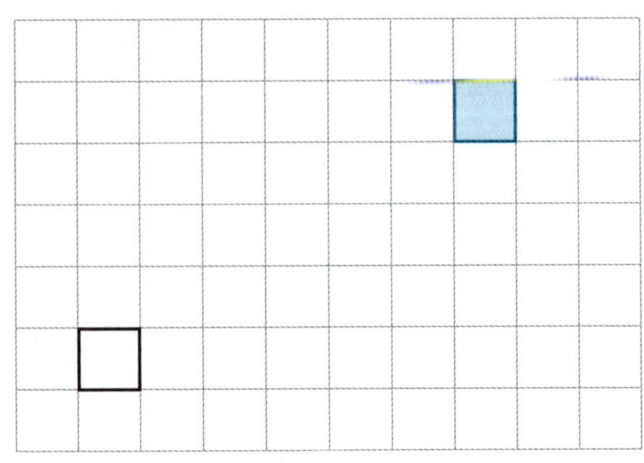

ISBN: 9780170416016

Decide whether these figures show translation, reflection, both or neither.

- If they show translation, draw a line around one unit which has been translated.
- If they show reflection, draw the mirror line(s).
- If they show both, do both of the above.

7 Translation/Reflection/Both/Neither

____

8 Translation/Reflection/Both/Neither

____

9 Translation/Reflection/Both/Neither

____

10 Translation/Reflection/Both/Neither

____

11 Translation/Reflection/Both/Neither

____

Rotation

- Rotation is the **turning** of a figure around a point.
- The **size** and **shape** of the figure stay **the same**.
- The **orientation** and **position** of the figure **change**.

Example:

Complete the table for translation:

	Stays the same	Changes
Size	✓	
Shape		
Orientation		
Position		

 ISBN: 9780170416016

Describing rotations

In order to describe a rotation, **two** pieces of information are required:
1 the **angle** of rotation
2 the **centre** of rotation.

1 Finding the angle of rotation

- In this book rotations are always **clockwise** unless stated.

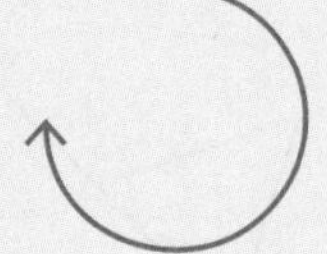

The main angles that you will use are:

45° or an eighth of a turn

90° or a quarter turn

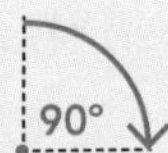

135° or three-eighths of a turn

180° or a half turn

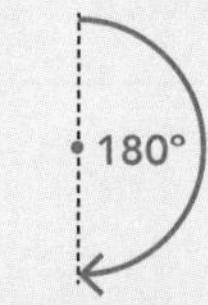

225° or five-eighths of a turn

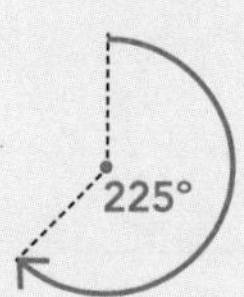

270° or a three-quarter turn

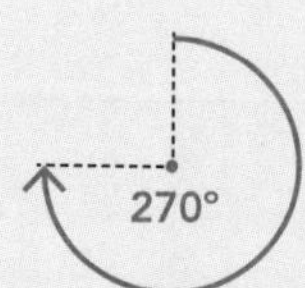

315° or a seven-eighths of a turn

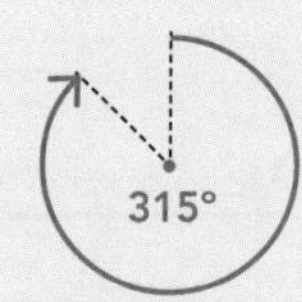

360° or a whole turn

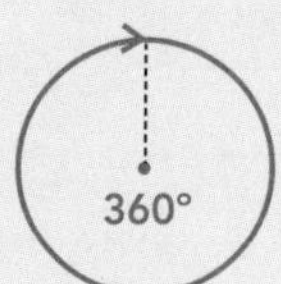

1 Rotations from an attached point

Example: Find how far this figure has been rotated.

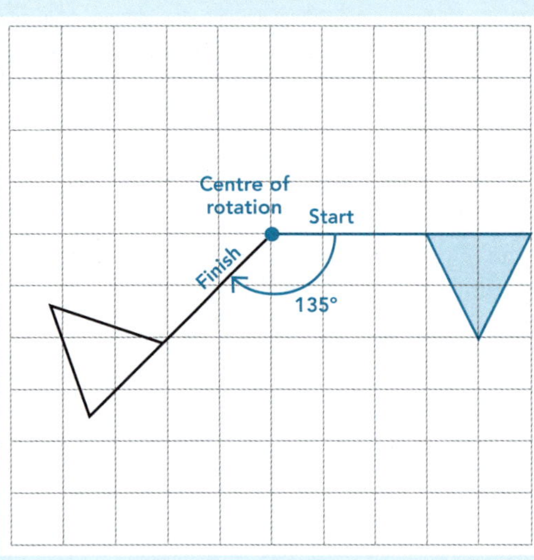

The figure has been rotated by 135° around the teal dot.

How far have these shapes been rotated in a clockwise direction?

1

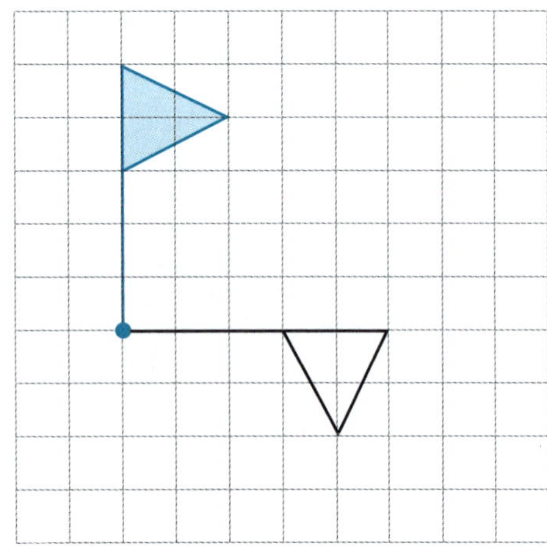

____

2

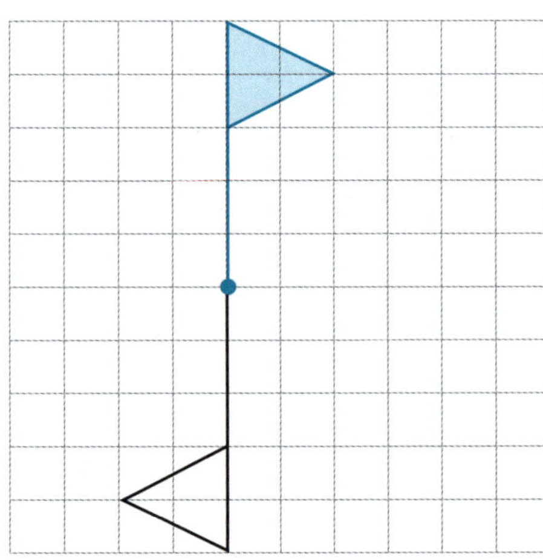

____

3

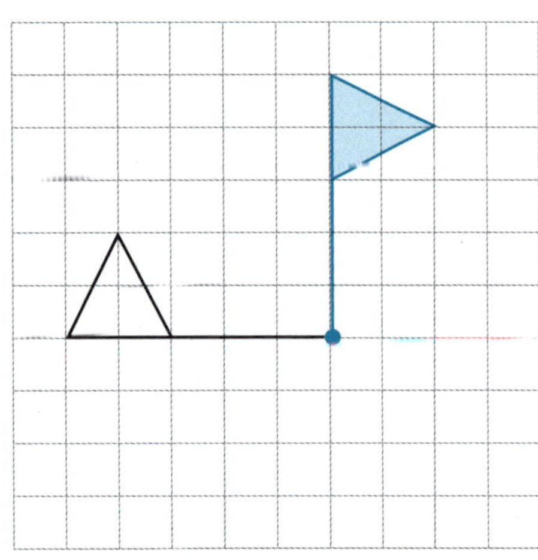

____

4

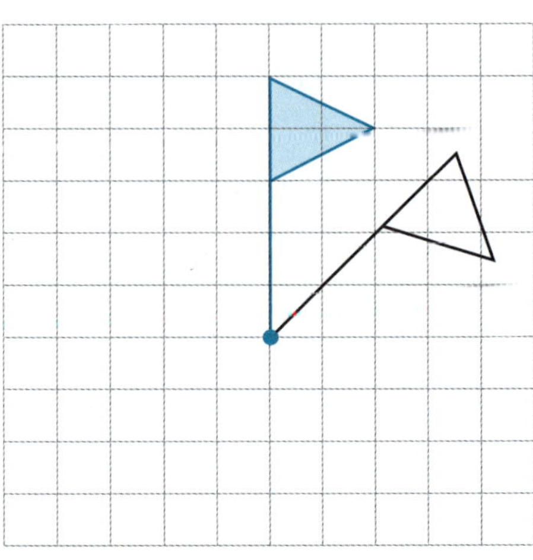

____

 ISBN: 9780170416016

5

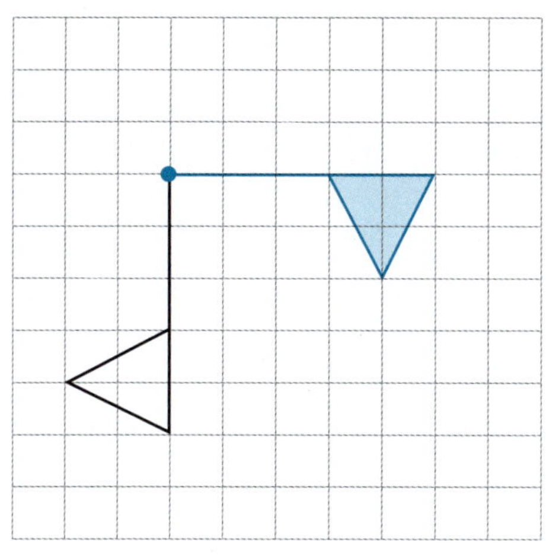

6

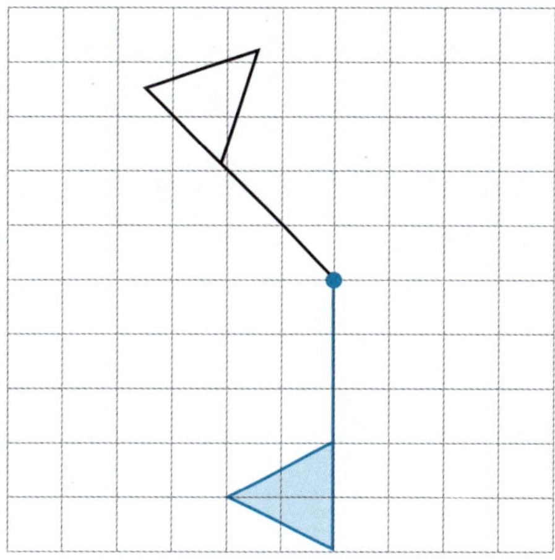

7

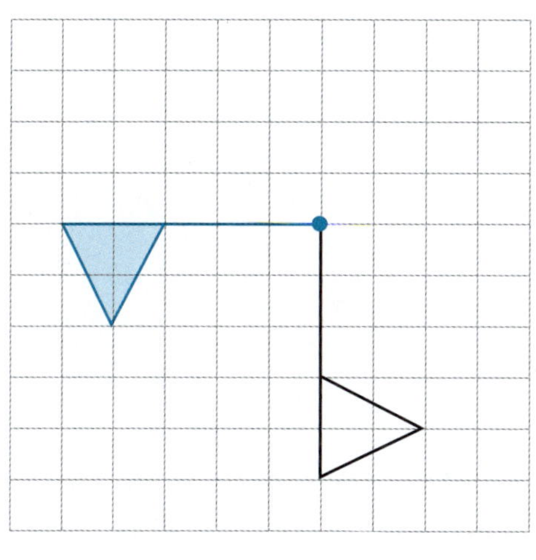

8

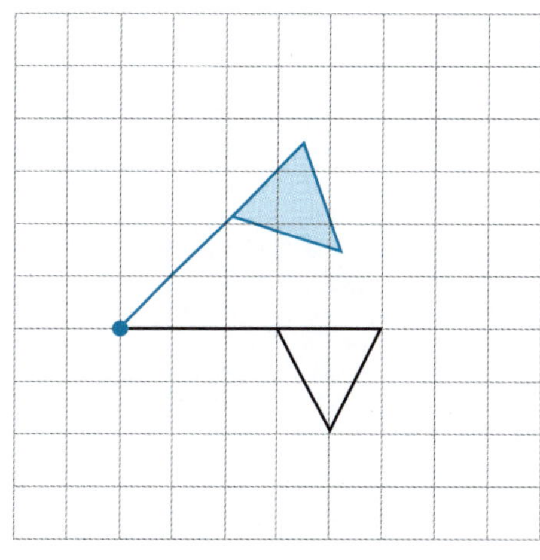

9

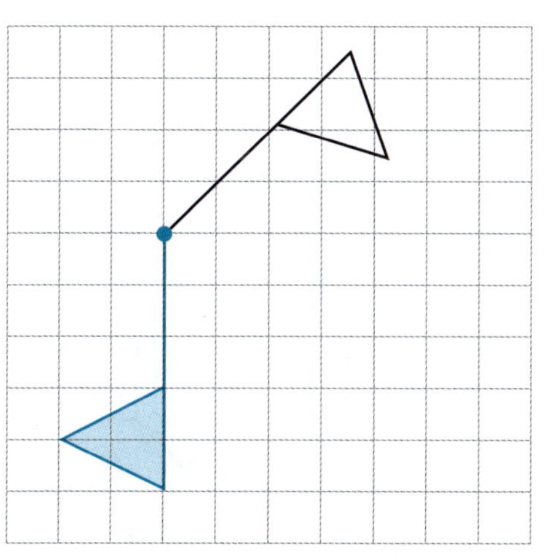

10

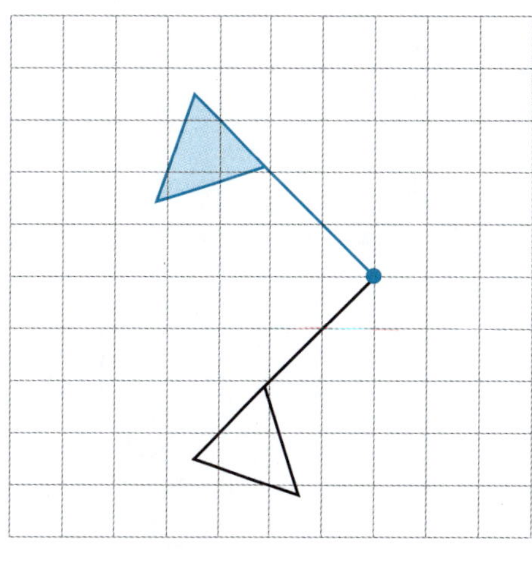

2 Rotations from an unattached point

Step 1
Rule lines (------) from the centre of rotation to a significant point on the original figure and on the image (often the closest point).

Step 2
Work out the angle of rotation of these two lines.

Examples: Find how far the following figures have been rotated in a clockwise direction.

1

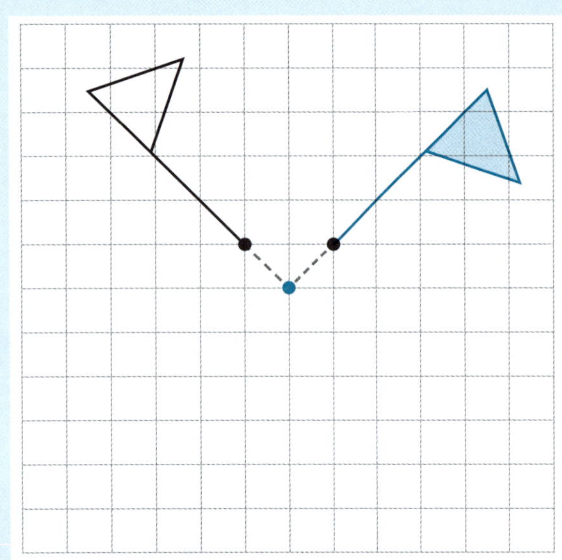

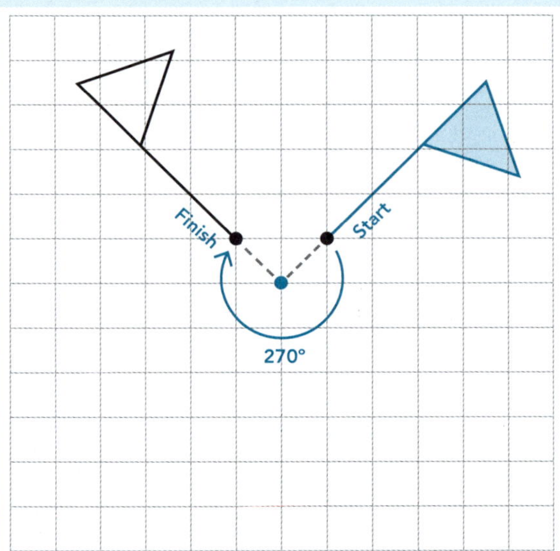

The figure has been rotated by 270° clockwise around the teal dot.

2

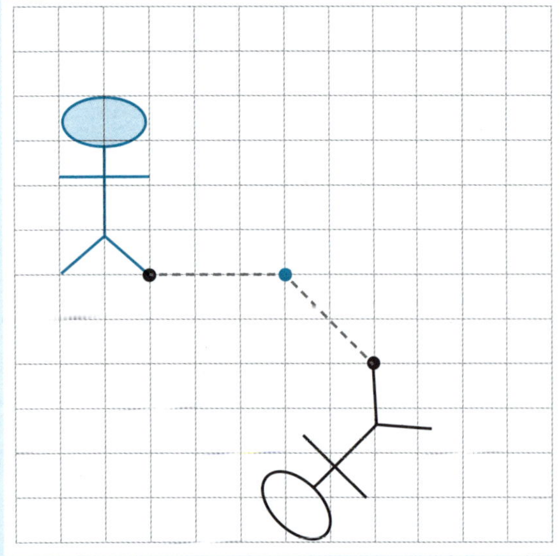

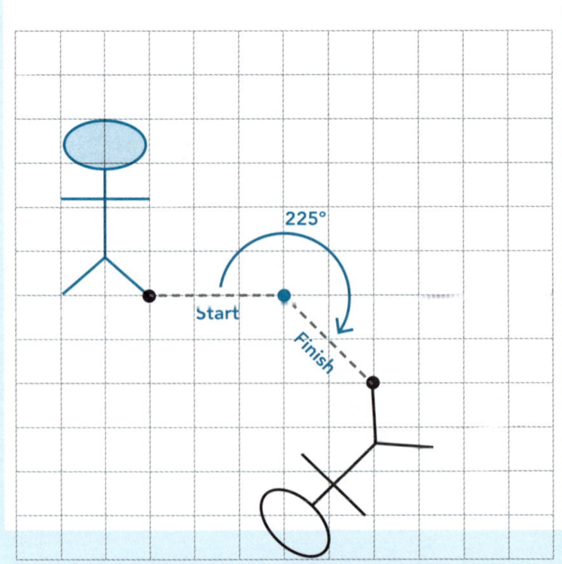

The figure has been rotated by 225° clockwise around the teal dot.

ISBN: 9780170416016

How far have these shapes been rotated in a clockwise direction?

1 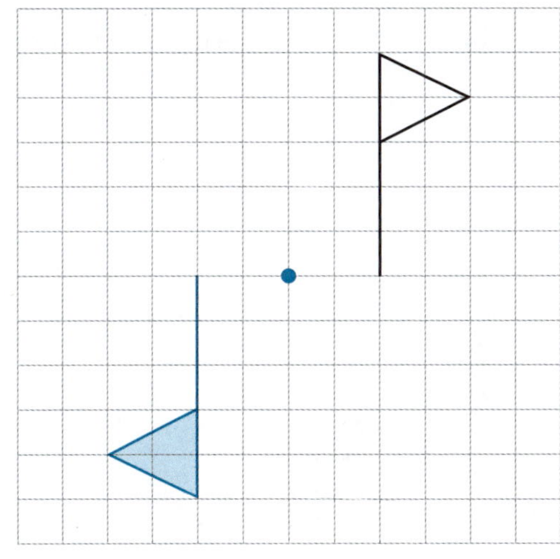

____

2 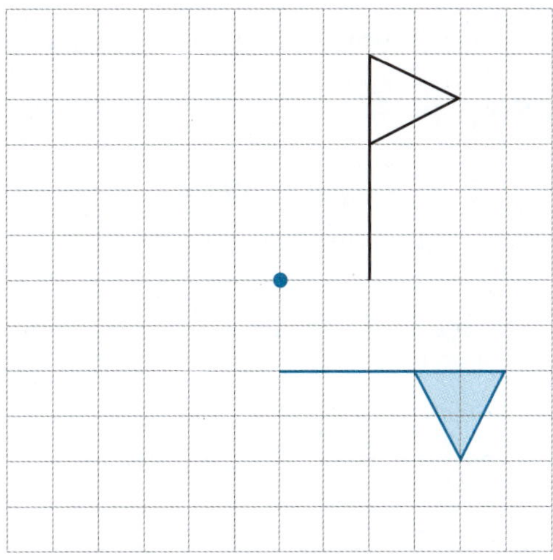

____

3 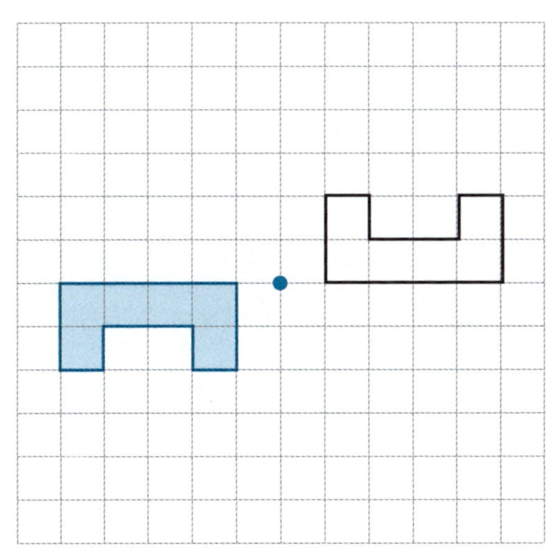

____

4 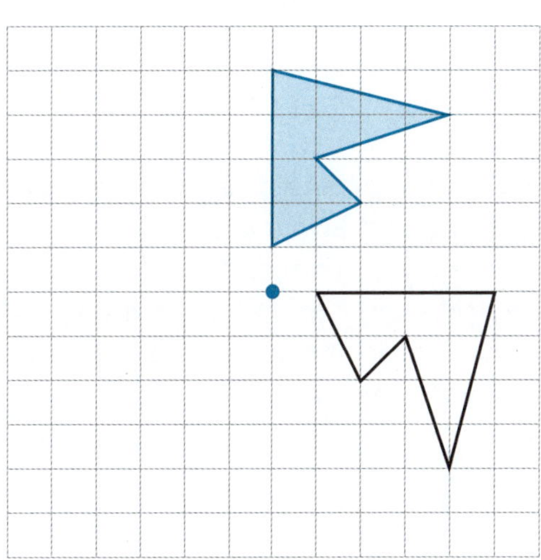

____

5 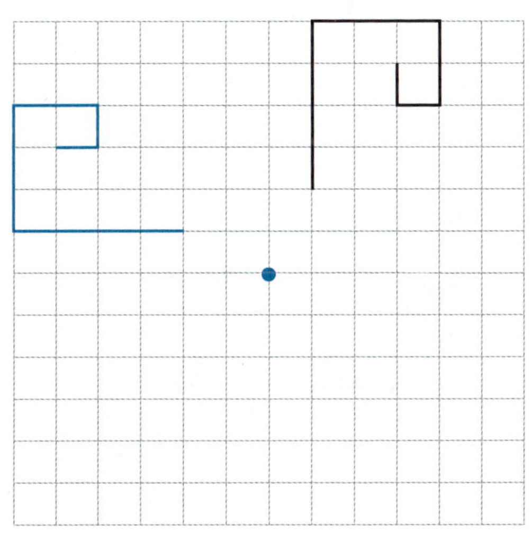

____

6 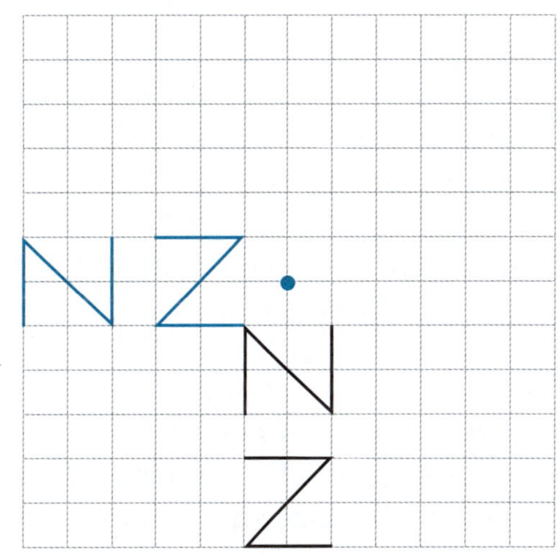

____

ISBN: 9780170416016

2 Finding the centre of rotation

- When you have a figure and its image, you may need to find the centre of rotation.

Step 1

Select a critical point on the figure and the equivalent point on the image.

Draw a line between the two points.

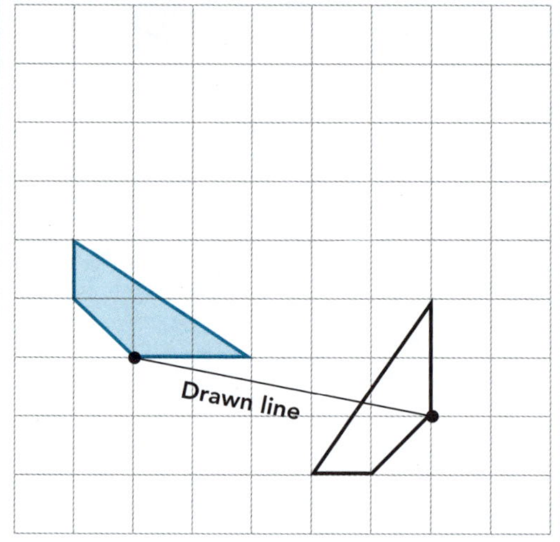

Step 2

Draw a perpendicular bisector to the line you have drawn by:
- finding the midpoint
- drawing a line through the midpoint which is at right angles to the line that you have drawn.

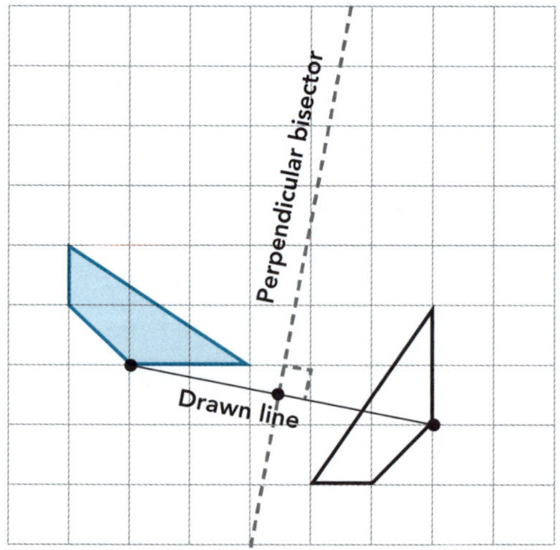

Step 3

Repeat the process with at least one more point.

The centre of rotation is where the perpendicular bisectors meet.

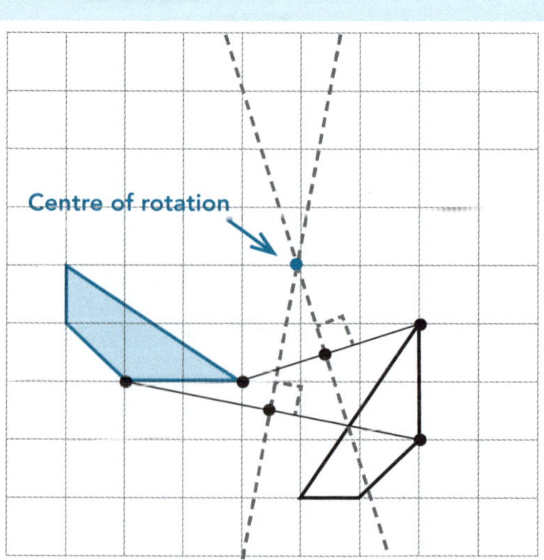

Note: Your teacher may provide you with tracing paper to help you find centres of rotation so you can guess and check.

ISBN: 9780170416016

Find the centre of rotation for each of the following.

1

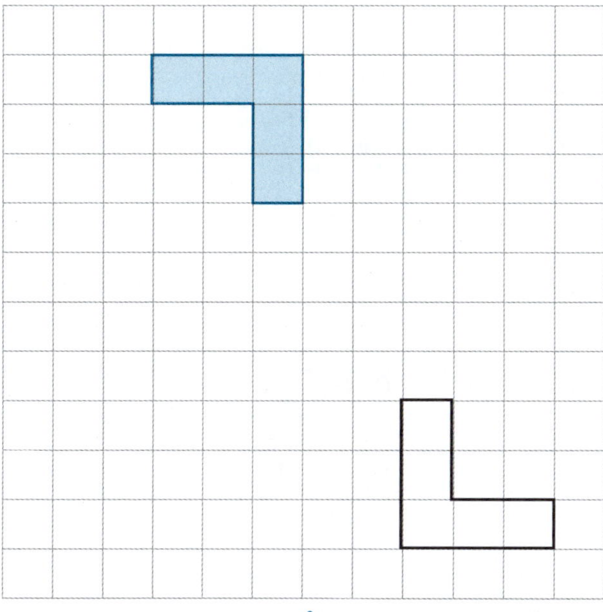

2

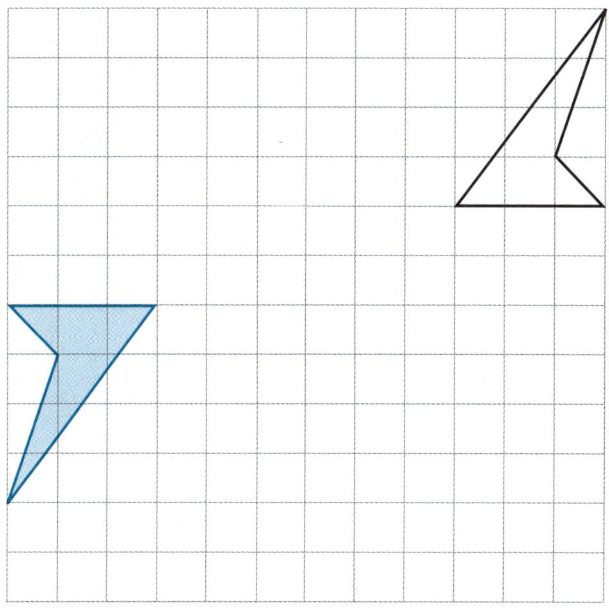

Note: If the rotation is by 180°, then you will not need to draw the perpendicular bisectors — just join equivalent points, and these lines will pass through the centre of rotation.

3

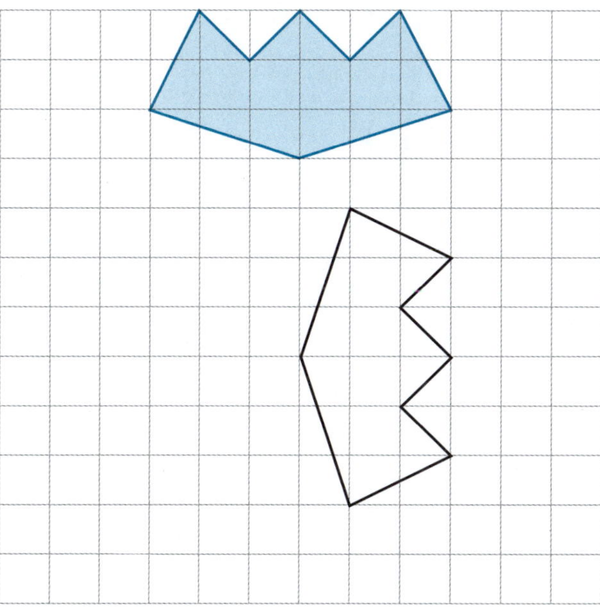

4

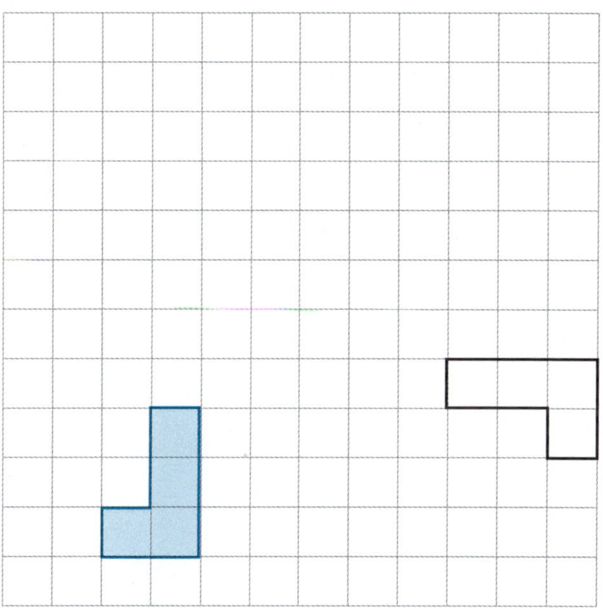

5

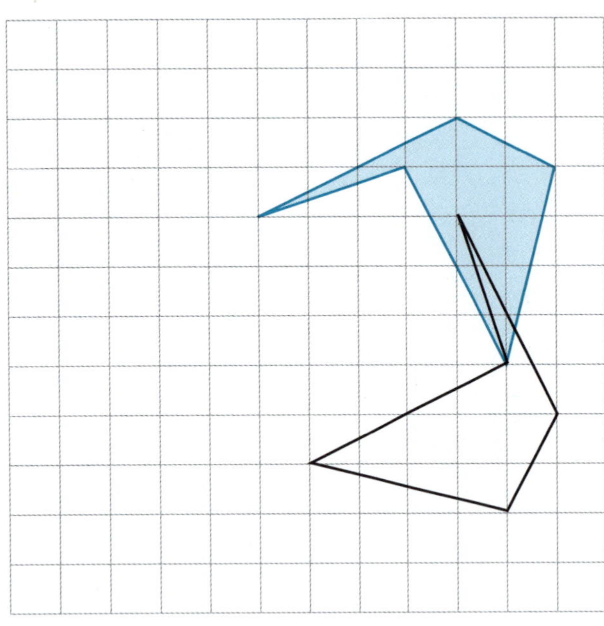

6

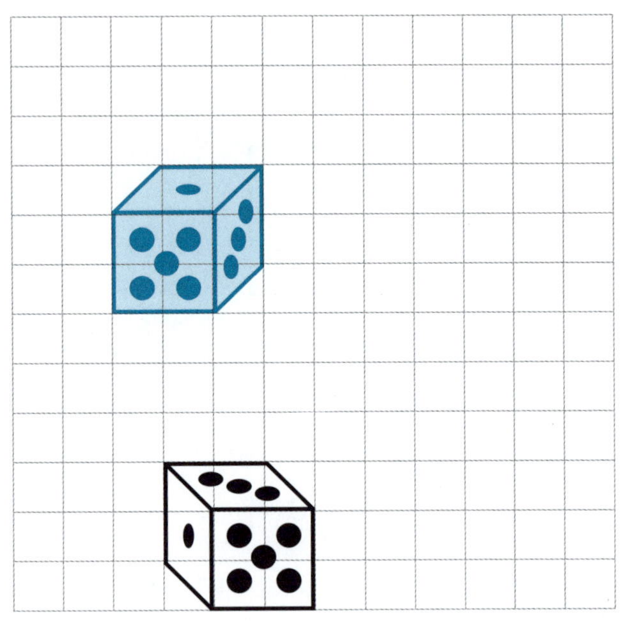

7

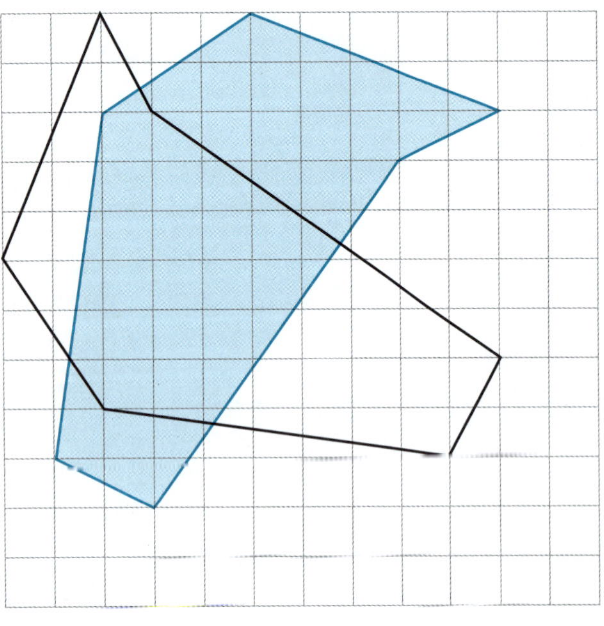

8

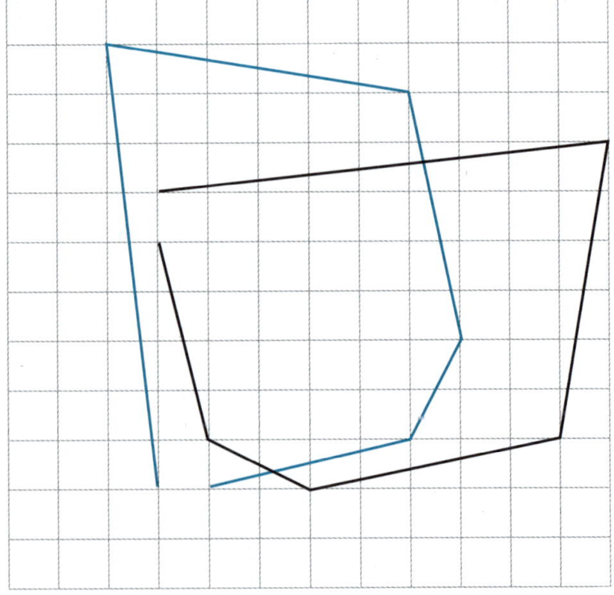

ISBN: 9780170416016

Drawing rotations

1 Rotations from an attached point

Example: Rotate this figure clockwise by 225° around the teal dot.

Step 1

Select a critical point on the figure.

Draw a line between it and the centre.

Rotate the line by the required angle.

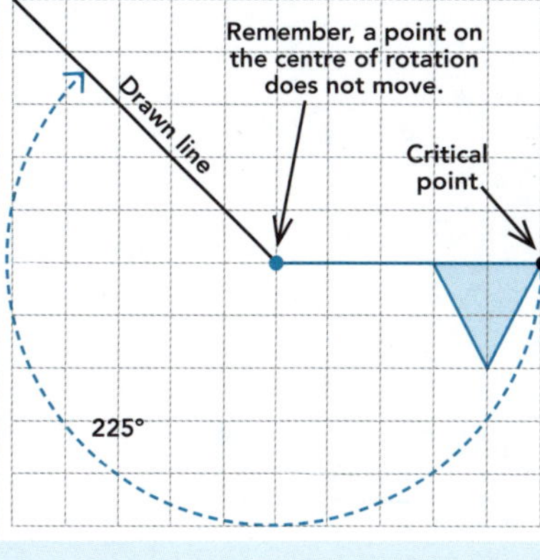

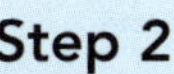

Step 2

Measure the distances from the centre to critical points along this line.

Mark the positions of the critical points on the image by measuring along the drawn line.

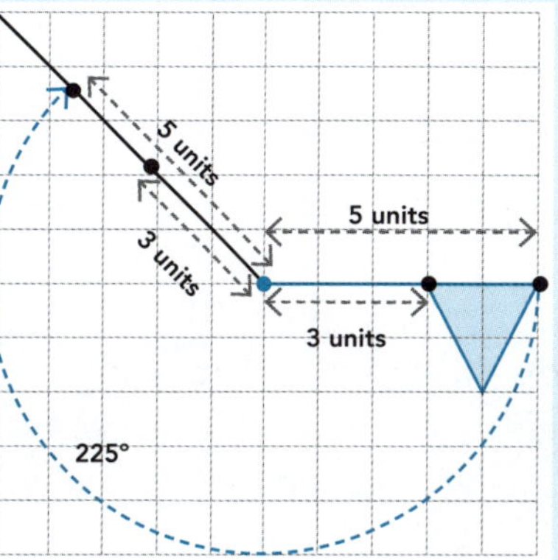

Step 3

Repeat the process with other critical points.

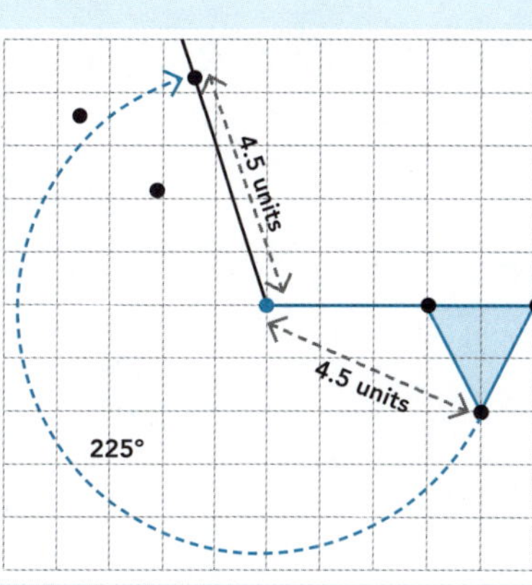

Step 4

Join the points.

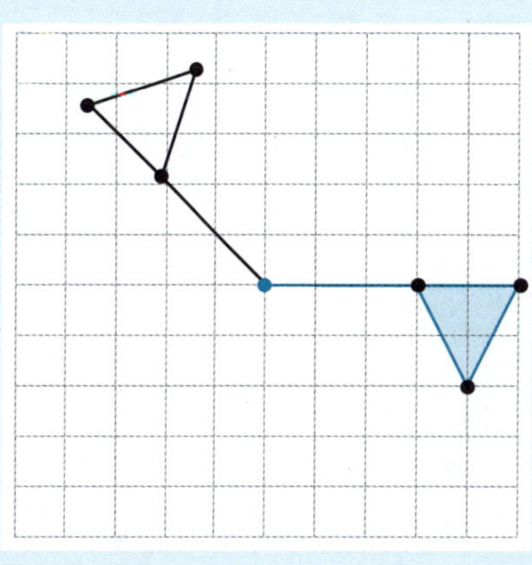

Note: Your teacher may provide you with tracing paper to help you do steps **2** and **3**.

ISBN: 9780170416016

Draw the rotated images of the following figures.

1 Rotate this figure 180° clockwise about the point.

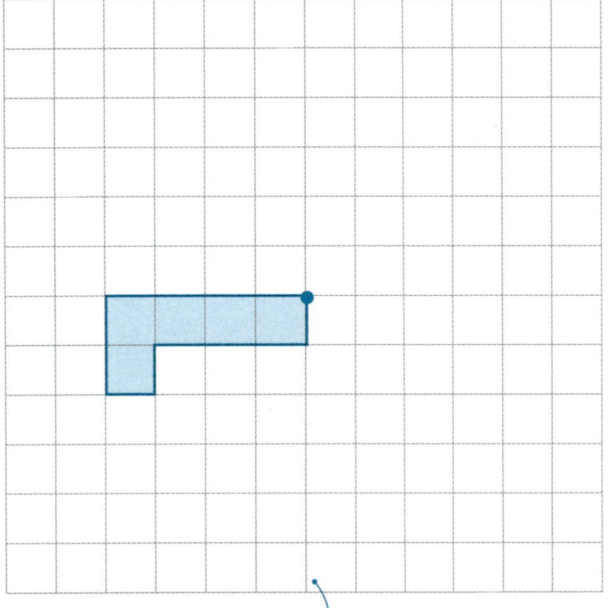

Hint: When you are rotating by 90°, 180° or 270°, you can work out where the critical points are by counting squares.

2 Rotate this figure 90° clockwise about the point.

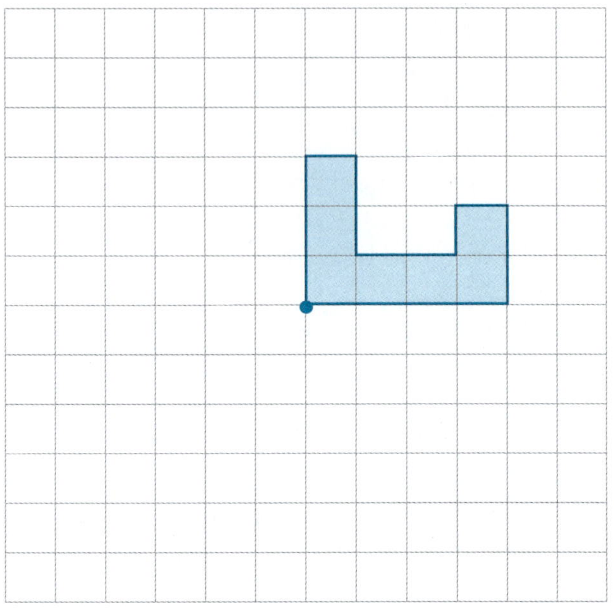

3 Rotate this figure 270° clockwise about the point.

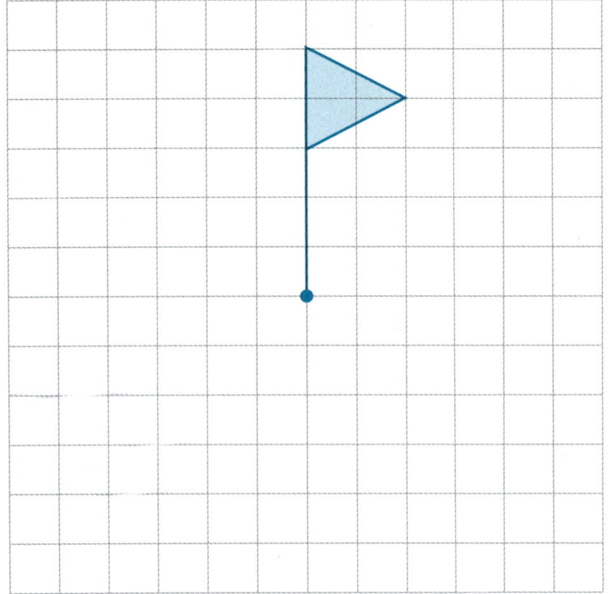

4 Rotate this figure 90° clockwise about the point.

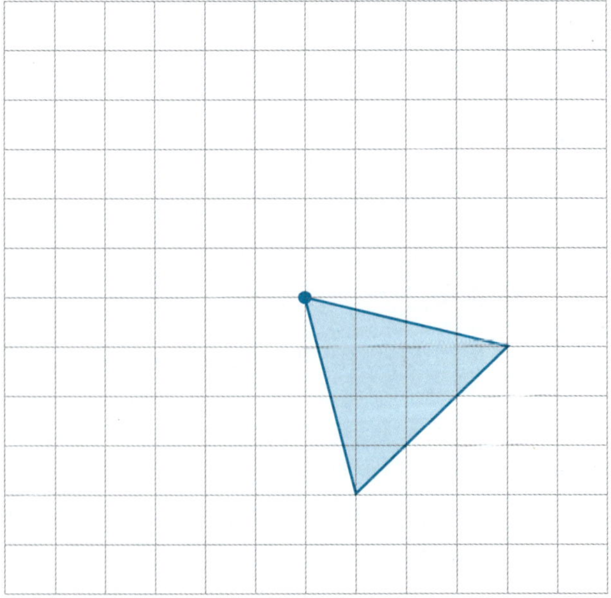

 ISBN: 9780170416016

5 Rotate this figure 180° clockwise about the point.

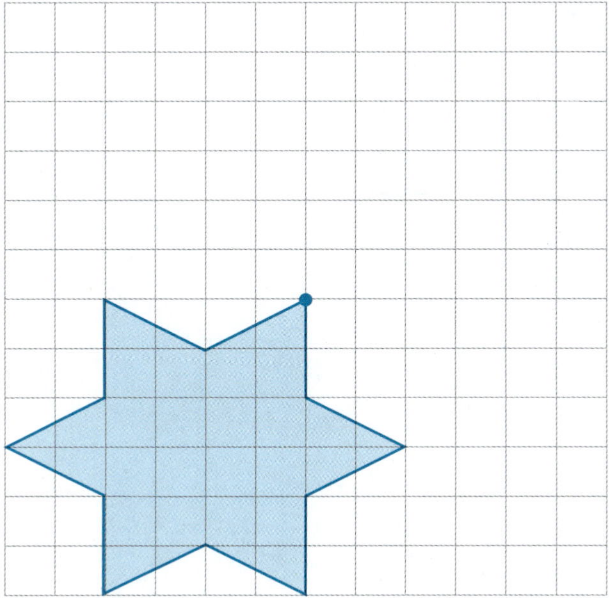

6 Rotate this figure 225° clockwise about the point.

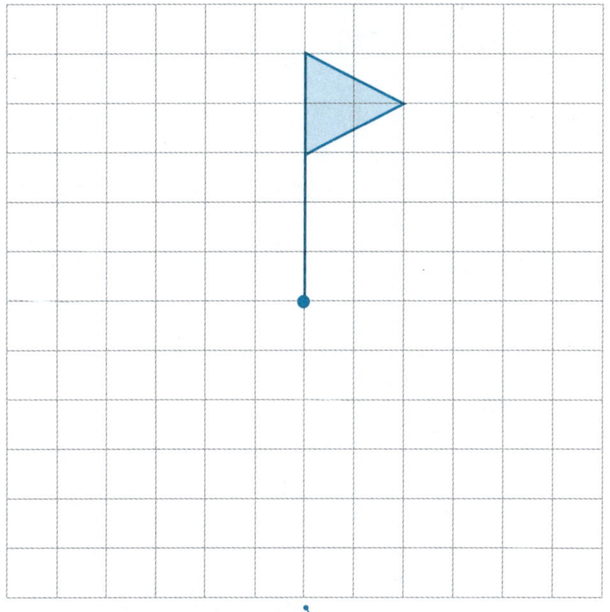

Hint: You will need to **measure** the lengths for question numbers **6–8**. Do not count squares.

7 Rotate this figure 45° clockwise about the point.

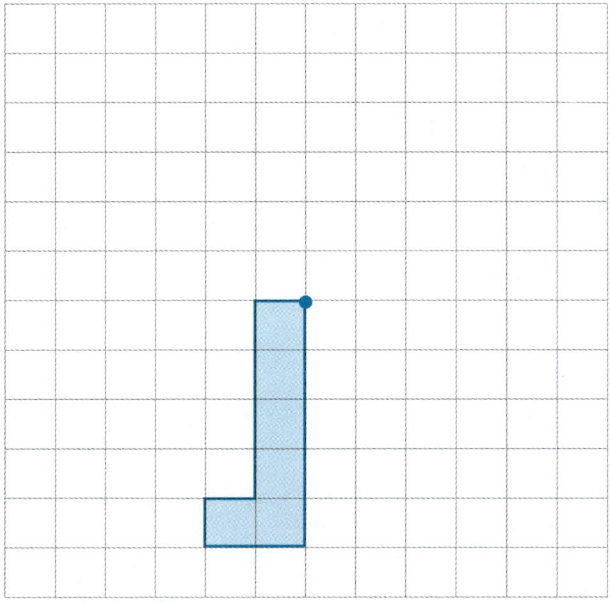

8 Rotate this figure 225° clockwise about the point.

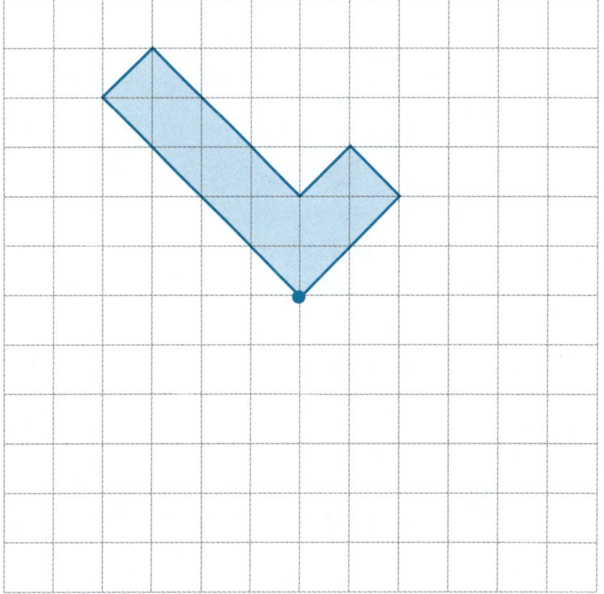

ISBN: 9780170416016

2 Rotations from an unattached point

Example: Rotate this figure clockwise by 270°.

Step 1

Select a critical point on the figure.

Draw a line between it and the centre.

Rotate the line by the required angle.

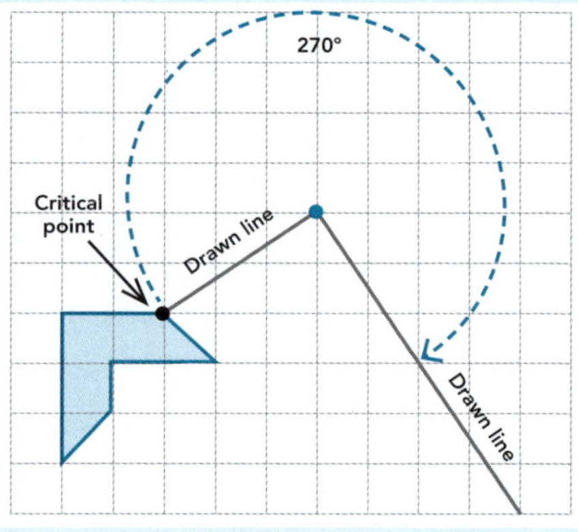

Step 2

Measure the distances or count squares from the centre to the critical point along this line.

Mark the position of this critical point on the image by measuring or counting squares along the drawn line.

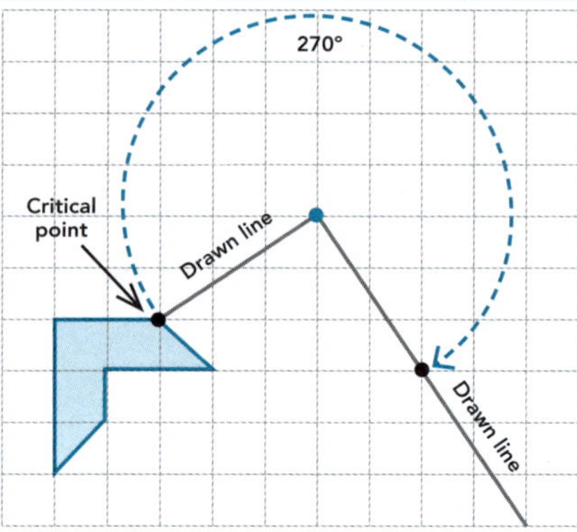

Step 3

Repeat the process with other critical points.

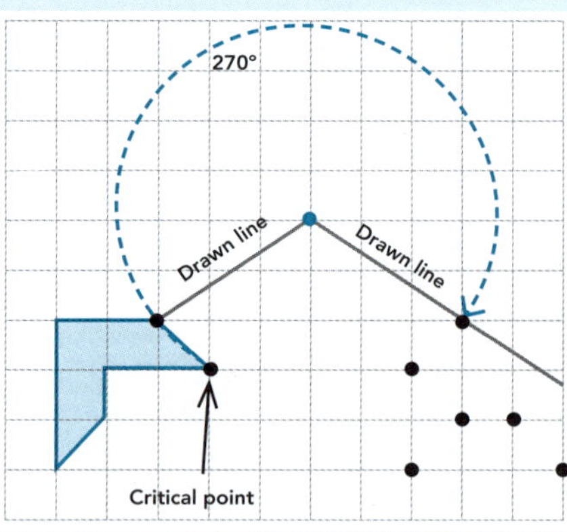

Step 4

Join the points.

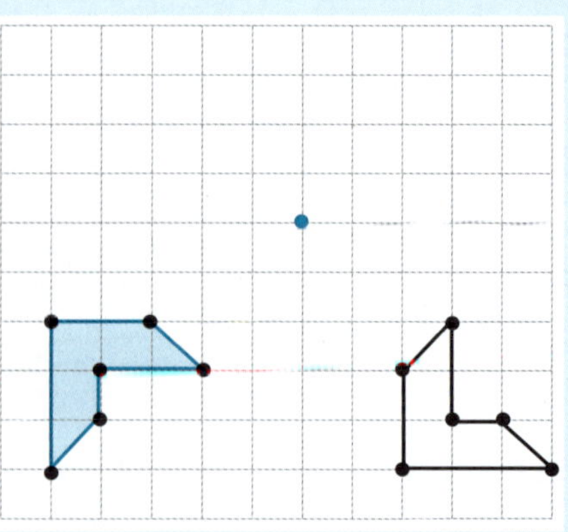

Note: Your teacher may provide you with tracing paper to help you do steps **2** and **3**.

 ISBN: 9780170416016

Draw the rotated images of the following figures.

1 Rotate this figure 180° clockwise about the point.

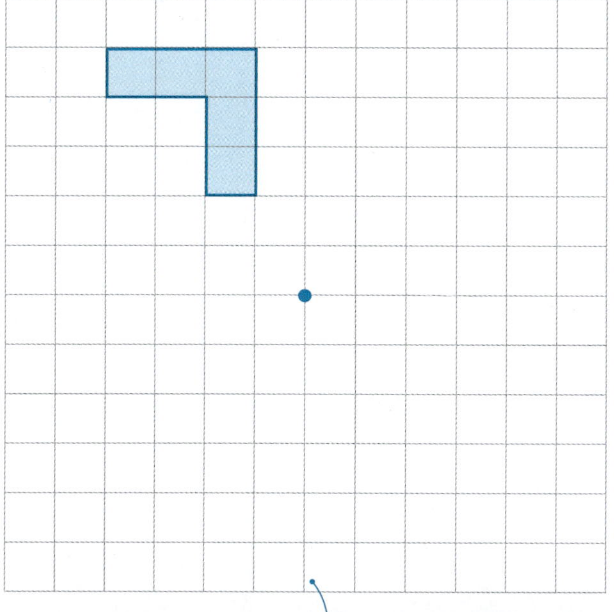

Don't forget, when you are rotating by 90°, 180° or 270°, you can work out where the critical points are by counting squares.

2 Rotate this figure 180° clockwise about the point.

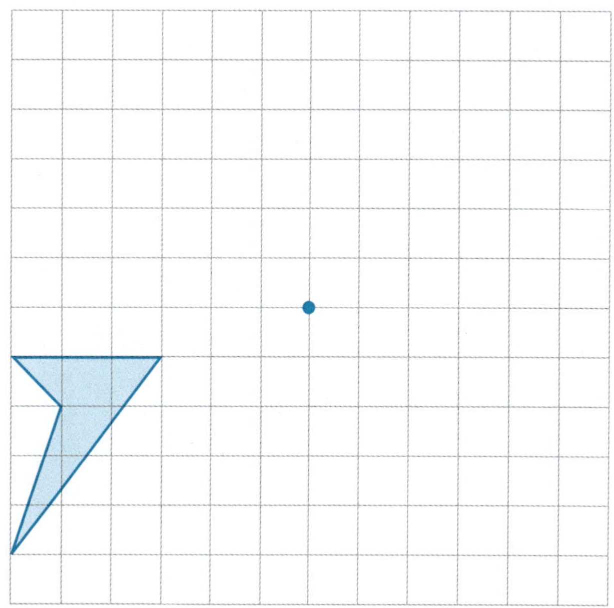

3 Rotate this figure 270° clockwise about the point.

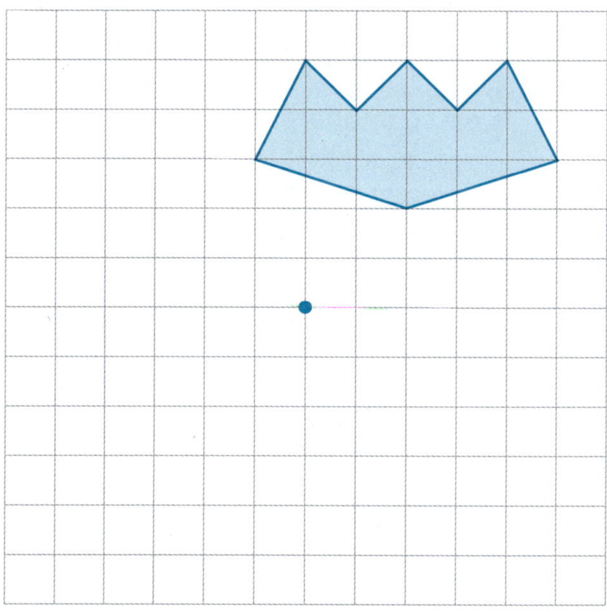

4 Rotate this figure 90° clockwise about the point.

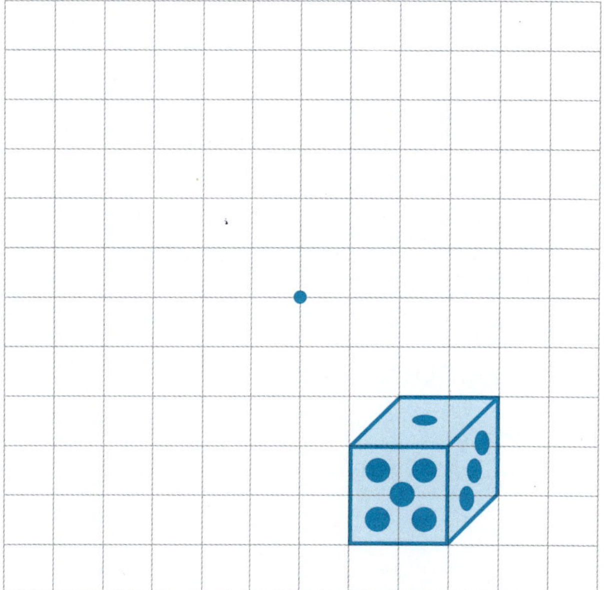

ISBN: 9780170416016

5 Rotate this figure 180° clockwise about the point.

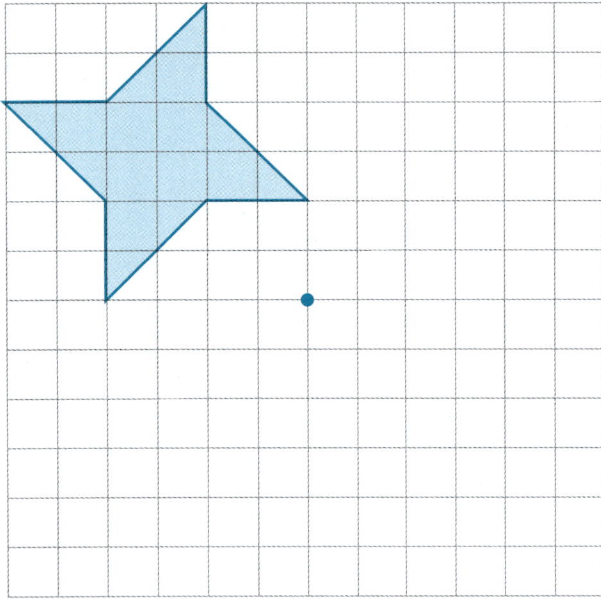

6 Rotate this figure 270° clockwise about the point.

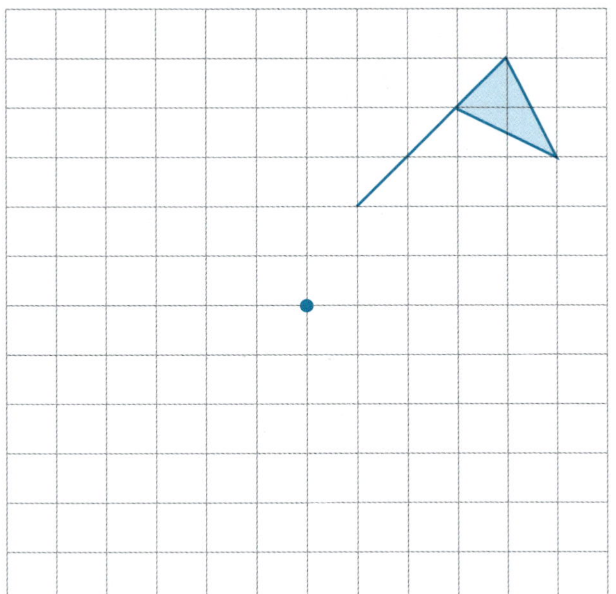

7 Rotate this figure 90° clockwise about the point.

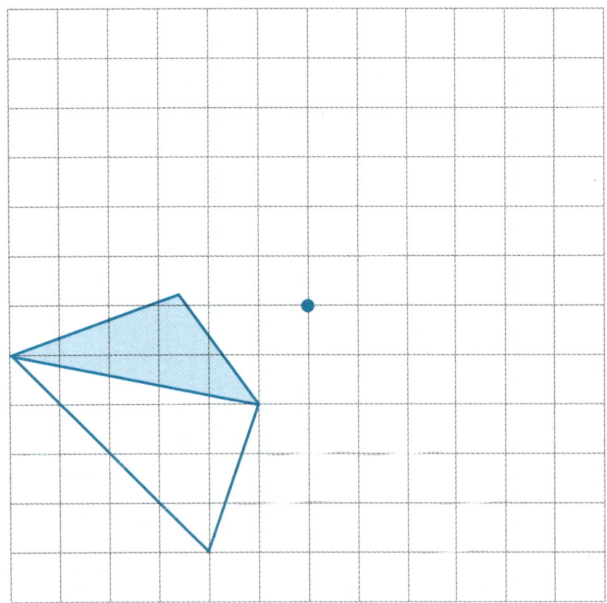

8 Rotate each of these lines by 90°, 180° and 270° clockwise about the point.

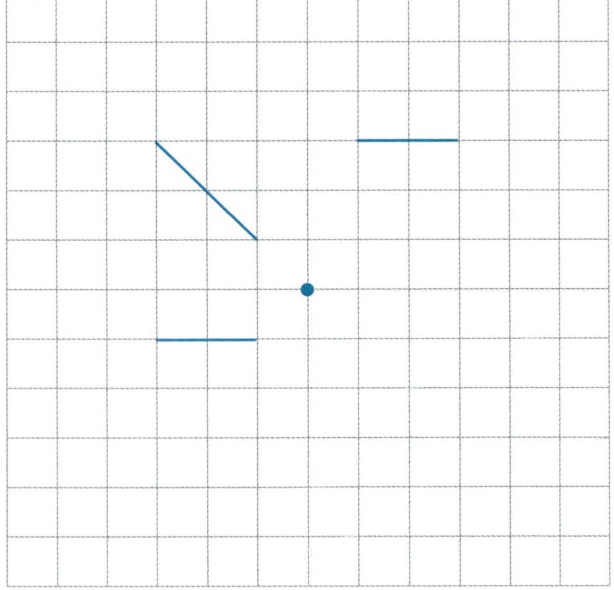

ISBN: 9780170416016

Rotational symmetry

- All figures can be rotated so they map onto themselves.
- The **number** of times that a figure can be rotated onto itself **within 360°** gives the **order of rotational symmetry**.
- Therefore **all** figures have, at least, **rotational symmetry** of order **1**.

Examples:

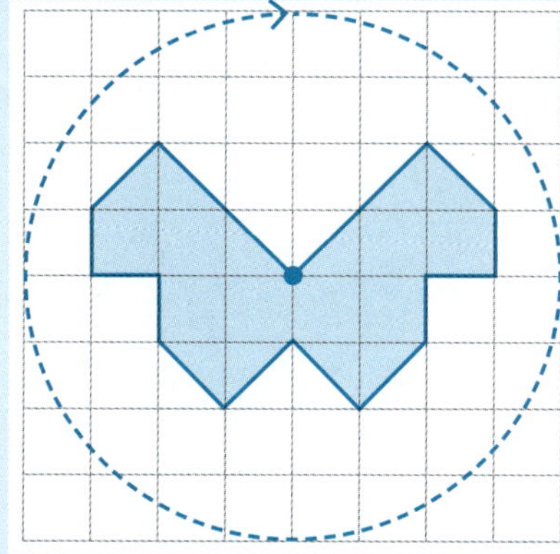

Order of rotational symmetry: 1

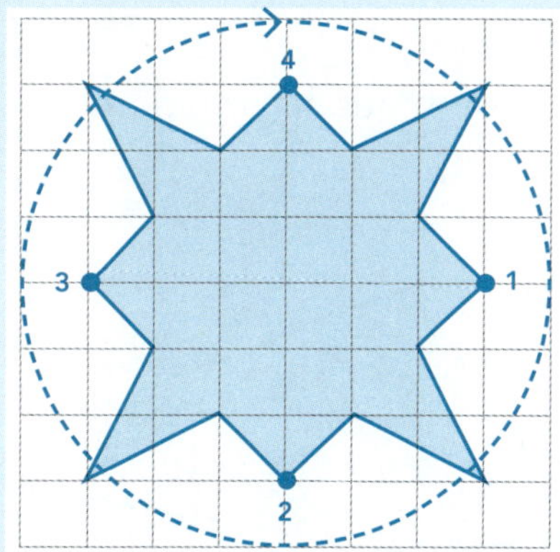

Order of rotational symmetry: 4

State the order of rotational of symmetry.

1

Order of rotational symmetry: ______

2

Order of rotational symmetry: ______

3

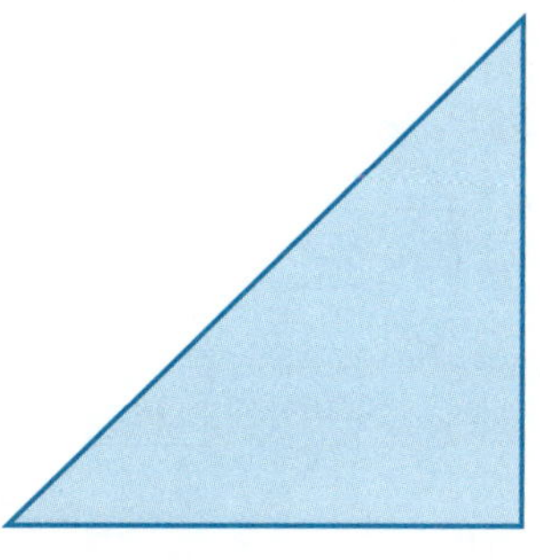

Order of rotational symmetry: ______

4

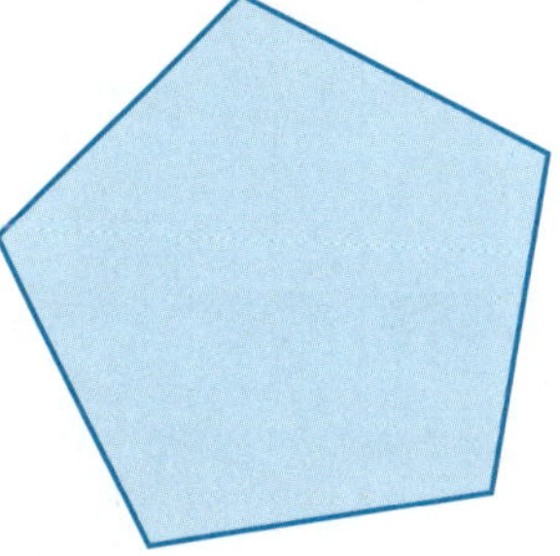

Order of rotational symmetry: ______

ISBN: 9780170416016

5

Order of rotational symmetry: ______

6

Order of rotational symmetry: ______

7

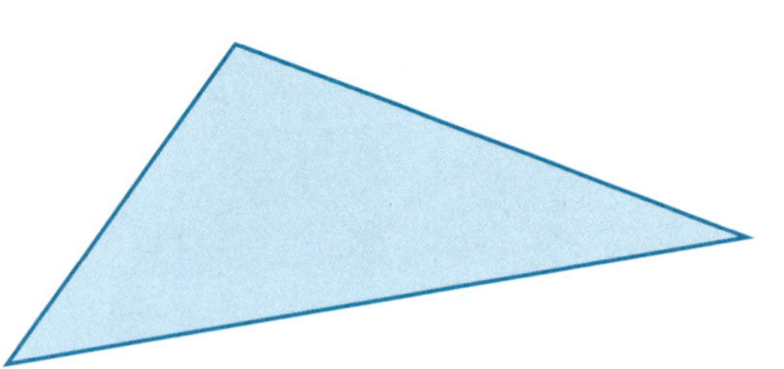

Order of rotational symmetry: ______

8

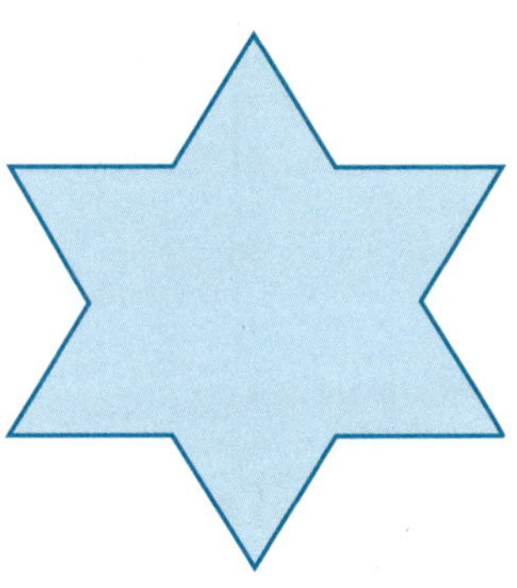

Order of rotational symmetry: ______

9

Order of rotational symmetry: ______

10

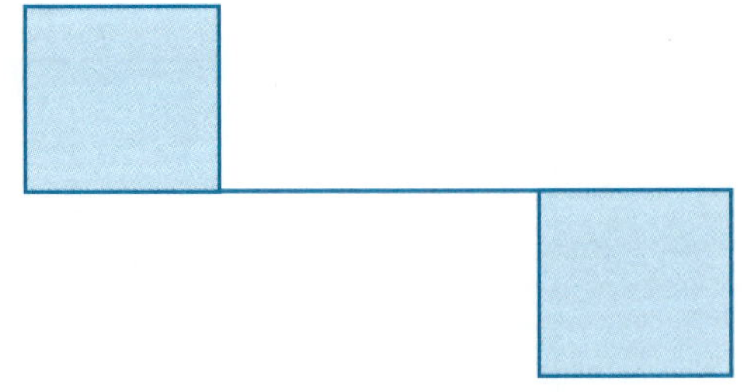

Order of rotational symmetry: ______

11

Order of rotational symmetry: ______

12

Order of rotational symmetry: ______

ISBN: 9780170416016

Challenges

1 Draw a figure with rotational symmetry of order 1.

2 Draw a figure with rotational symmetry of order 3.

3 Write the order of rotational symmetry for each of the following figures.

ISBN: 9780170416016

Mixing it up

Decide whether these figures have been translated, reflected or rotated. Remember the teal figure is the original.

- If they show translation, write a vector.
- If they show reflection, draw the mirror line(s).
- If they show rotation, mark the centre and write down the clockwise angle of rotation.
- Some could be more than one – give all possible transformations for these.

1 Translation/Reflection/Rotation

___

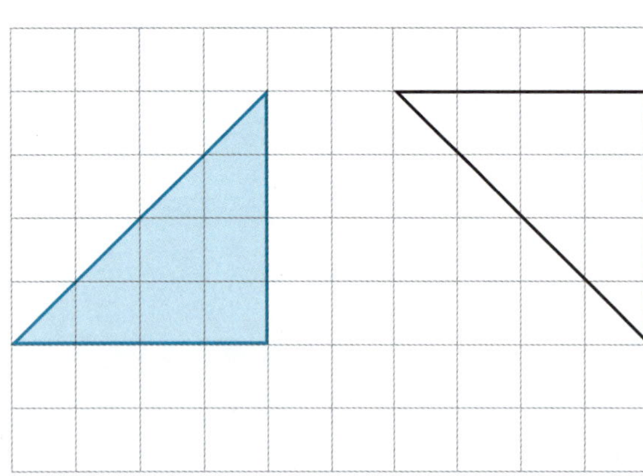

2 Translation/Reflection/Rotation

___

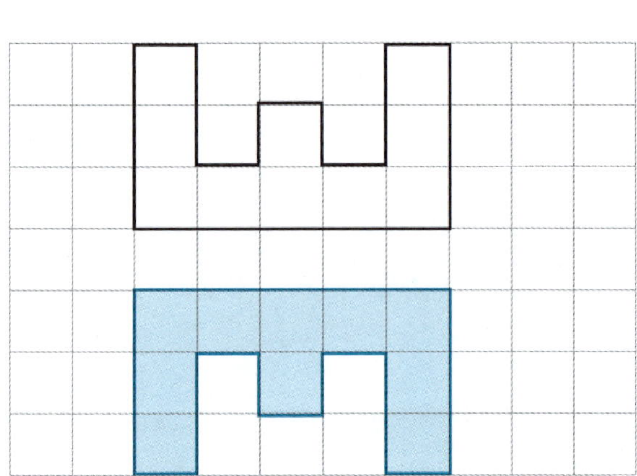

3 Translation/Reflection/Rotation

___

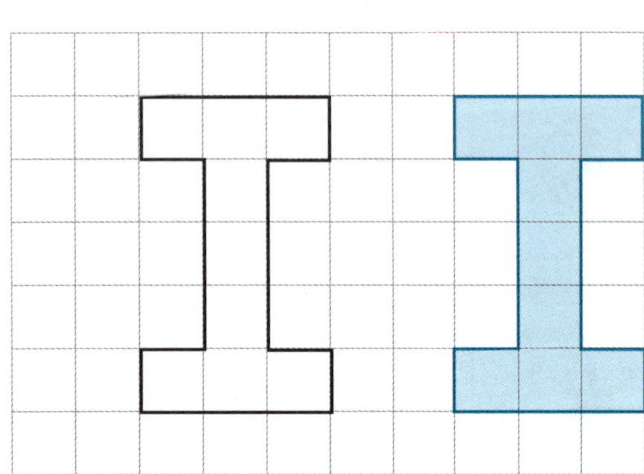

4 Translation/Reflection/Rotation

___

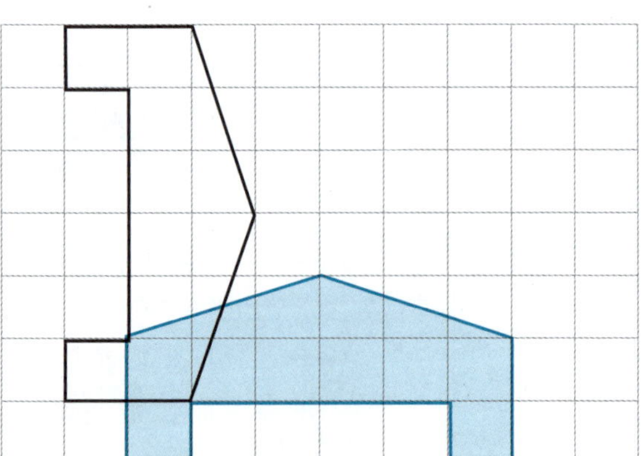

5 Translation/Reflection/Rotation

___

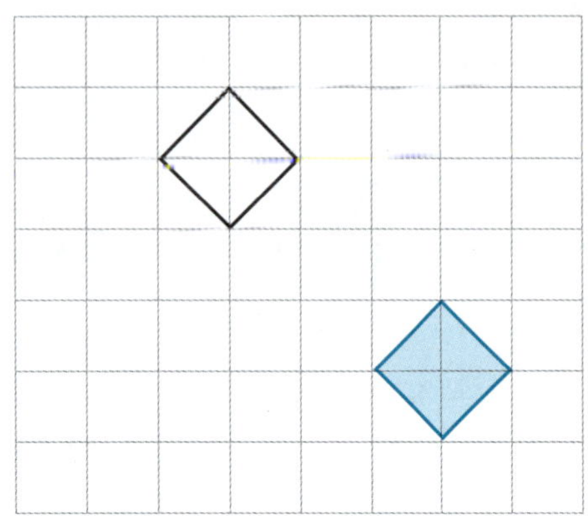

6 Translation/Reflection/Rotation

___

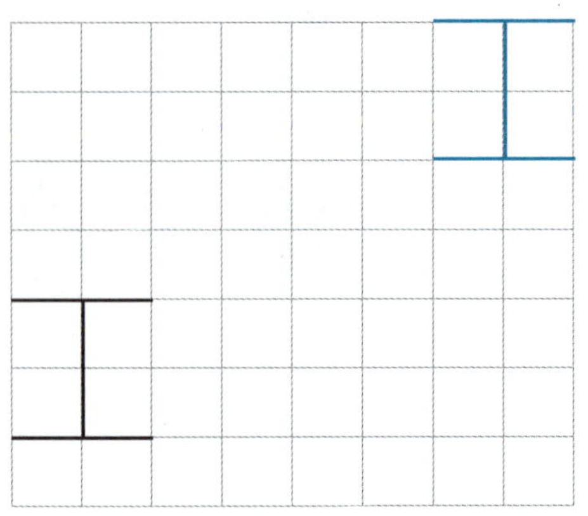

 ISBN: 9780170416016

Decide whether these figures show translation, reflection or rotation.

- If they show translation, draw a line around one unit which has been translated.
- If they show reflection, draw the mirror line(s).
- If they show rotation, mark the centre and write down the angle of rotation.

7

8

9

10

ISBN: 9780170416016

Enlargement

- Enlargement is changing the **size** and **position** of a figure.
- The **shape** and **orientation** of the figure stay **the same**.
- The **position** and **size** of the figure **change**.

Example:

Complete the table for enlargement:

	Stays the same	Changes
Size		✓
Shape		
Orientation		
Position		

 ISBN: 9780170416016

Describing enlargements

In order to describe an enlargement, **two** pieces of information are required:

1 the **scale factor**

2 the **centre** of enlargement.

1 Finding the scale factor

- The **scale factor (sf)** is the **ratio** of a length on the image to an equivalent length on the original figure.
- These are usually expressed as **whole numbers** or **fractions**.

$$\textbf{scale factor} = \frac{\textbf{length on image}}{\textbf{length on original figure}}$$

- Scale figure size: scale factor > 1 ⇒ image gets **larger**
  scale factor = 1 ⇒ image stays **the same size**
  scale factor > **0 and < 1** ⇒ image gets **smaller**

Examples:

1 Original figure

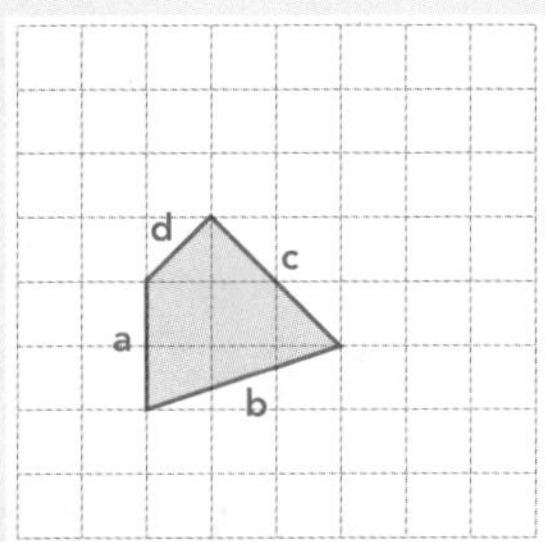

Image

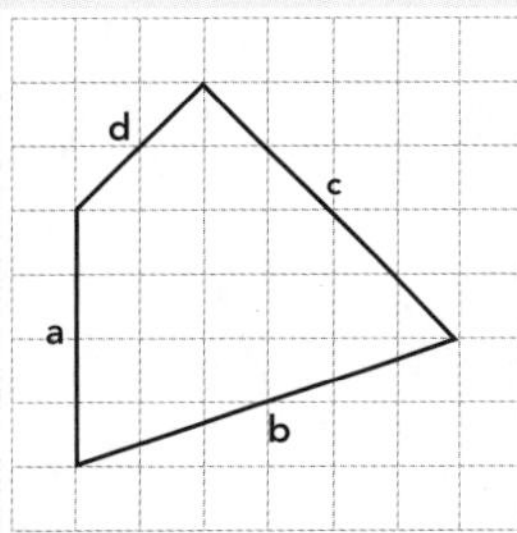

Note: It doesn't matter which sides you use for your calculation:

Side a: scale factor = $\frac{\text{4 units up}}{\textbf{2 units up}}$ **= 2**

Side b: scale factor = $\frac{\text{6 units across and 2 units up}}{\textbf{3 units across and 1 unit up}}$ **= 2**

Side c: scale factor = $\frac{\text{4 diagonal units}}{\textbf{2 diagonal units}}$ **= 2**

Side d: scale factor = $\frac{\text{2 units across and 2 units up}}{\textbf{1 units across and 1 unit up}}$ **= 2**

2 Original figure

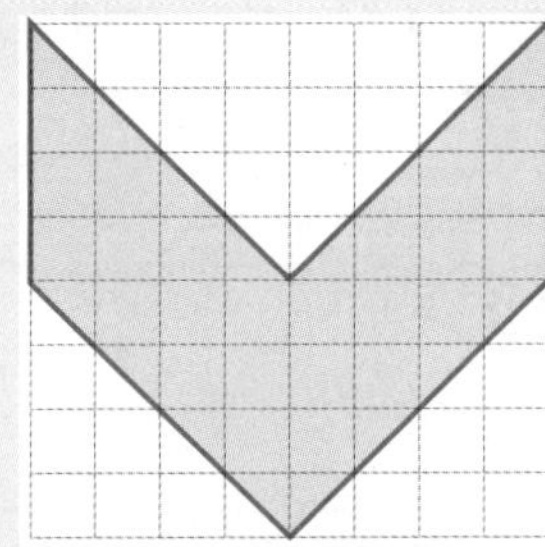

Image

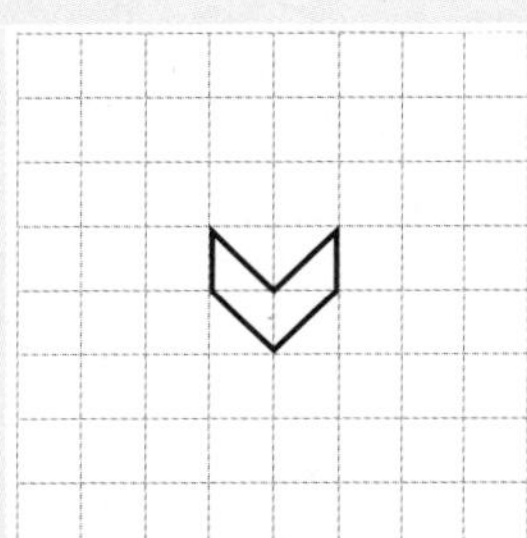

scale factor = $\frac{\text{1 unit}}{\textbf{4 units}} = \frac{1}{4}$

ISBN: 9780170416016

Write down the scale factor for each of these images.

1

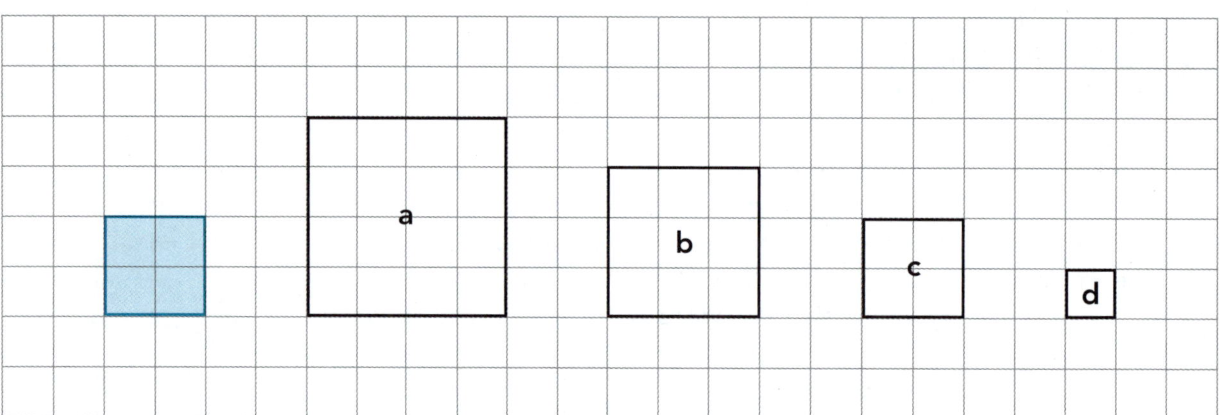

a sf = $\frac{4}{2}$ = ______ **b** sf = ______ **c** sf = ______ **d** sf = ______

2

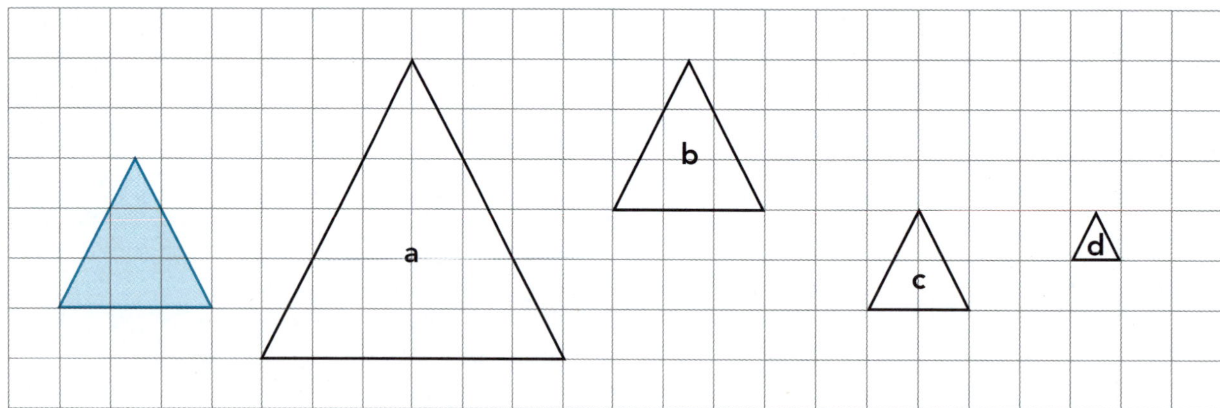

a sf = ______ **b** sf = ______ **c** sf = ______ **d** sf = ______

3

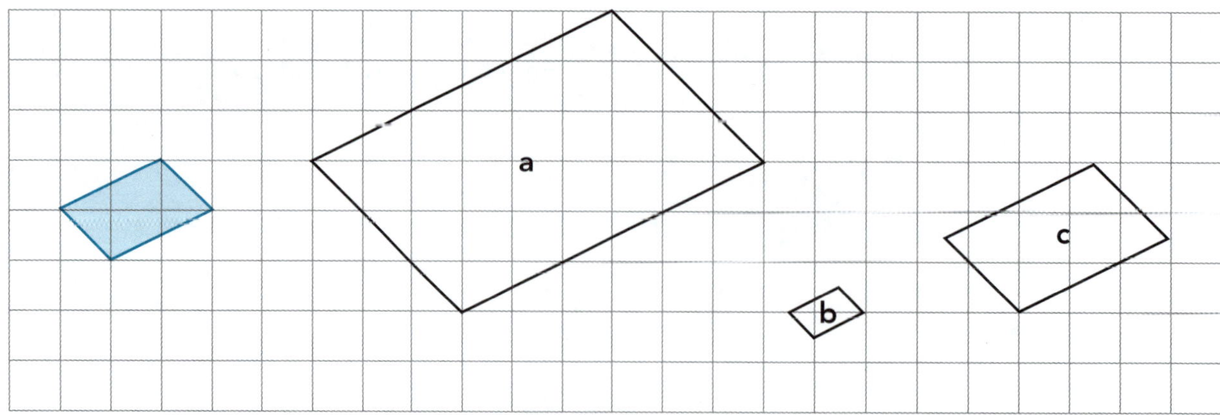

a sf = ______ **b** sf = ______ **c** sf = ______

ISBN: 9780170416016

2 Finding the centre of enlargement

- Enlargement is always done from a focal point called the **centre of enlargement**.

To find the centre of enlargement:

Step 1: Rule lines through **equivalent** points on the original figure and the image (-----).

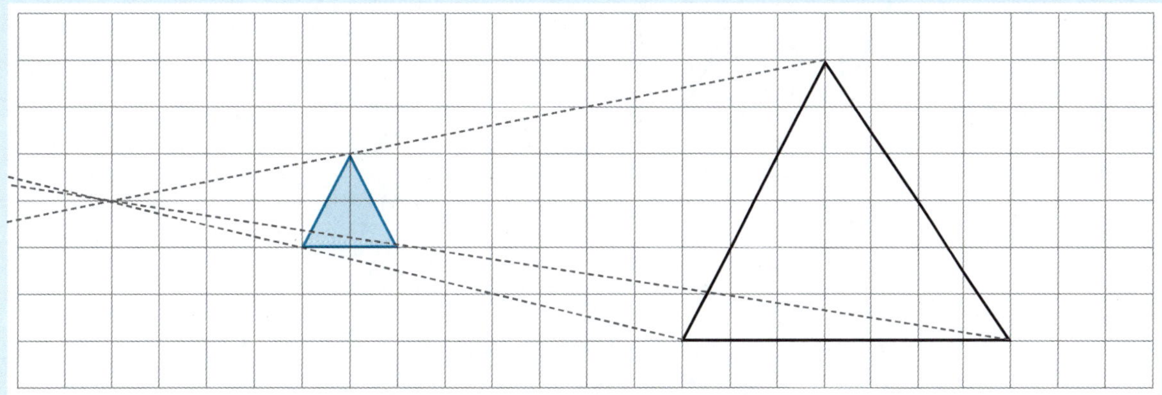

Step 2: The centre of enlargement is the point where they all meet.

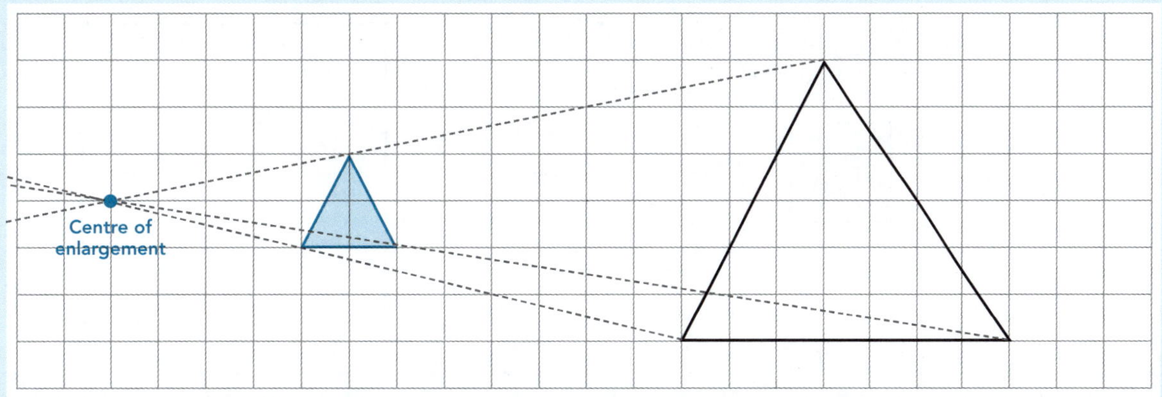

In this case, the image is **larger** than the original figure, so the **image** is on the **far** side of the centre of enlargement and the original figure.

In the case below, the image is **smaller** than the original figure, so the **image** is **between** the centre of enlargement and the original figure.

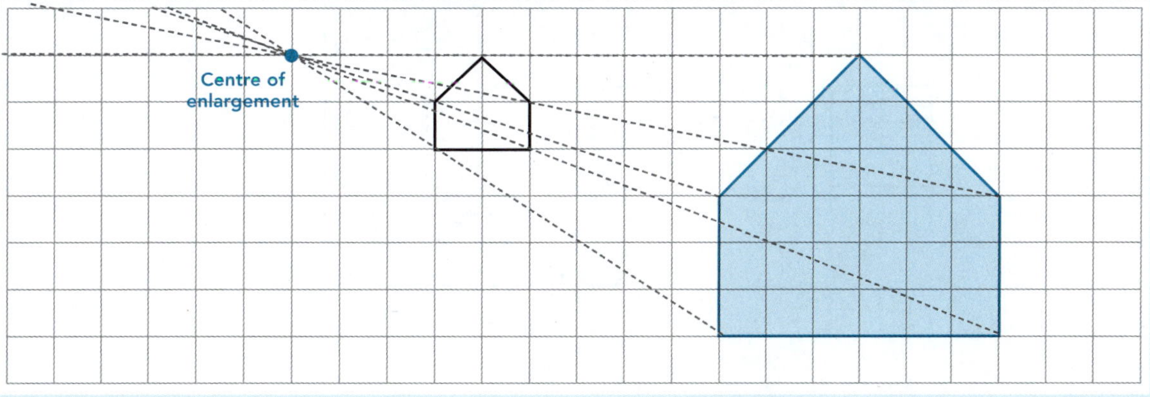

ISBN: 9780170416016

Find the centre of enlargement for the following figures and their images. Write down the scale factor in each case.

1

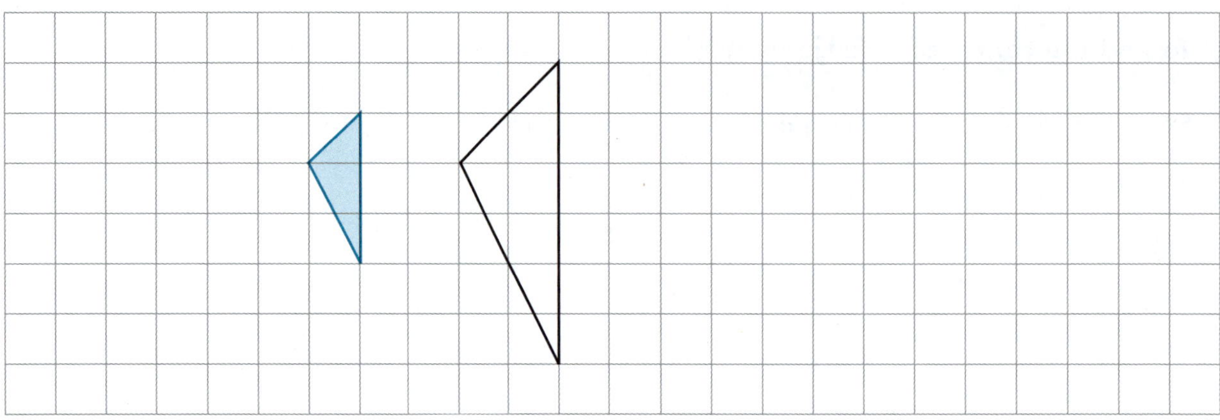

Scale factor = ______

2

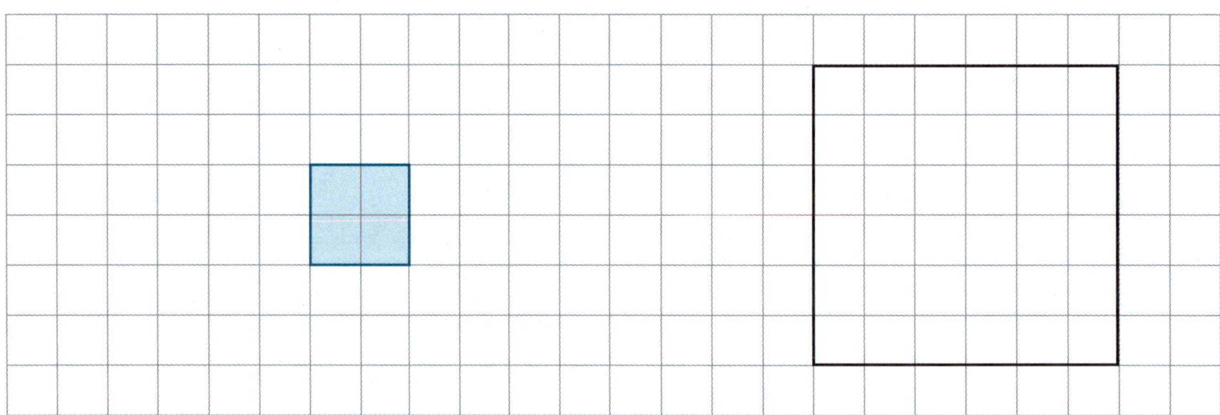

Scale factor = ______

3

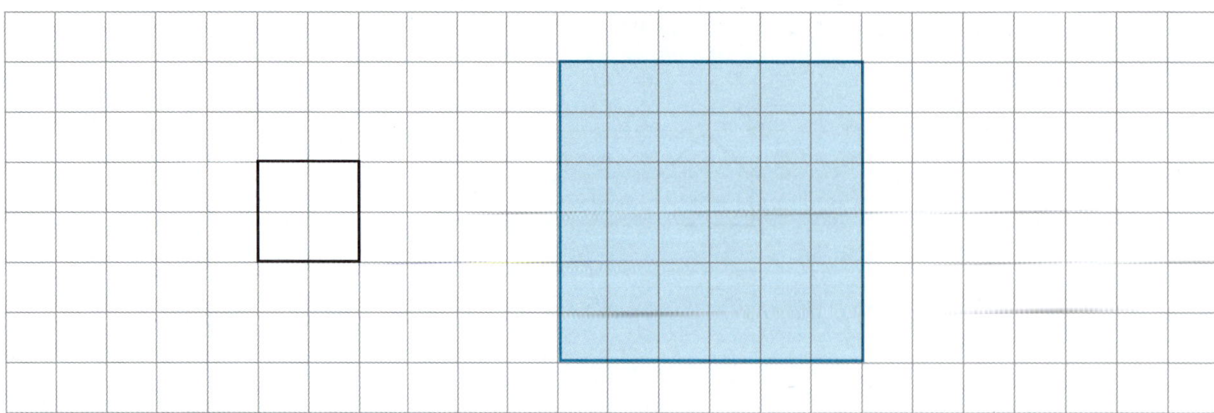

Scale factor = ______

 ISBN: 9780170416016

4

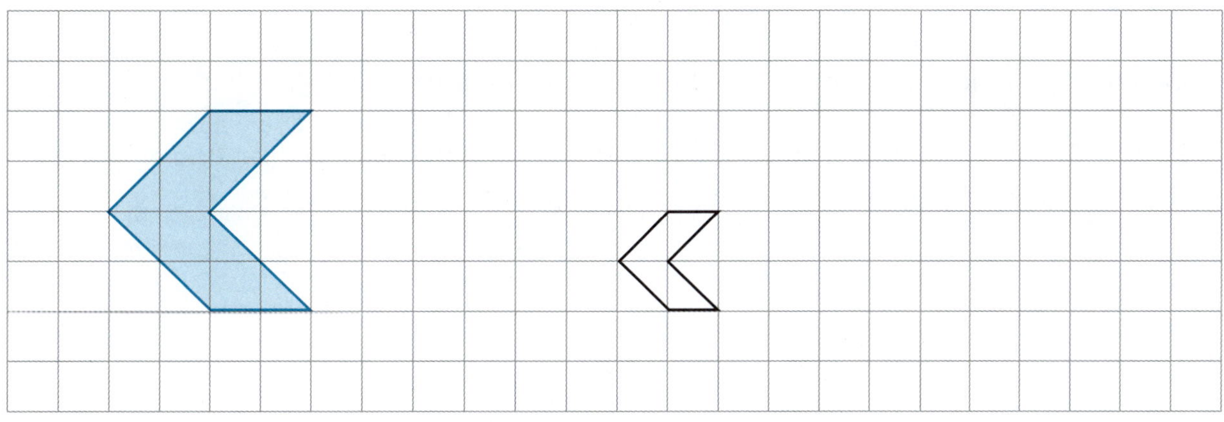

Scale factor = ______

5

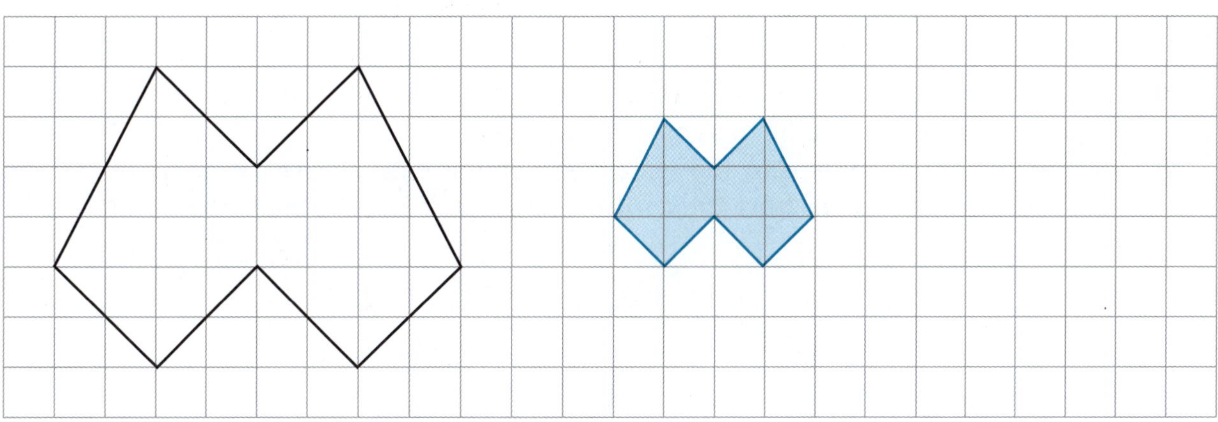

Scale factor = ______

6

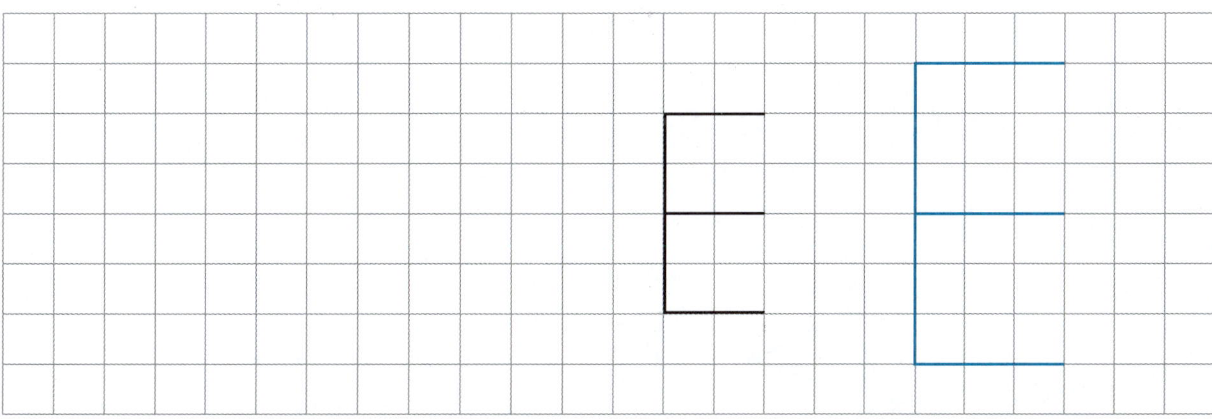

Scale factor = ______

ISBN: 9780170416016

Drawing enlargements

Example: Enlarge the figure from centre A, by a scale factor of 3.

Step 1: Rule lines from the centre of enlargement through each significant point on the original figure.

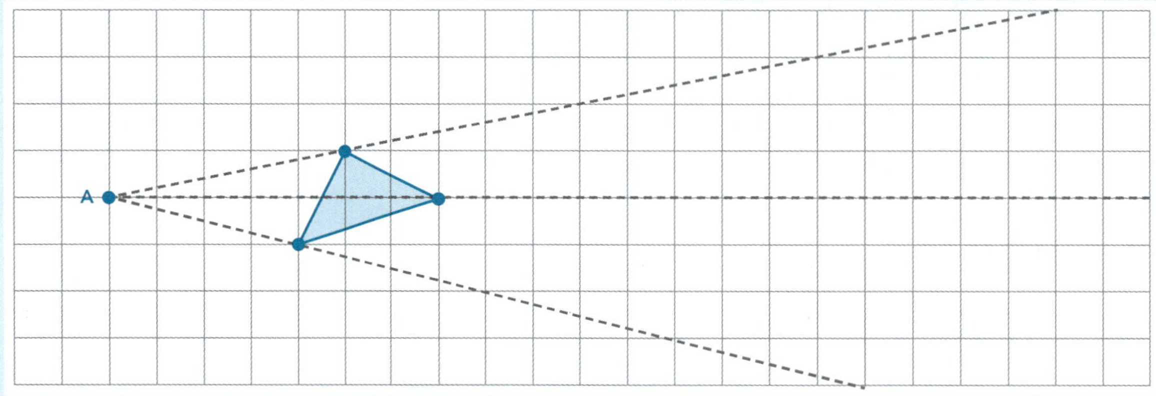

Step 2: Count the number of squares between the centre of enlargement and a significant point on the figure (in this case, across 5 and up 1).
Multiply the number of squares by the scale factor (in this case across 15 and up 3).
Count this number of squares from the **centre** of enlargement, and mark the point.

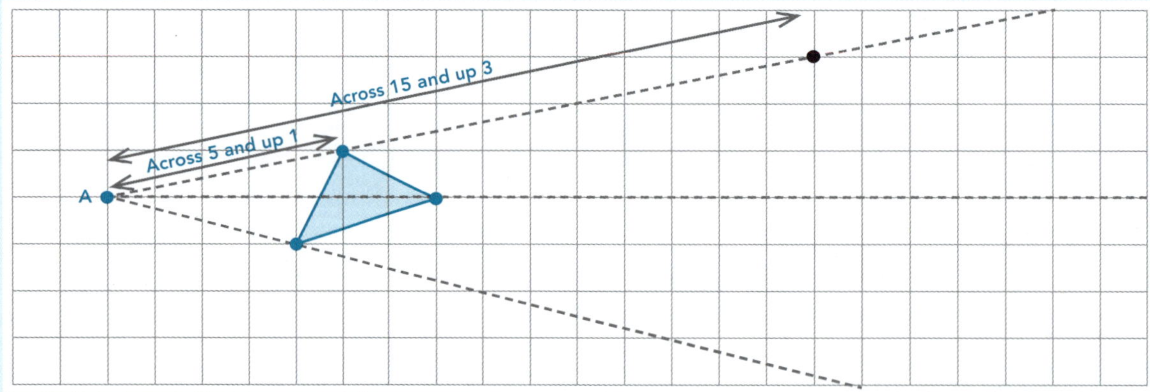

Step 3: Repeat with the remaining significant points.

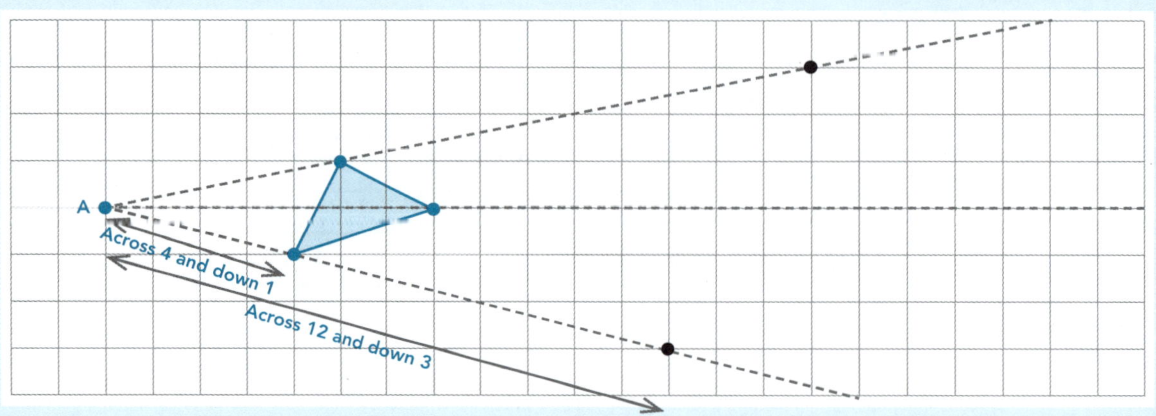

ISBN: 9780170416016

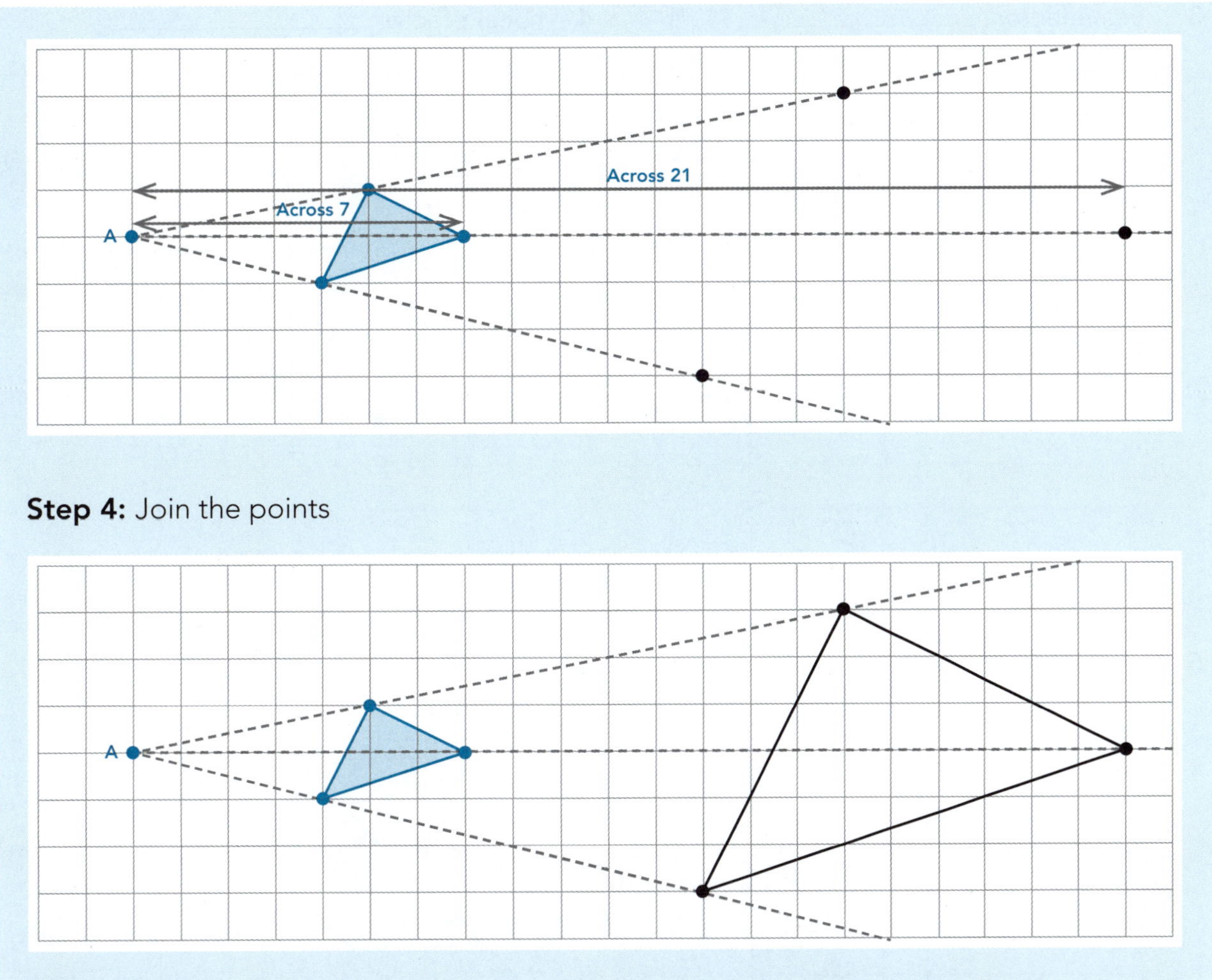

Step 4: Join the points

Note: If you don't have grid paper, you will need to **measure** every length.

Draw all the lines and points required to complete these enlargements (some have been done for you). State the scale factor for each.

1 Scale factor ____________

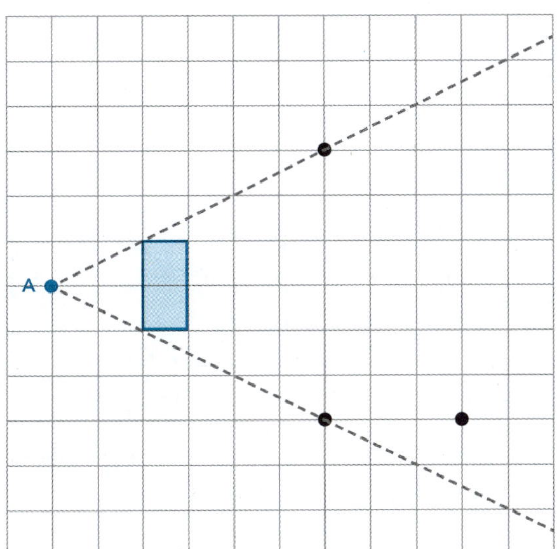

2 Scale factor ____________

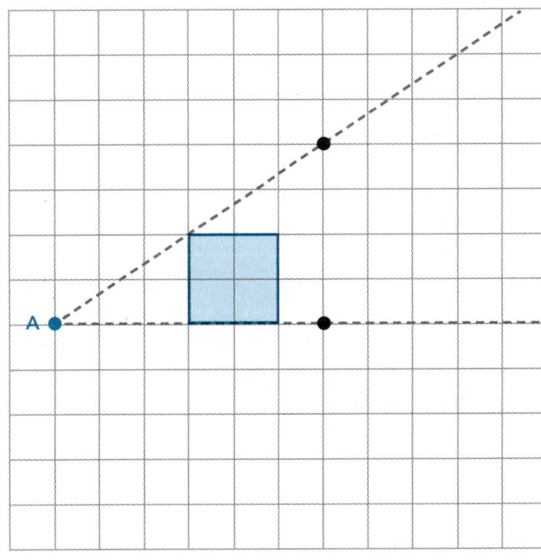

ISBN: 9780170416016

3 Scale factor ____________

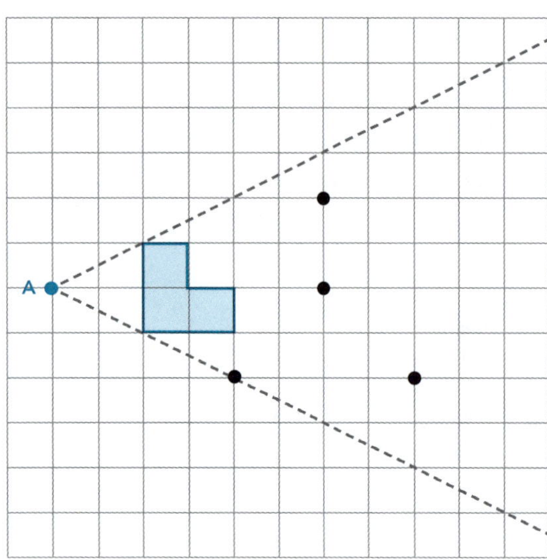

4 Scale factor ____________

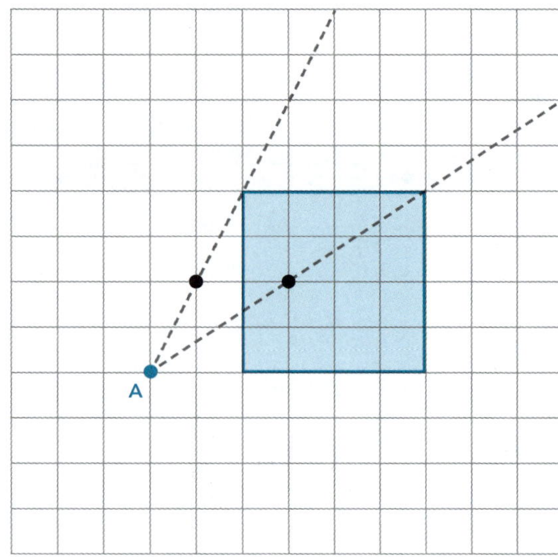

5 Scale factor ____________

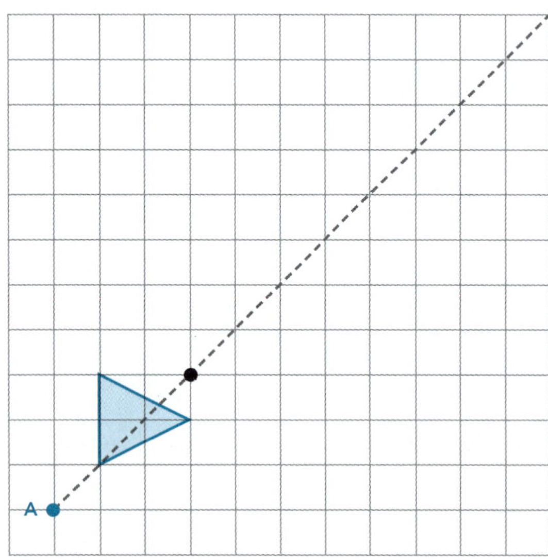

6 Scale factor ____________

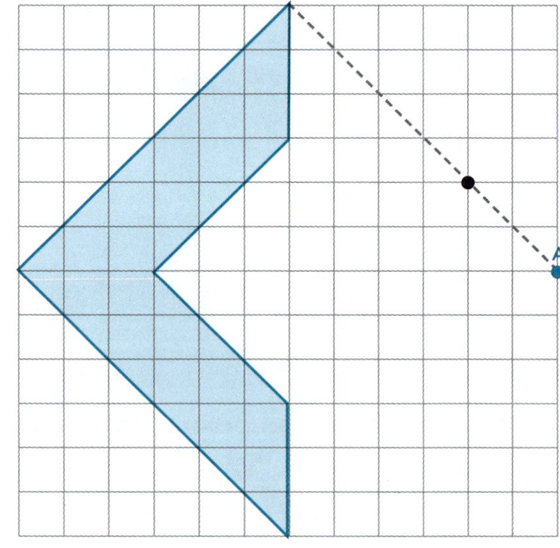

Draw the following enlargements.

7 Scale factor = 3

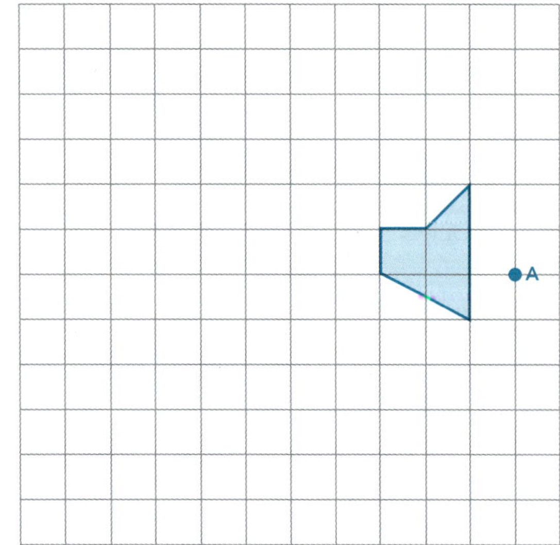

8 Scale factor = $\frac{1}{2}$

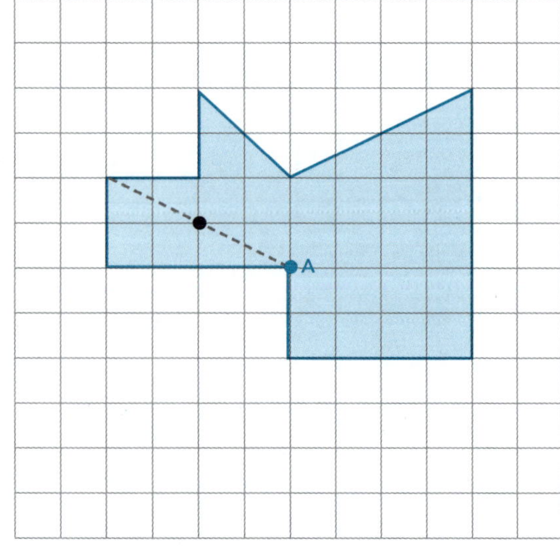

 ISBN: 9780170416016

9 Scale factor = 3

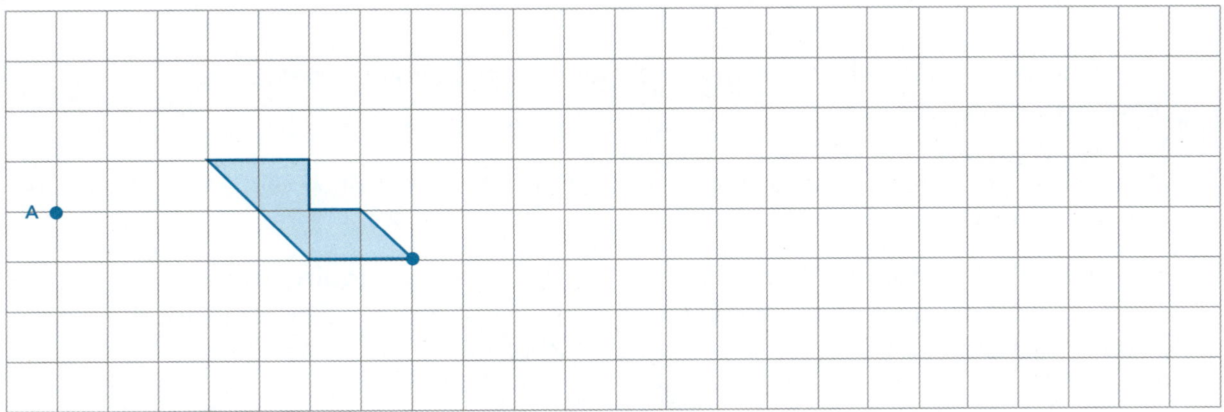

10 Scale factor = $\frac{1}{3}$

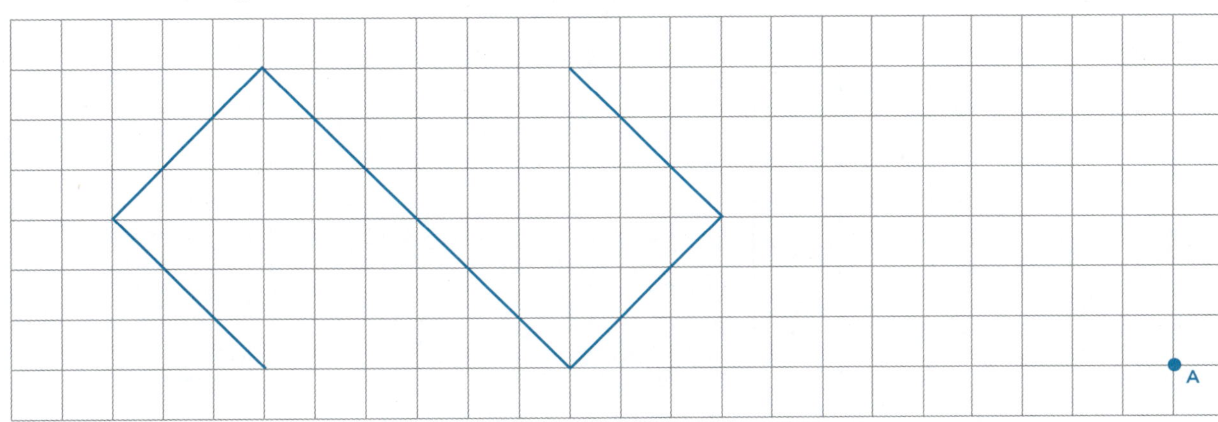

11 Scale factor = 2

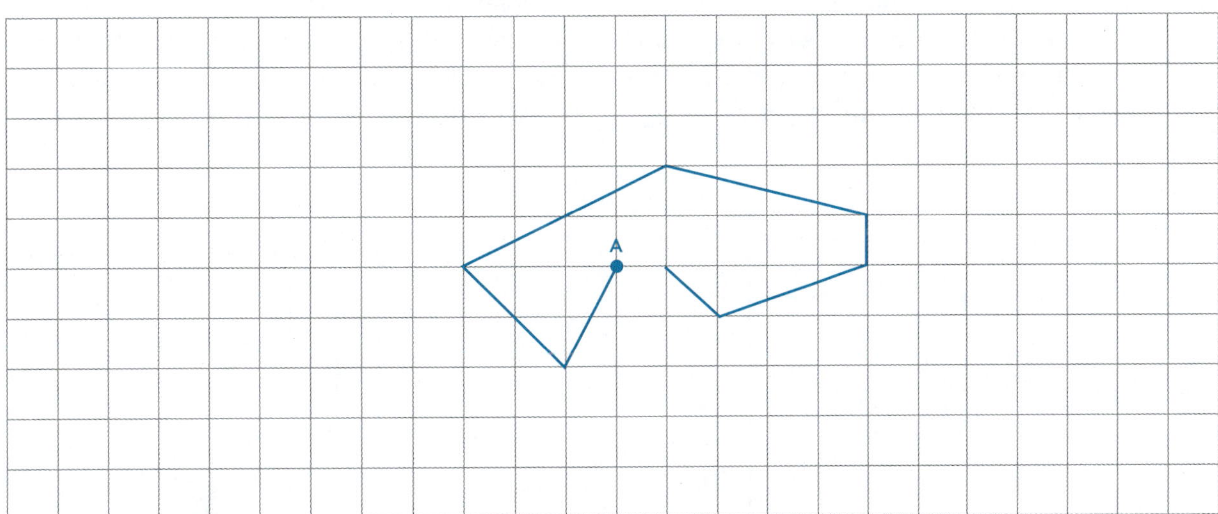

Recognising enlargements

There are two factors which you must consider when deciding whether figures are enlargements of each other:

1 Is the **scale factor** the **same** for all parts of the figures? In other words, are the figures the **same shape**?

These figures **could** be enlargements because the scale factor is the **same** for both sides:

$\frac{6}{3} = \frac{2}{1} \Rightarrow$ Scale factor = 2

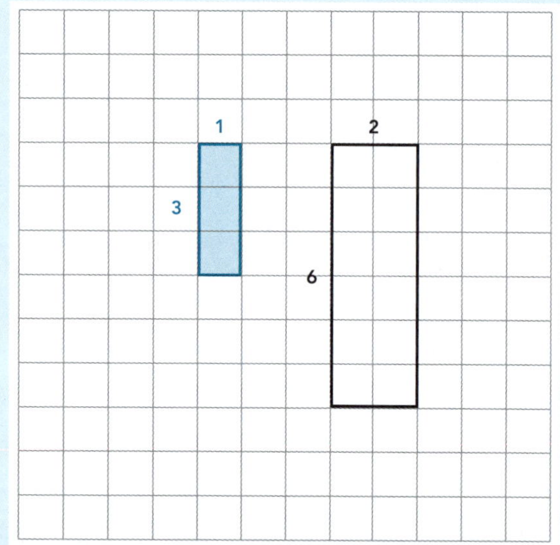

These figures **could not** be enlargements because the scale factor is **not** the **same** for both sides:

$\frac{7}{3} \neq \frac{2}{1}$

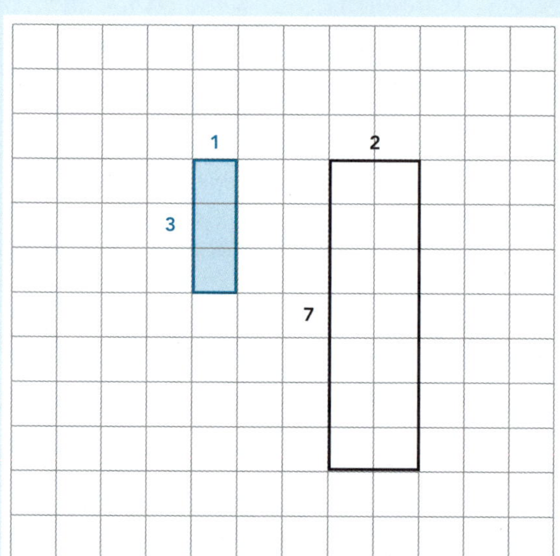

2 Are the figures **orientated** the **same** way?

These figures **could** be enlargements as they are orientated the **same** way and because lines drawn through equivalent points all meet at **one** point.

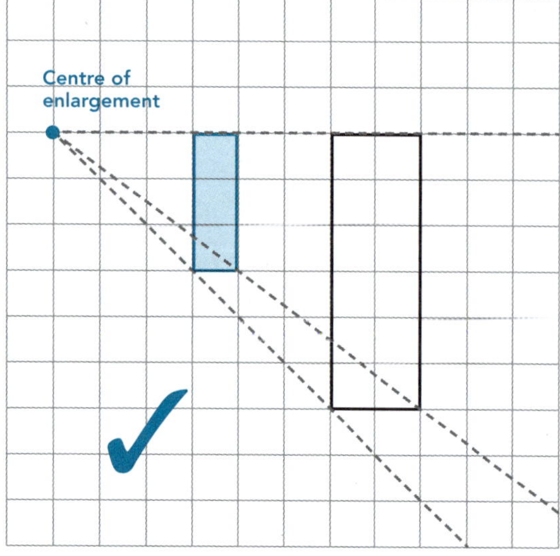

These figures **could not** be enlargements because they are **not** orientated the same way, so lines drawn through equivalent points **do not** all meet at **one** point.

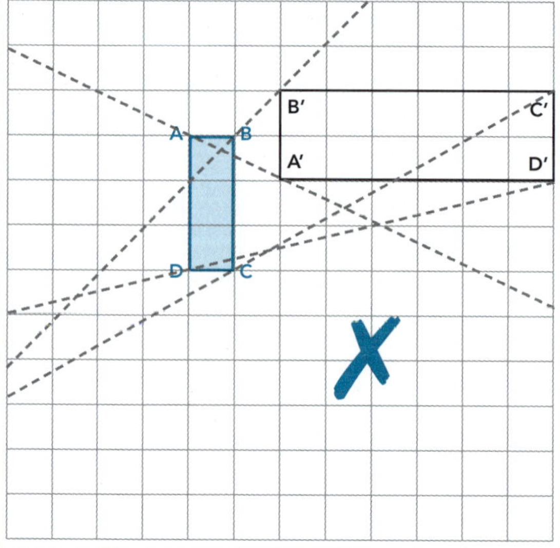

 ISBN: 9780170416016

Decide whether these figures have been enlarged or not. If they have, write the scale factor. Give reasons for your answers.

1

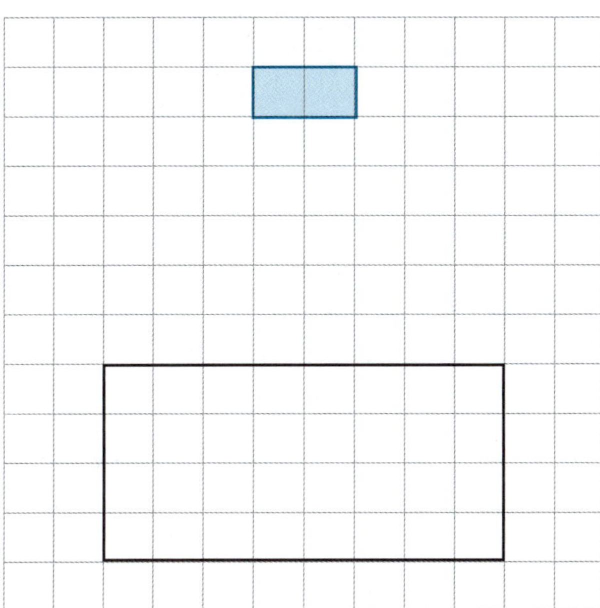

Enlargement/Not an enlargement

Reason: ______________________________

____

____

2

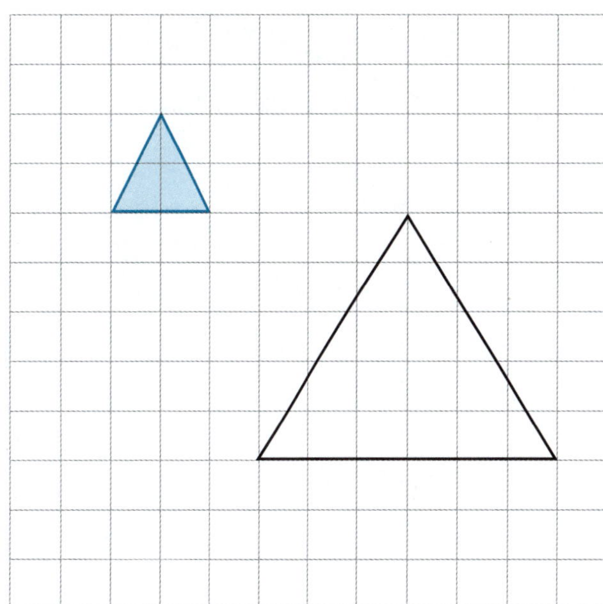

Enlargement/Not an enlargement

Reason: ______________________________

____

____

3

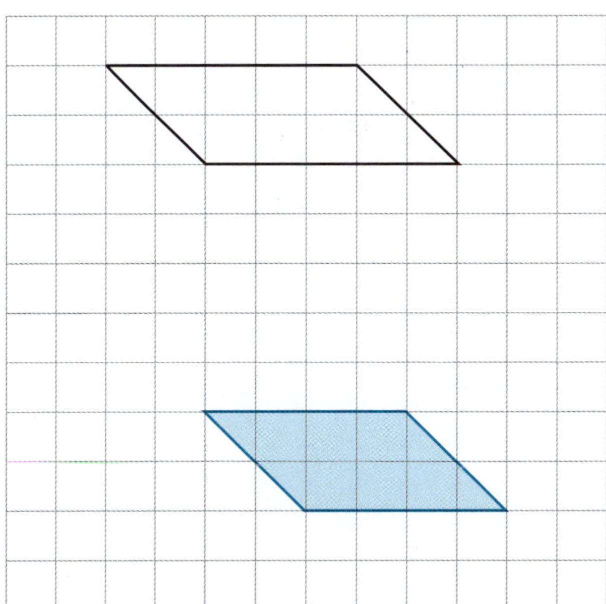

Enlargement/Not an enlargement

Reason: ______________________________

____

____

4

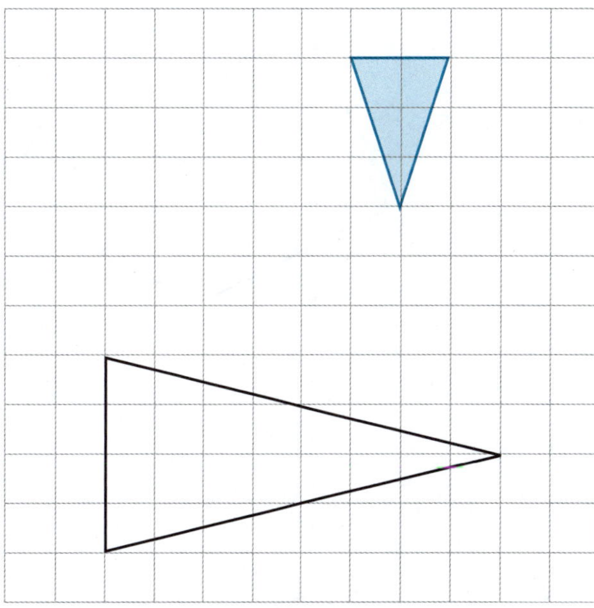

Enlargement/Not an enlargement

Reason: ______________________________

____

____

ISBN: 9780170416016

5

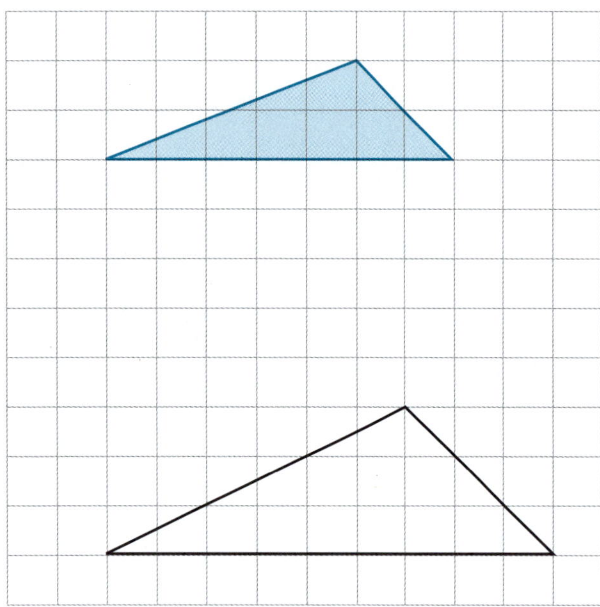

Enlargement/Not an enlargement

Reason: ______________________________

____

____

6

Enlargement/Not an enlargement

Reason: ______________________________

____

____

7

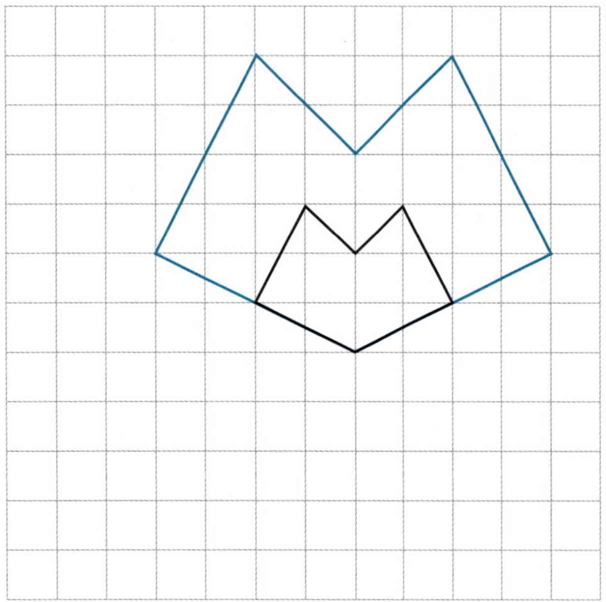

Enlargement/Not an enlargement

Reason: ______________________________

____

____

8

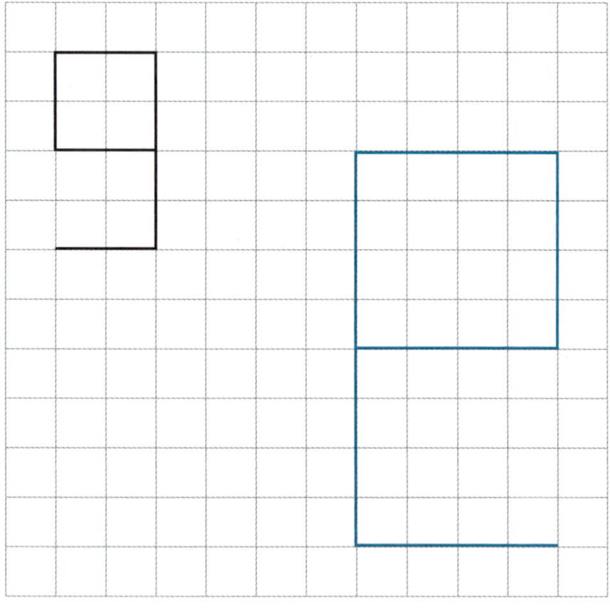

Enlargement/Not an enlargement

Reason: ______________________________

____

____

ISBN: 9780170416016

Challenges

Drawing enlargements without a grid

Draw the following enlargements by measuring lengths instead of counting squares.

1 Scale factor = 2

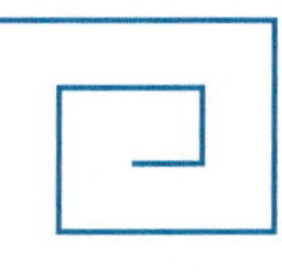

2 Scale factor = $\frac{1}{2}$

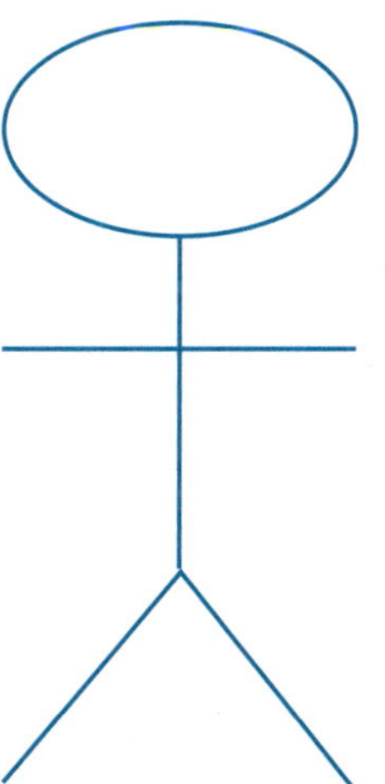

ISBN: 9780170416016

Negative scale factors

- A figure and its image have a **negative scale factor** if they are on the **opposite** side of the centre of enlargement.
- When the scale factor is **negative**, the image will appear **upside down** and **back to front** when compared with the original figure.

Examples:

Scale factor = –1

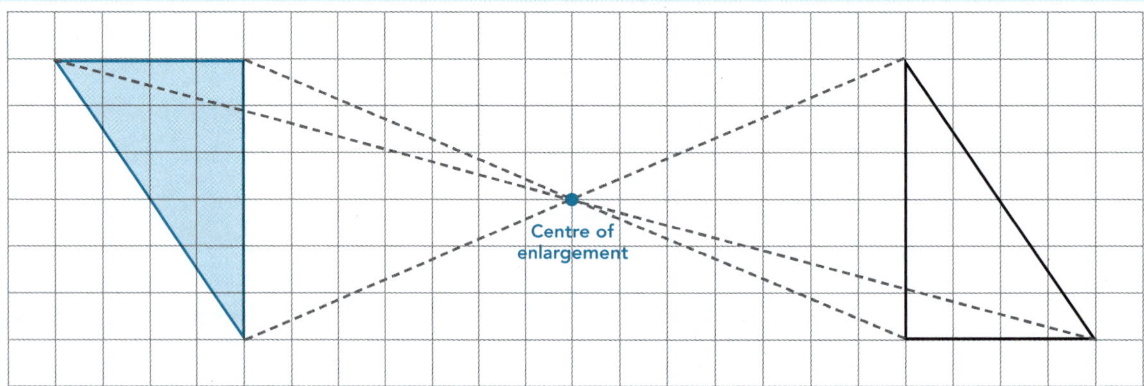

Notice: This is the same as a rotation of 180°.

Scale factor = $-\frac{1}{2}$

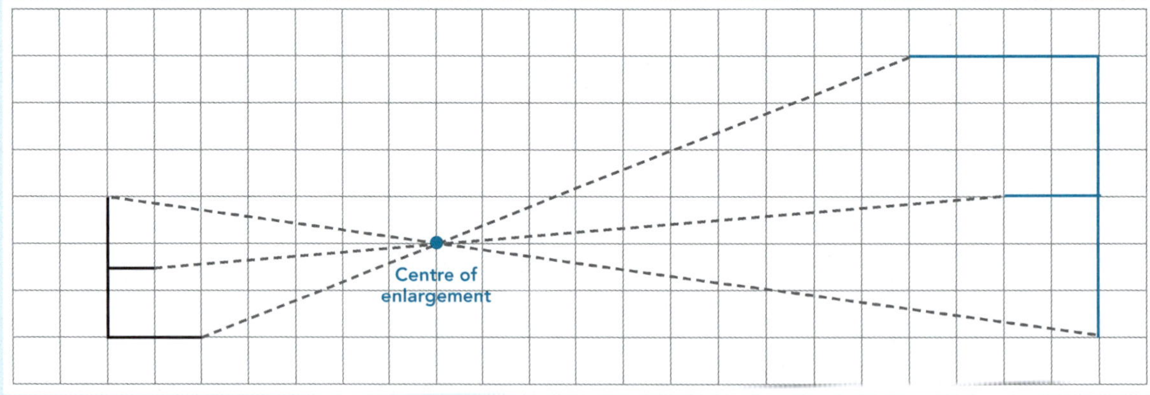

ISBN: 9780170416016

Write down the scale factor and mark the centre for the following enlargements. All scale factors are negative.

1

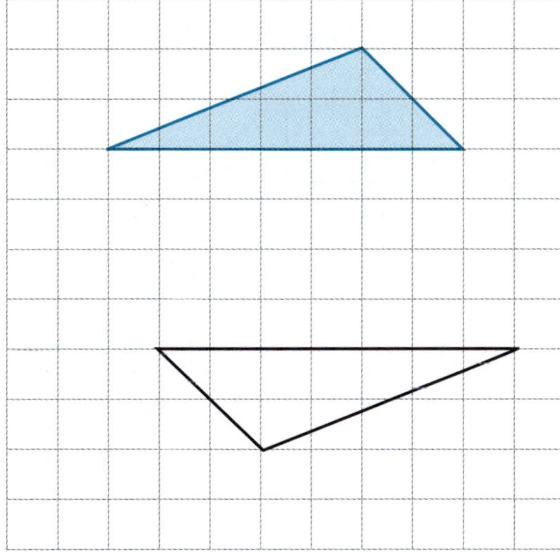

Scale factor = ______

2

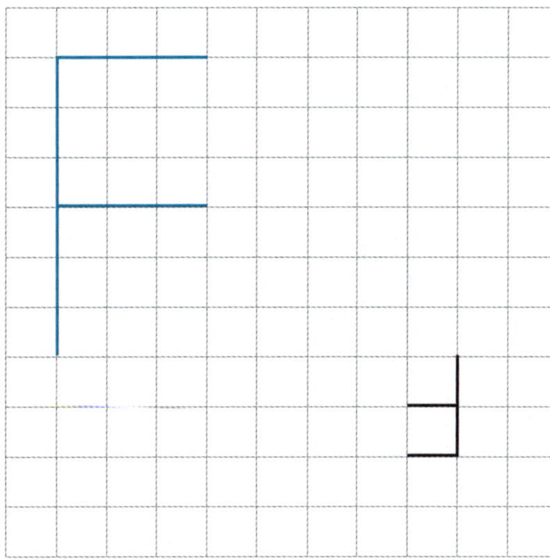

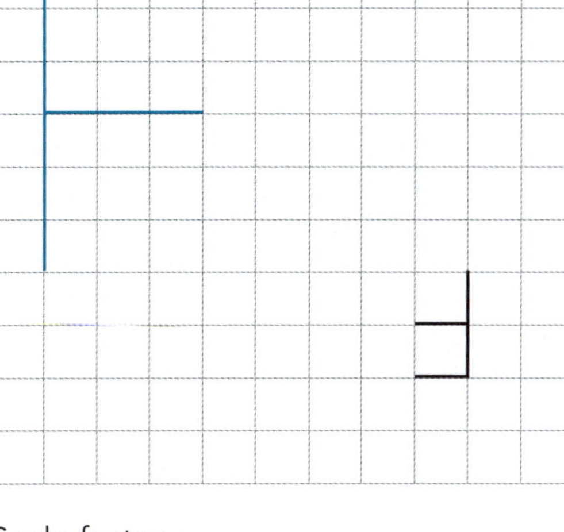

Scale factor = ______

3

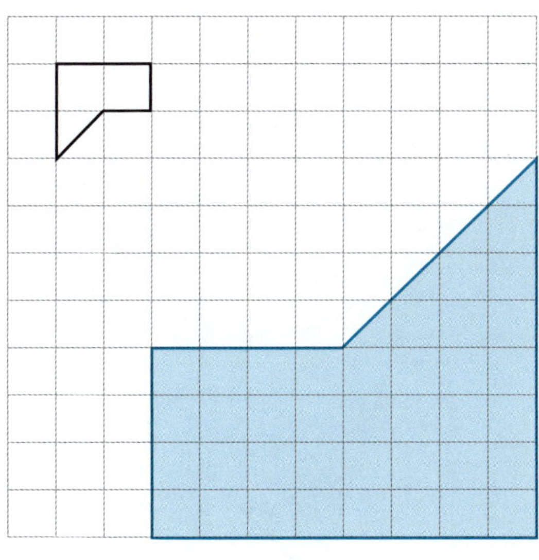

Scale factor = ______

4

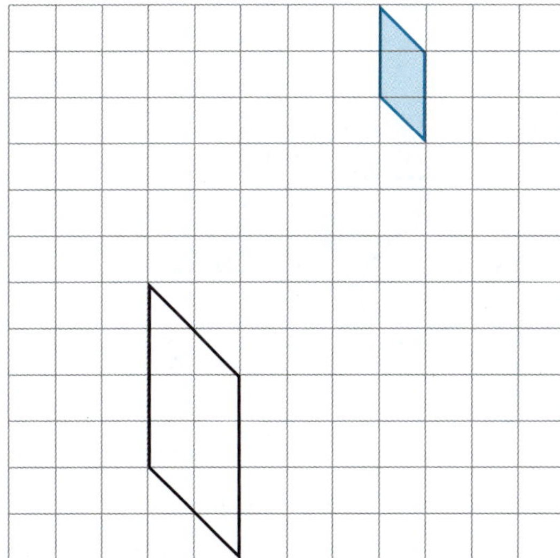

Scale factor = ______

5

Scale factor = ______

6

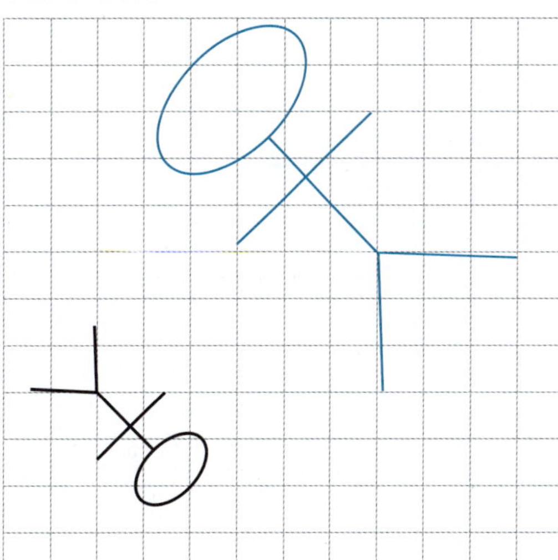

Scale factor = ______

ISBN: 9780170416016

Complete the following negative enlargements.

7 Scale factor = ______________

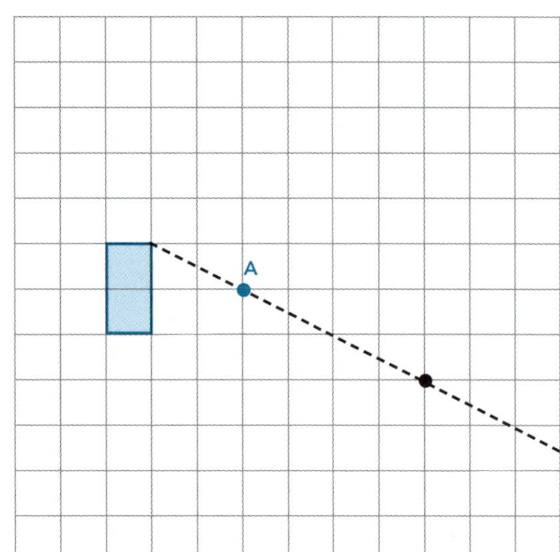

8 Scale factor = ______________

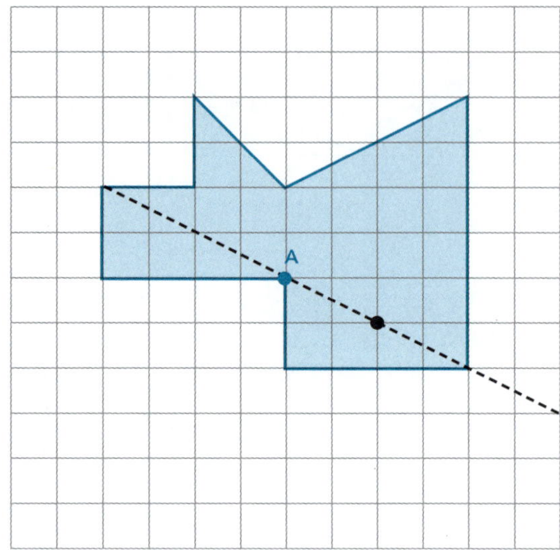

9 Scale factor = $-\frac{1}{2}$

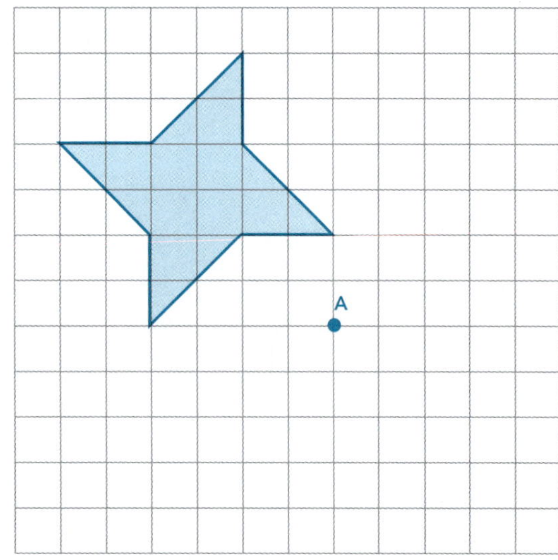

10 Scale factor = $-\frac{1}{3}$

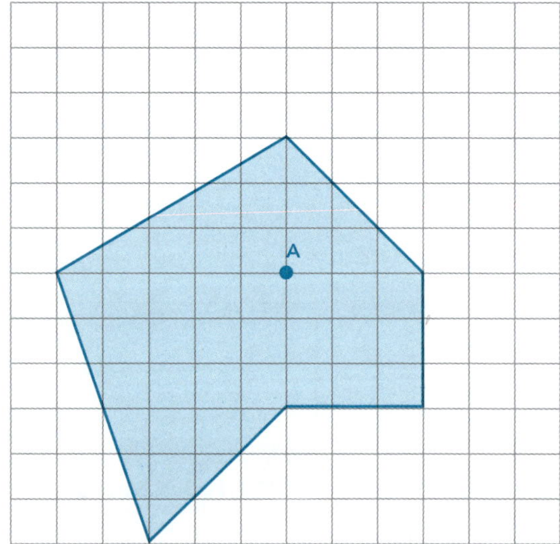

11 Scale factor = $-\frac{1}{2}$

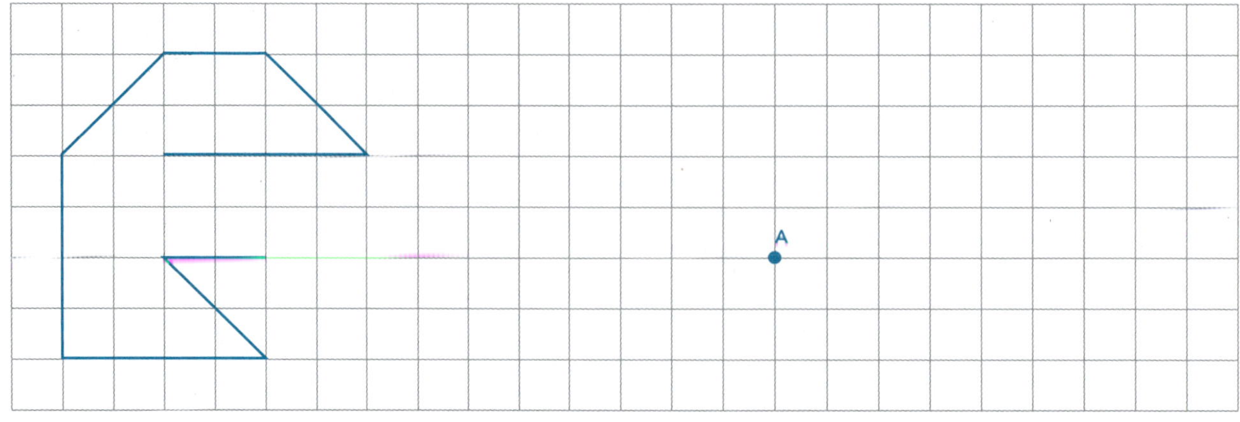

 ISBN: 9780170416016

Mixing it up

Decide whether these figures have been translated, reflected, rotated or enlarged.

- If they show translation, write a vector.
- If they show reflection, draw the mirror line(s).
- If they show rotation, mark the centre and write down the angle of rotation.
- If they show enlargement, mark the centre and write down the scale factor.

Some could be more than one — give all transformations for these.

1 Translation/Reflection/Rotation/Enlargement

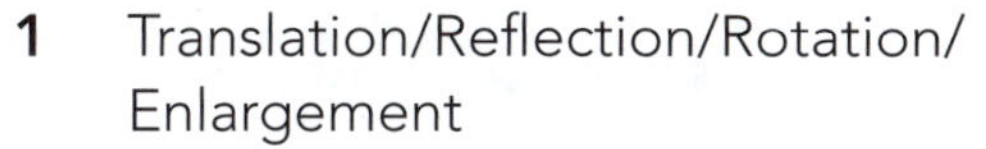

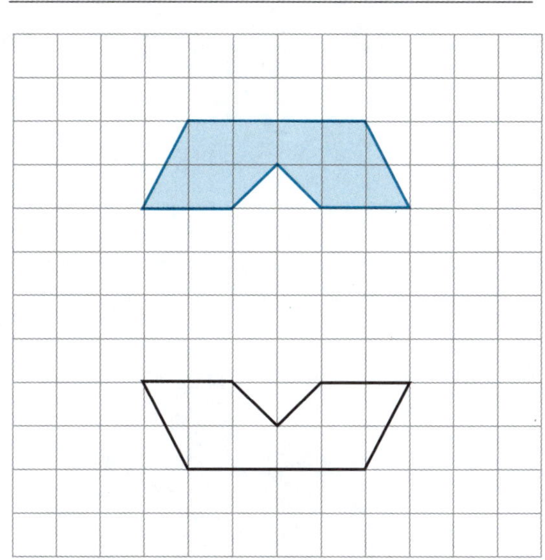

2 Translation/Reflection/Rotation/Enlargement

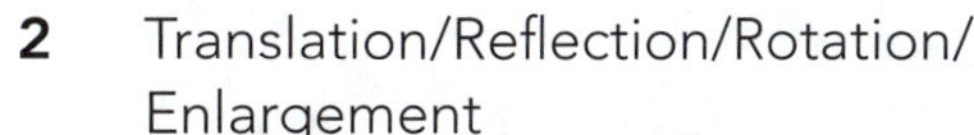

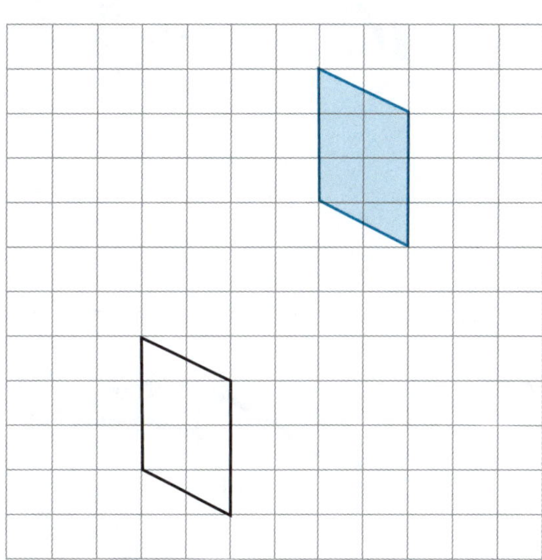

3 Translation/Reflection/Rotation/Enlargement

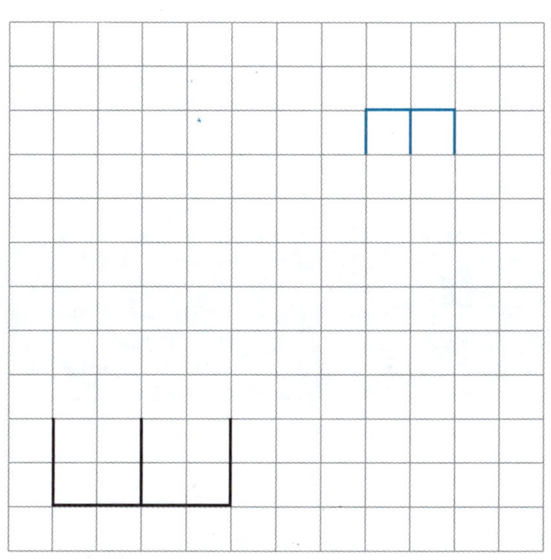

4 Translation/Reflection/Rotation/Enlargement

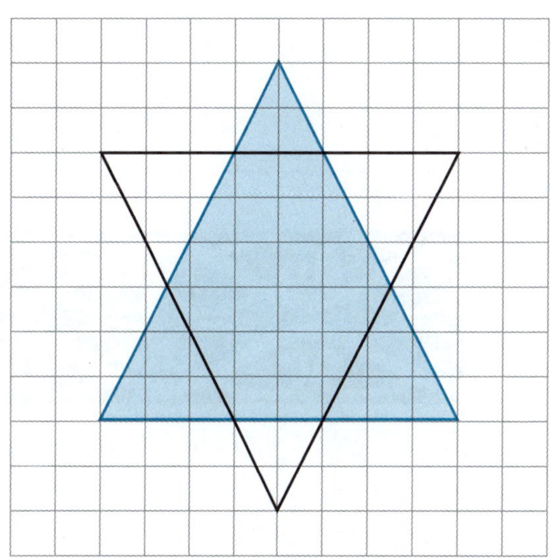

ISBN: 9780170416016

Decide whether these figures have show translation, reflection, rotation or enlargement.

- If they show translation, draw lines around one unit which is translated.
- If they show reflection, draw the mirror line(s).
- If they show rotation, mark the centre and write down the angle of rotation.
- If they show enlargement, mark the centre and write down the scale factor.

 ISBN: 9780170416016

Invariant points

- These are points that stay in the **same place** when a transformation is performed.

Translation: There are **no** invariant points — unless the translation is $\begin{pmatrix}0\\0\end{pmatrix}$.

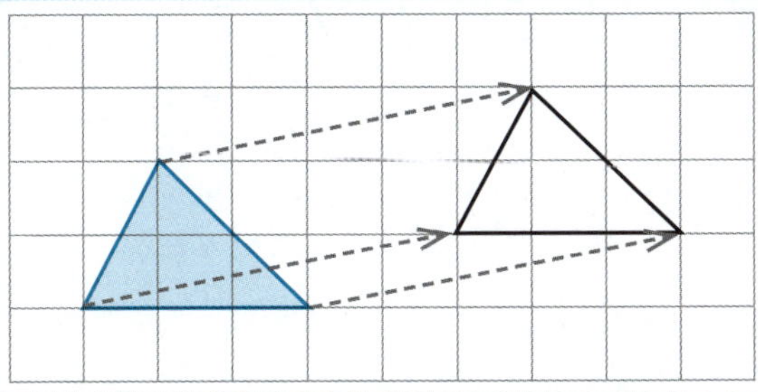

Reflection: Points **along the mirror line** are invariant.

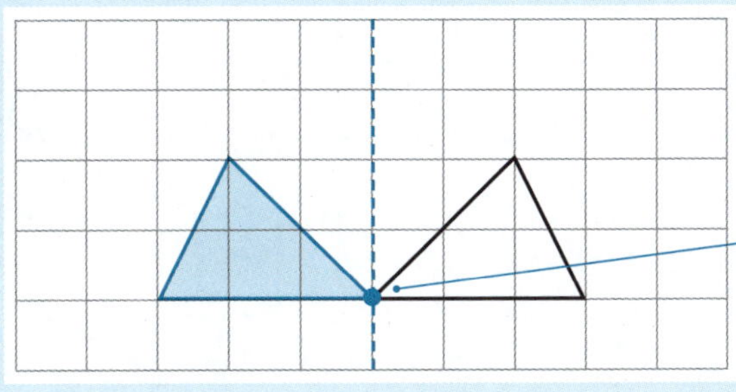

Rotation: Points that are **on the centre of rotation** are invariant.

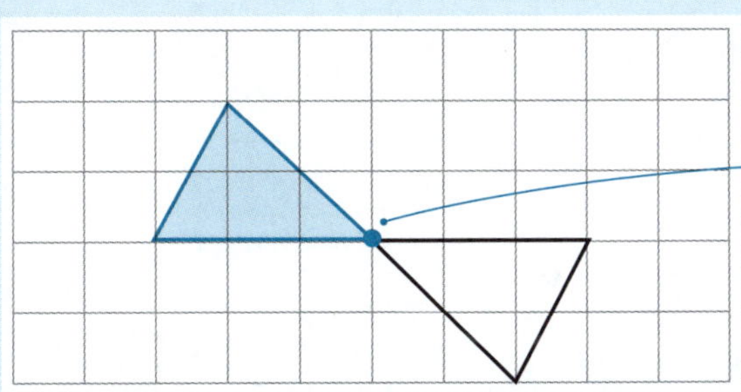

Enlargement: Points that are **on the centre of enlargement** are invariant.

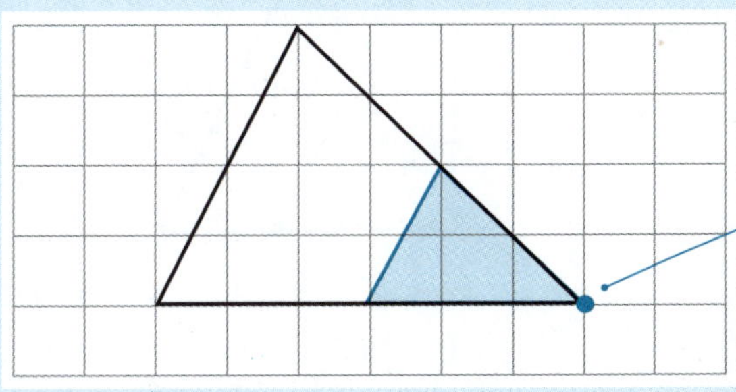

ISBN: 9780170416016

Describe the transformation in each of the following diagrams and label any invariant points.

1

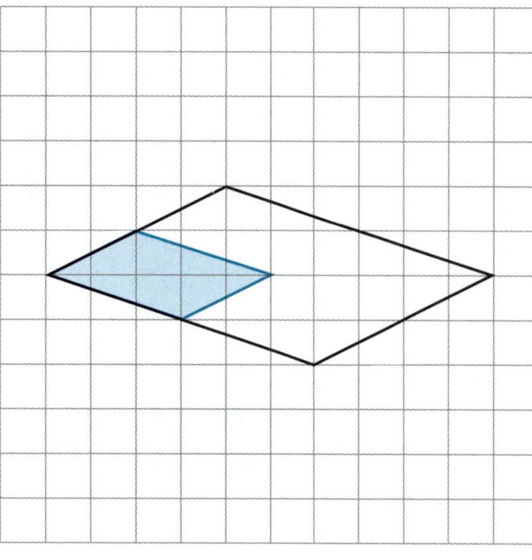

2

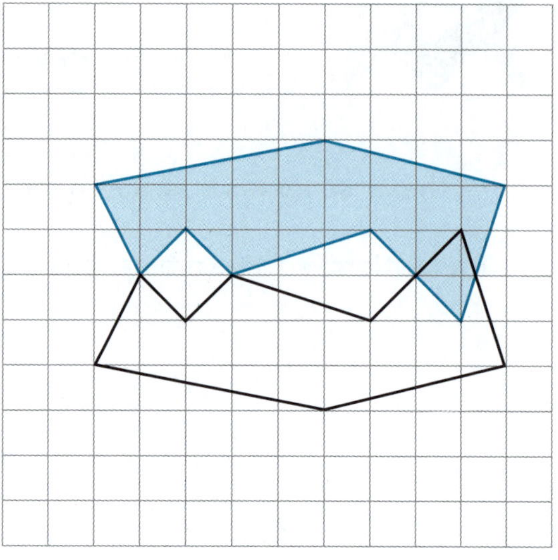

3

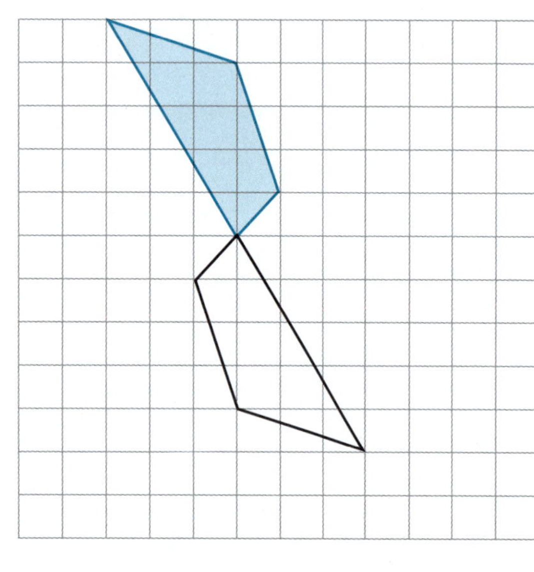

4

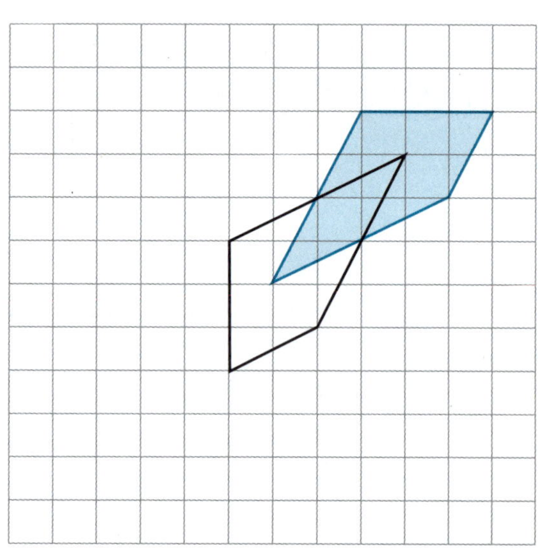

5

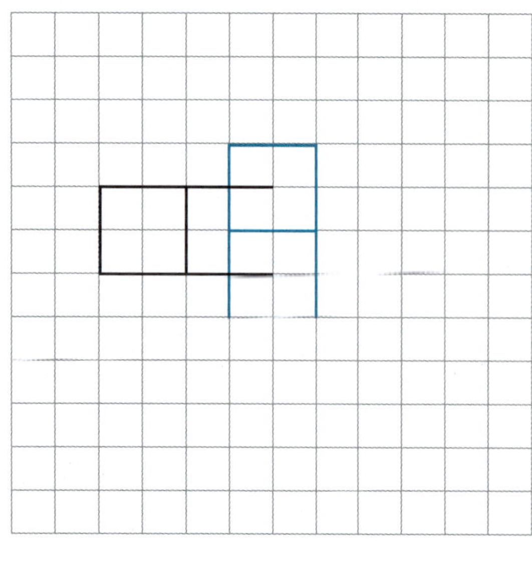

6

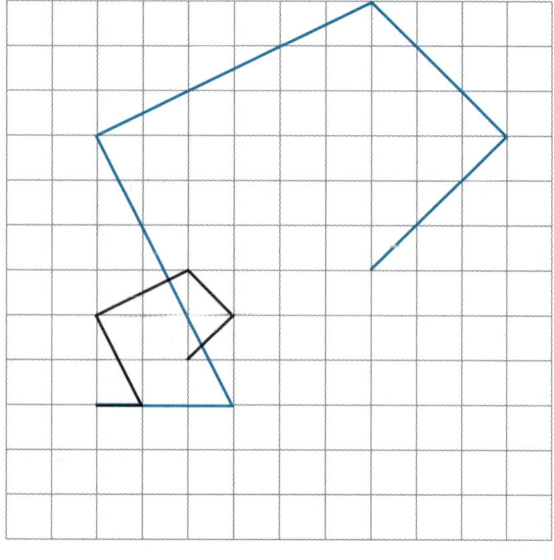

 ISBN: 9780170416016

Inverse transformations

- These are transformations that '**undo**' another transformation.
- An inverse transformation returns points and lines to their **original positions**.
- An inverse transformation turns an **image** into the **original figure**.

1 Translations

- To find an inverse translation: **change the sign** of each digit in the vector.

Example: For the vector $\begin{pmatrix}-4\\3\end{pmatrix}$, the inverse vector is $\begin{pmatrix}4\\-3\end{pmatrix}$.

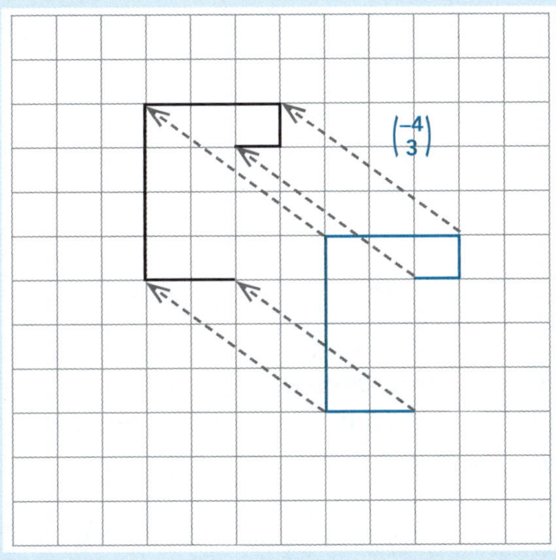

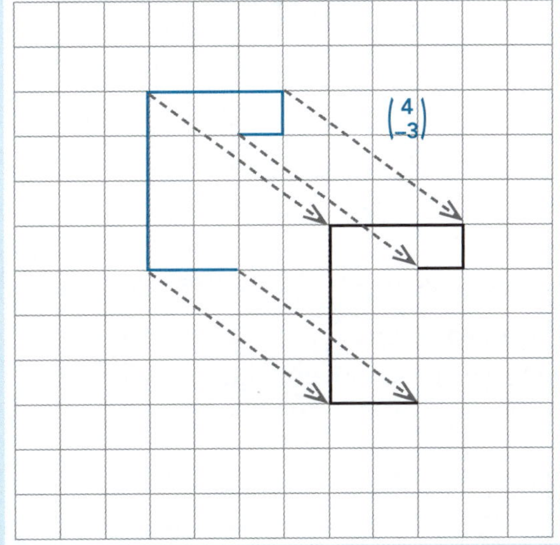

2 Reflections

- To find an inverse of a reflection: **reflect** the image in the **same mirror line**.

Example:

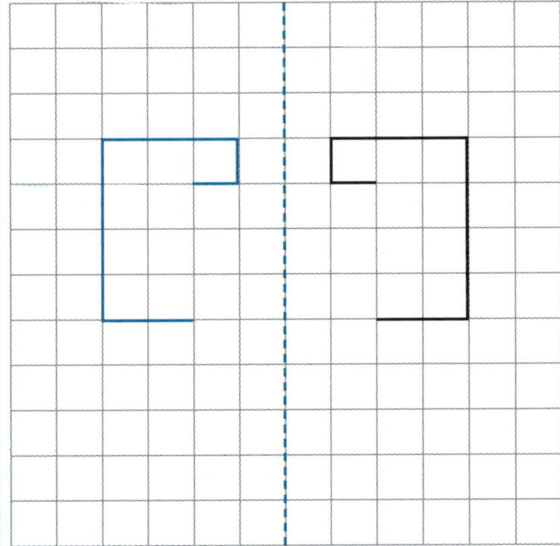

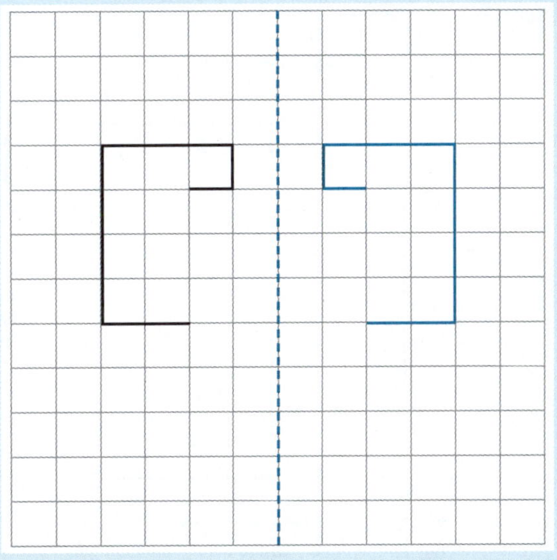

ISBN: 9780170416016

3 Rotations

- To find an inverse rotation: Use the **same centre** and **angle**. **Reverse** the **direction**.

Example: The inverse of a rotation of 270° in a clockwise direction is a rotation of 270° in an anticlockwise direction.

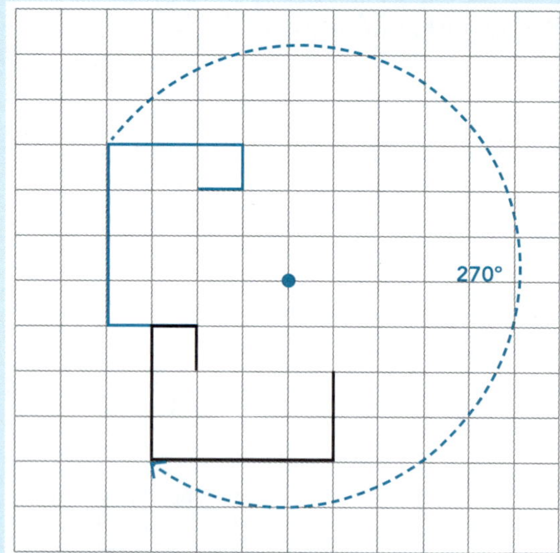

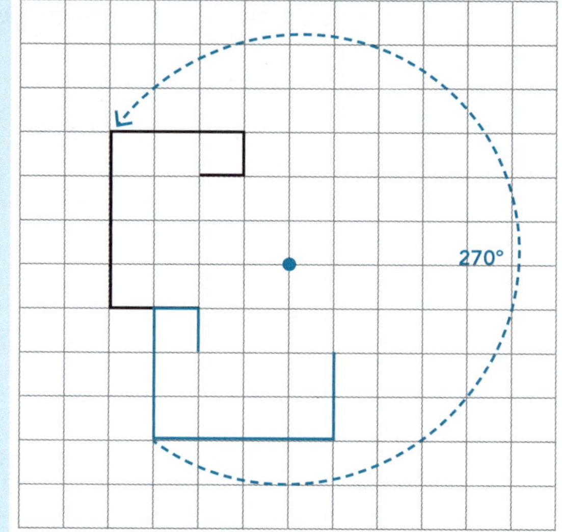

4 Enlargements

- To find an inverse enlargement: Use the **same centre**. Change the **scale factor** to the **reciprocal** of the original scale factor.

The **reciprocal** of a number = $\frac{1}{\text{number}}$

Examples: **1** Reciprocal of 6 is $\frac{1}{6}$

2 Reciprocal of $\frac{1}{9}$ is 9

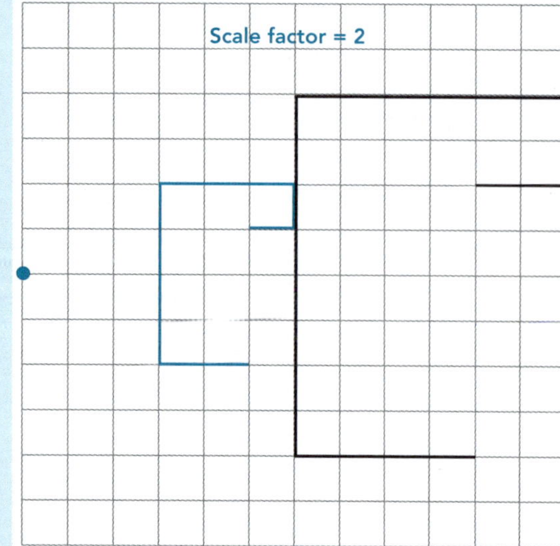

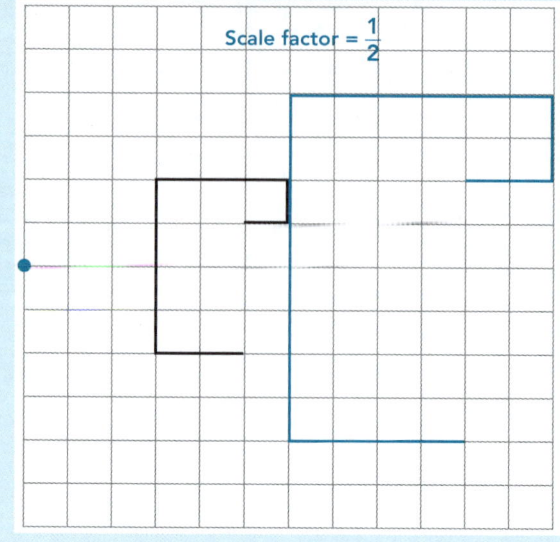

ISBN: 9780170416016

Write down the inverse transformations for the following. Mark any invariant points, mirror lines and centres on the diagrams. Be careful: there are several answers to some of these. Remember – you will be going from the black image to the teal one.

1

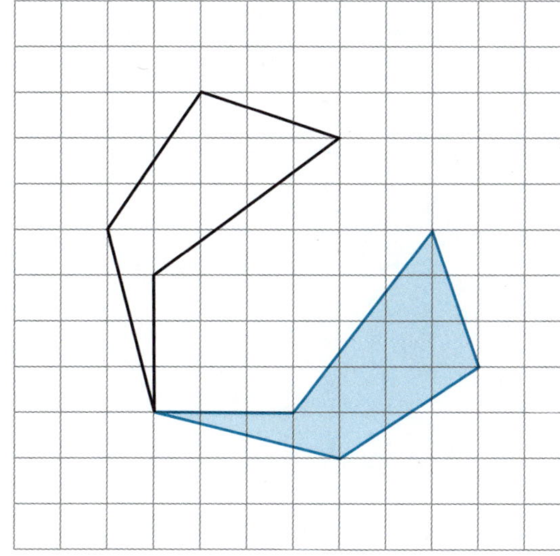

Inverse transformation(s):

2

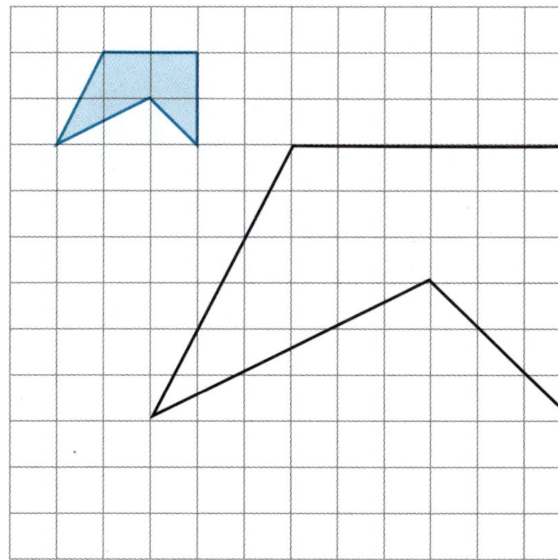

Inverse transformation(s):

3

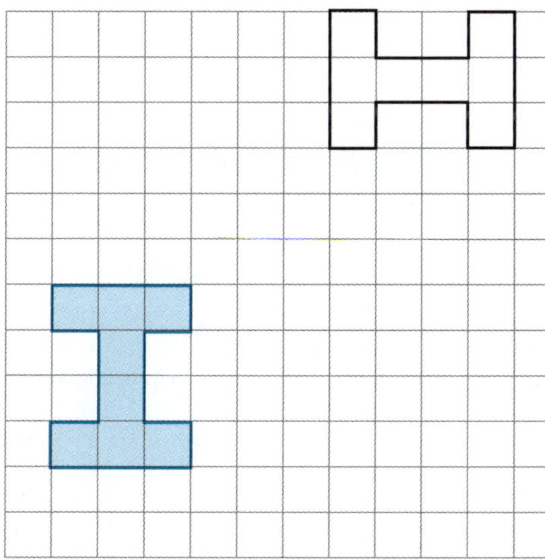

Inverse transformation(s):

ISBN: 9780170416016

4

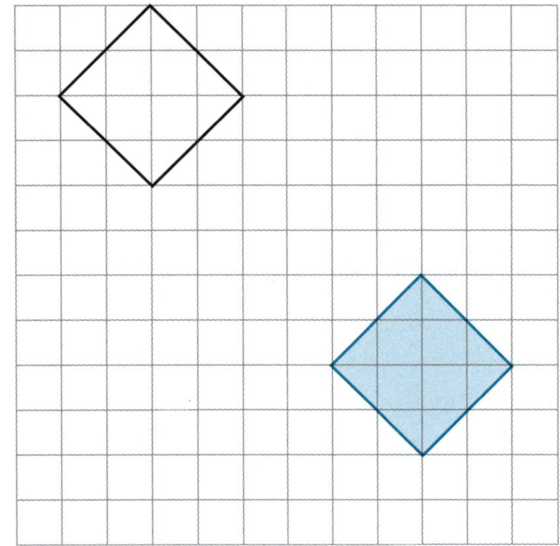

Inverse transformation(s):

5

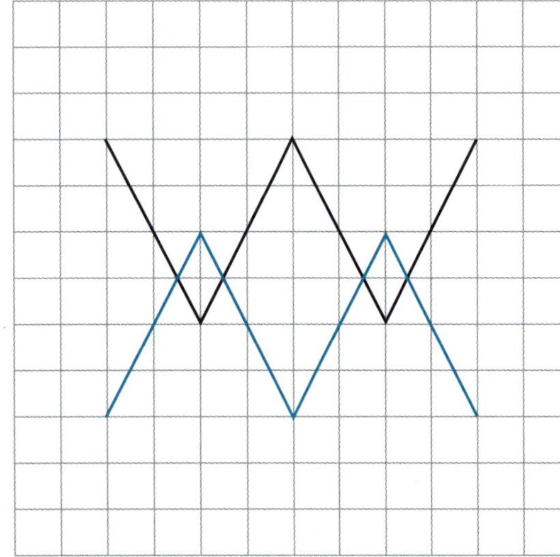

Inverse transformation(s):

6

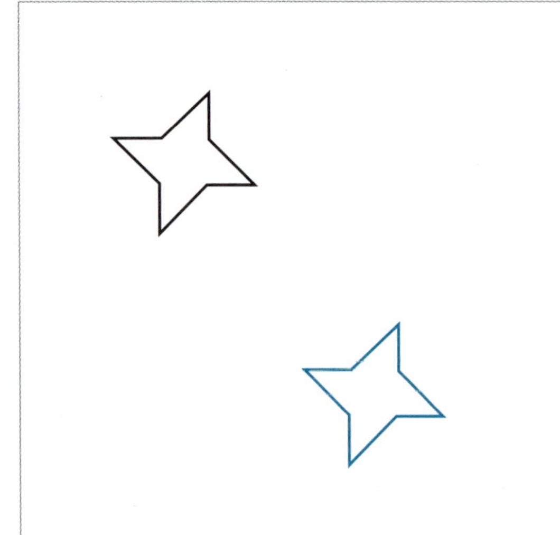

Inverse transformation(s):

 ISBN: 9780170416016

Mini tasks

1 Simon is creating a border pattern using his initials.
Fully describe each step required for its creation.

Starting point

Step 1

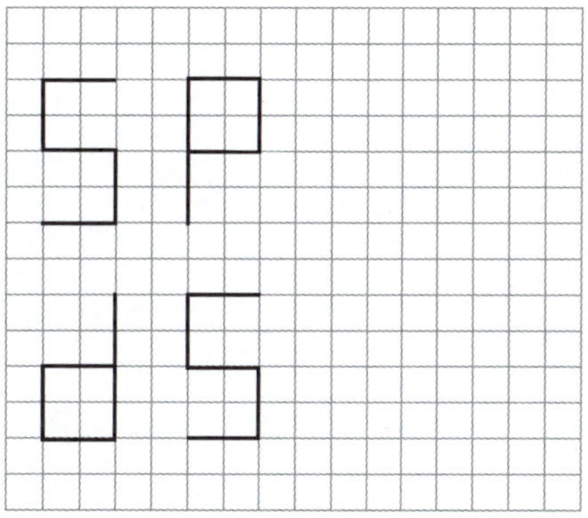

____

____

____

Step 2

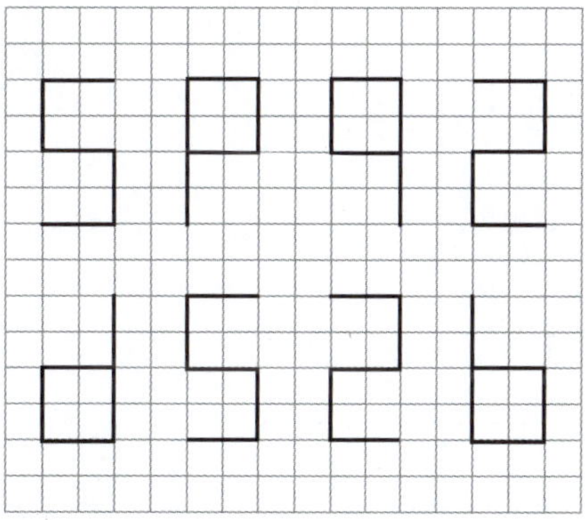

____

____

____

Step 3

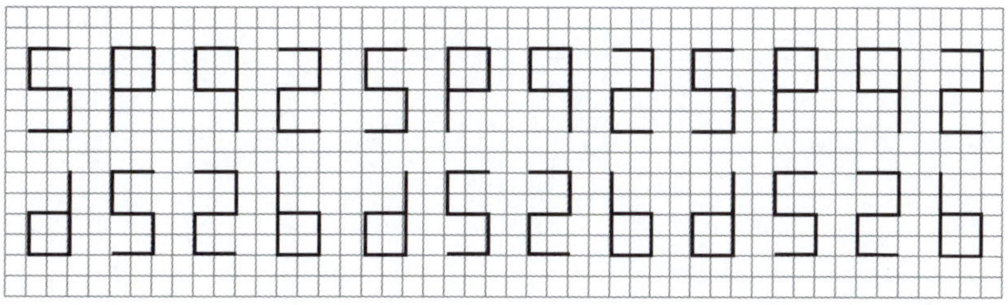

____

____

____

____

____

ISBN: 9780170416016

2 He was not satisfied with the first design, so he created a different one.
Complete the diagrams and fully describe each step required for its creation.

Starting point

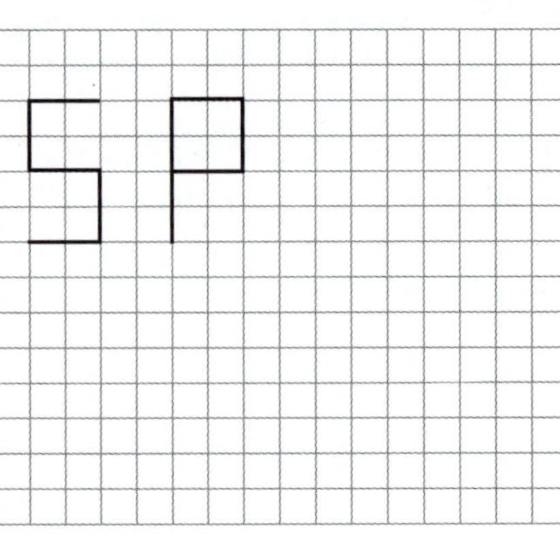

Step 1

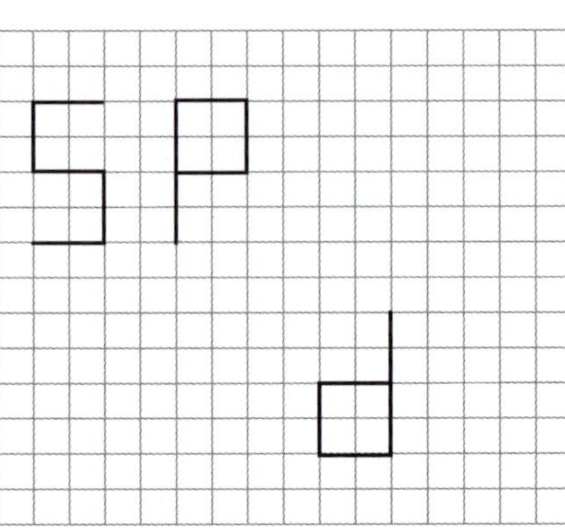

Step 2

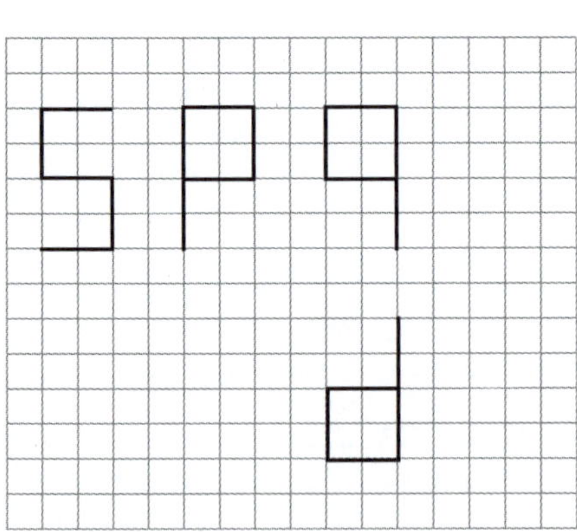

Step 3

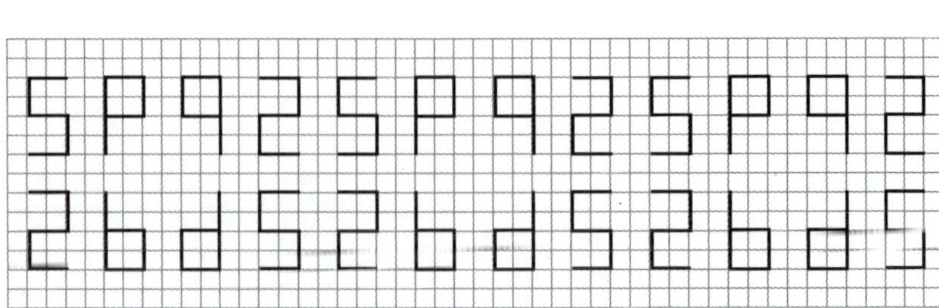

 ISBN: 9780170416016

3 Complete the diagrams and fully describe each step required for the creation of the pattern at the bottom of the page.

Start

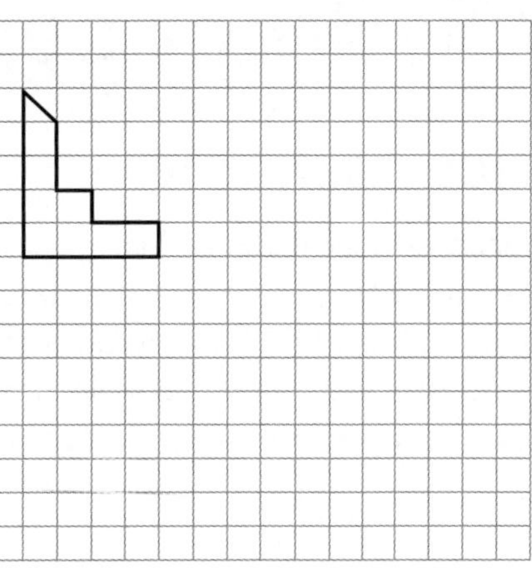

Step 1

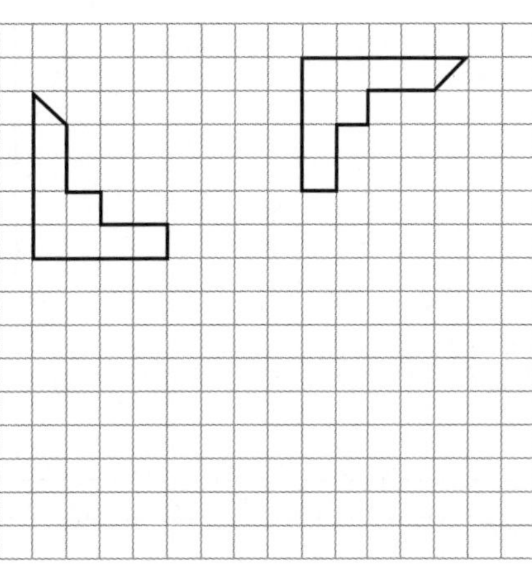

Step 2

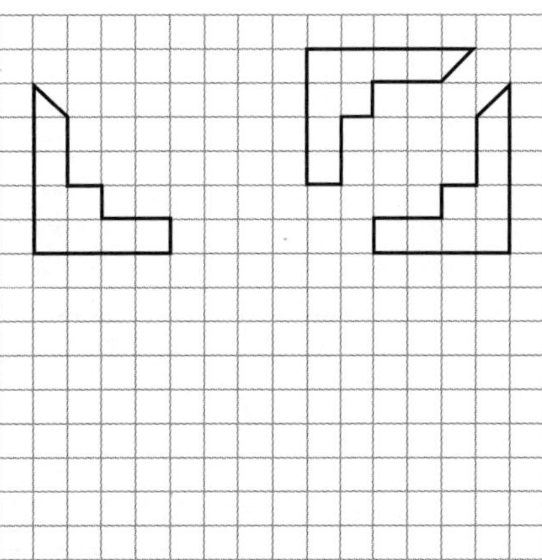

Step 3

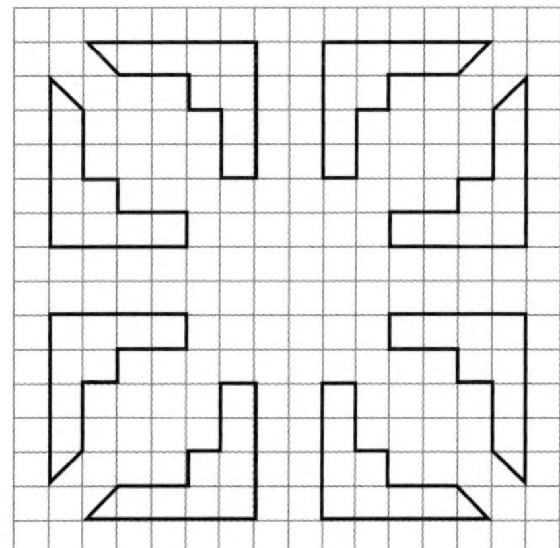

Practice task one

Snowboards and skateboards

You are required to investigate the different patterns possible using a single motif for the decoration of a new line of snowboards and skateboards.

You need to investigate possible patterns involving at least three transformations of the motif below, but performed in different orders.

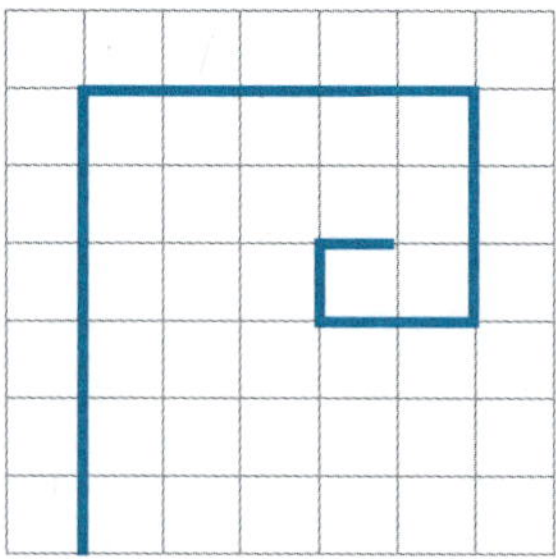

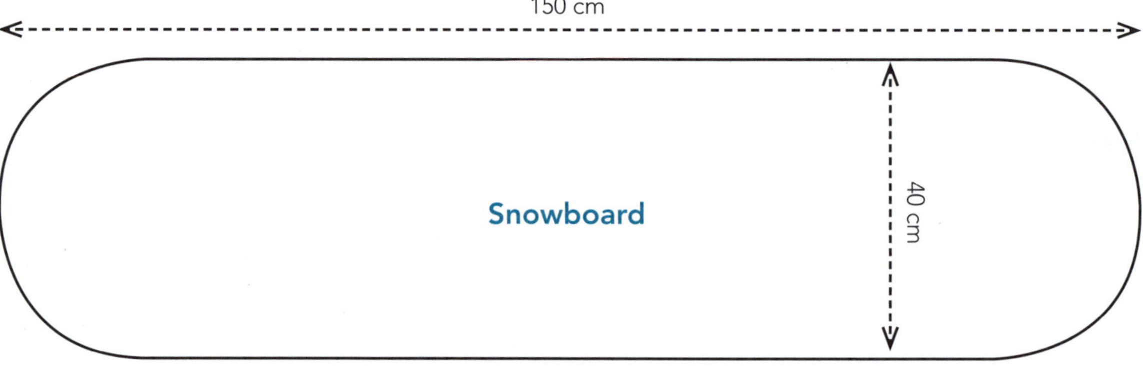

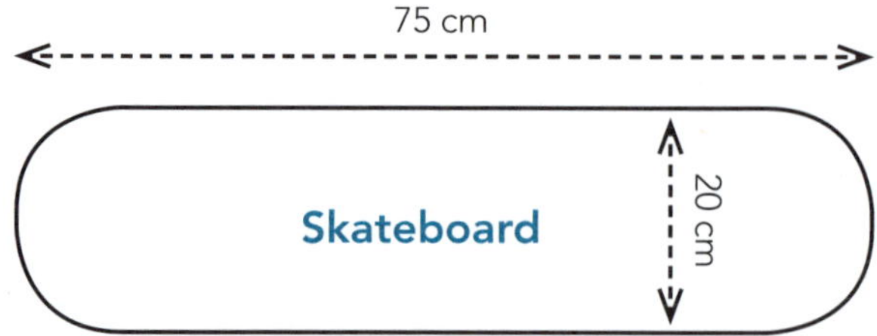

ISBN: 9780170416016

1 Rotation, then reflection, then translation.

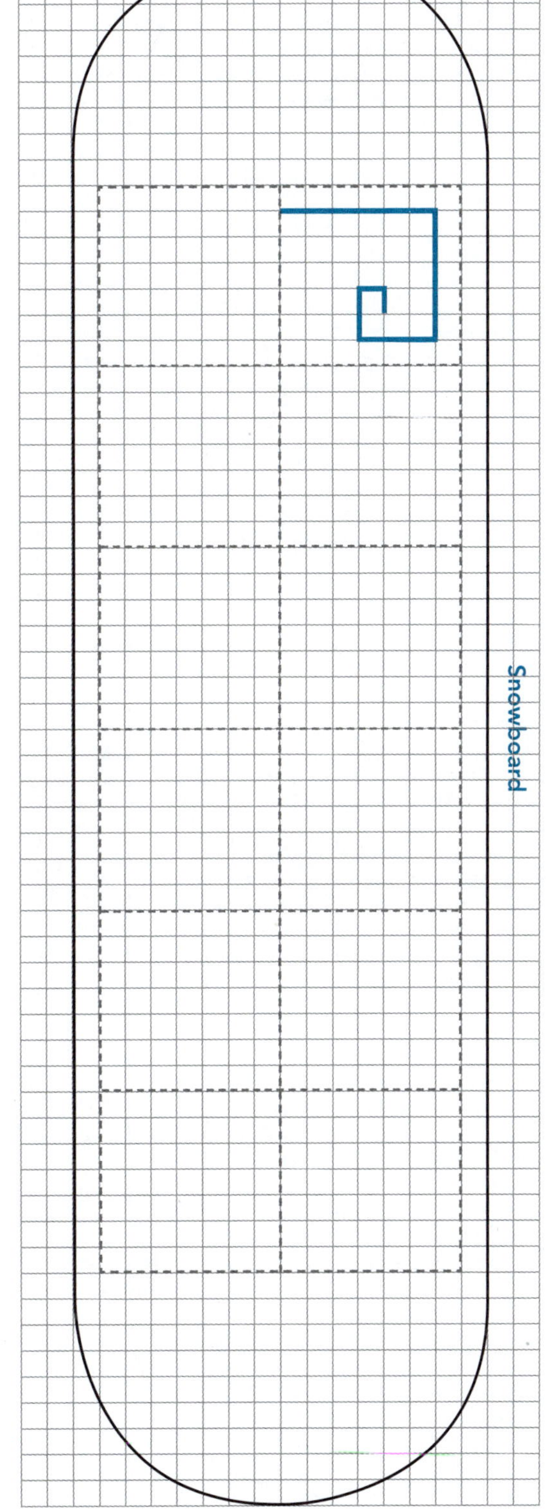

2 Reflection, then rotation, then translation.

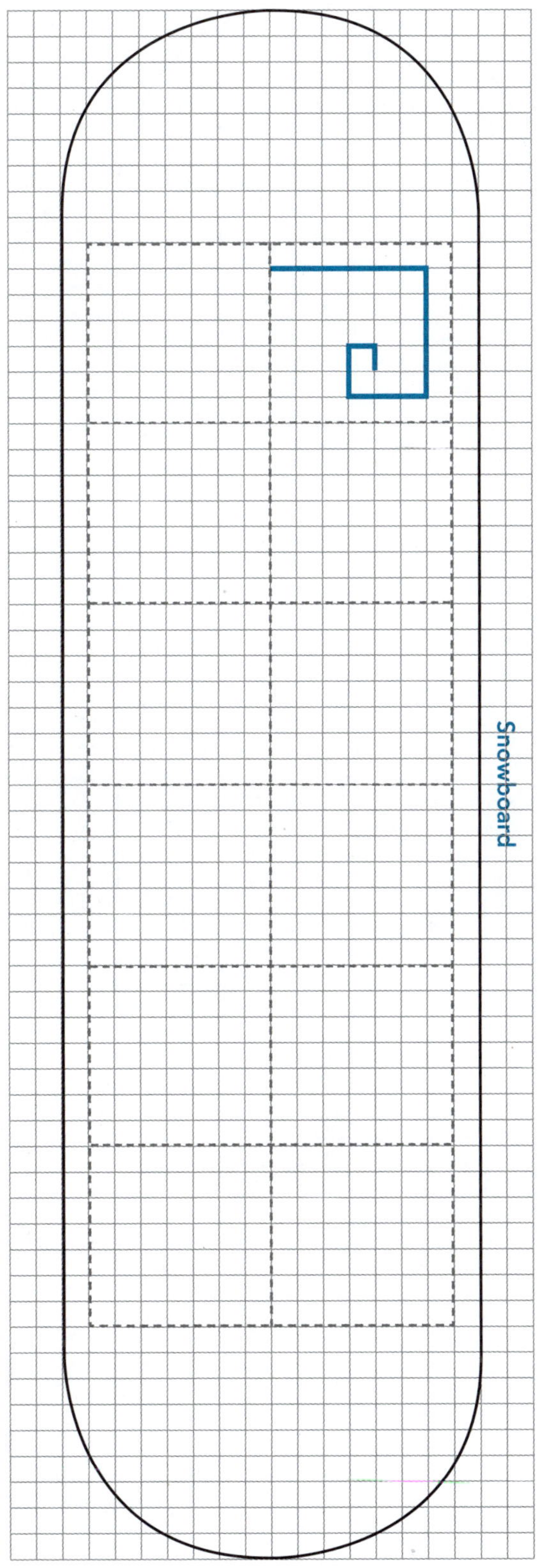

ISBN: 9780170416016

3 Create your own figure. Then rotate it, translate it and finally reflect it to complete your design.

Snowboard

4 Create your own starting figure. Then transform it three times to complete your design.

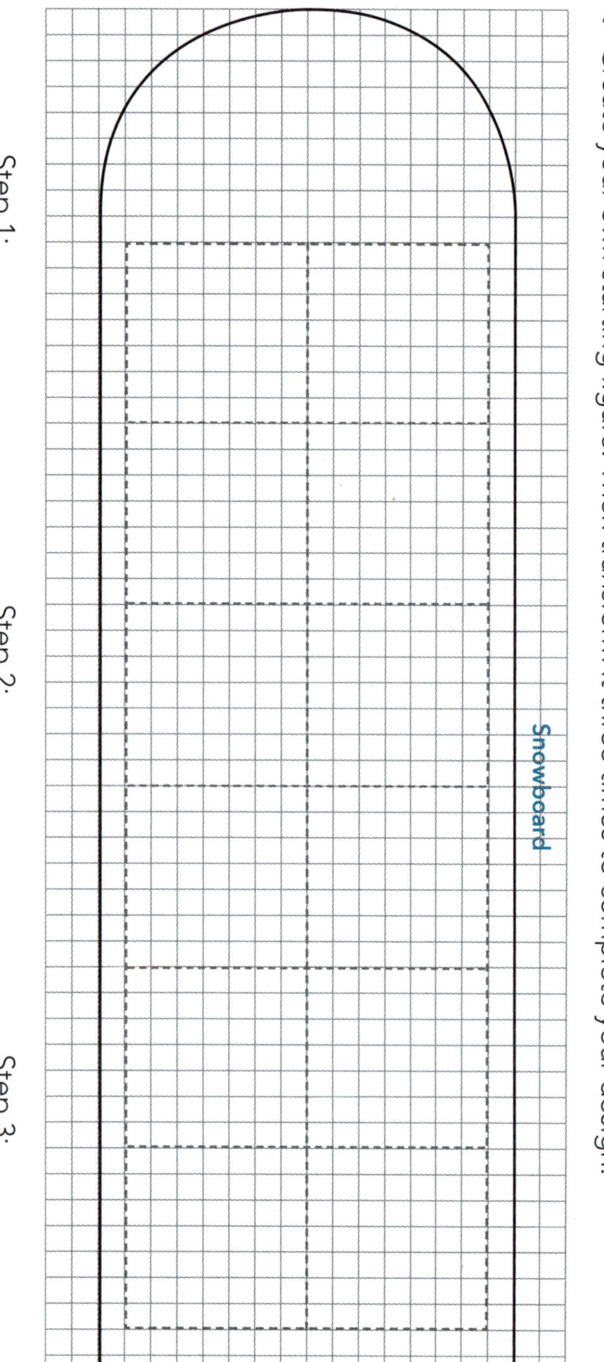

Step 1: __________ Step 2: __________ Step 3: __________

5 Select one of your designs, and describe the translation that would be required to alter its size so that it would fit on a skateboard.

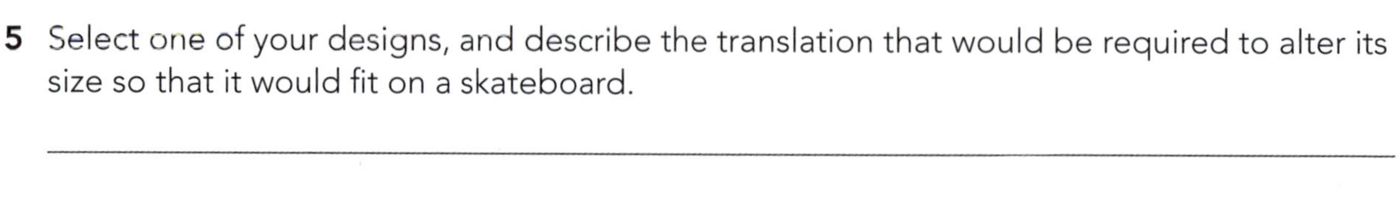

ISBN: 9780170416016

Practice task two

Cellphone and tablet covers

You are required to create a design suitable for use on a cellphone cover and matching tablet cover.

- Select or create a motif/picture and then use transformation geometry to create a design to be used on the cellphone cover.
- Your design must involve at least **three** different transformations.
- Show the steps used to create your design, from the beginning motif/picture through to the completed design.
- Write instructions for using your motif/picture to create your design. Your instructions need to include full descriptions of the transformations that have been used and enable your design to be reproduced accurately.
- Describe any symmetries and invariance in your completed design.
- The cellphone cover design is to be enlarged to be used for the tablet cover. The diagram below shows the relationship between the cellphone cover and the tablet cover.

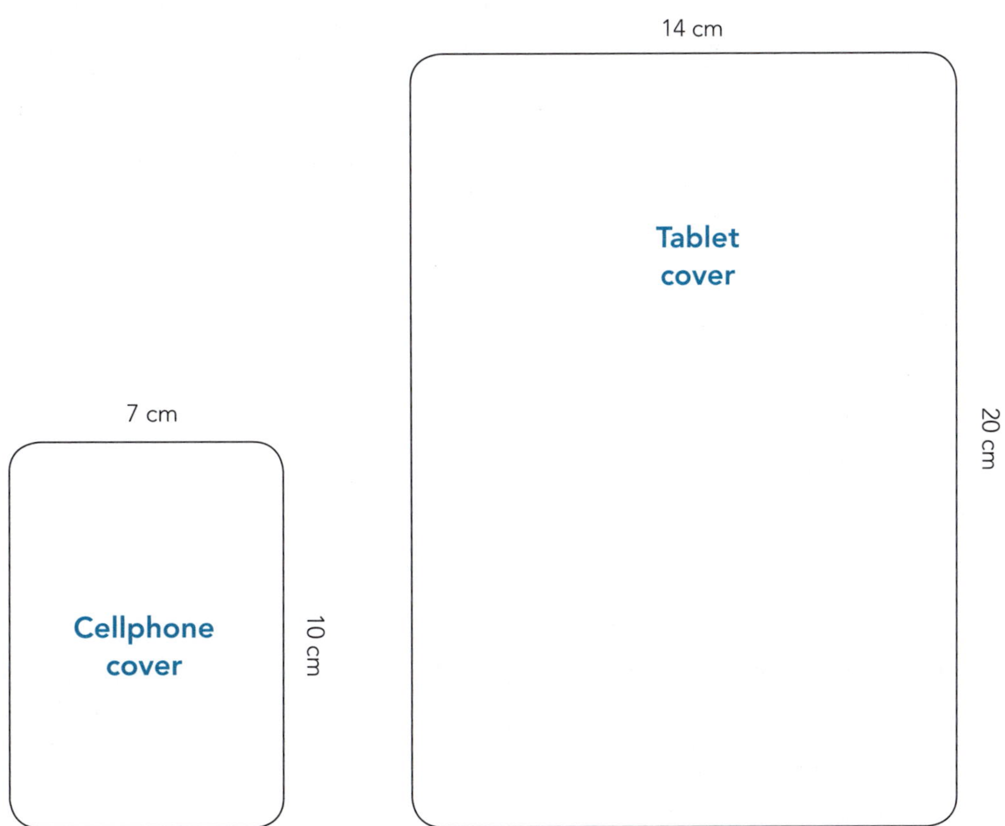

Using correct mathematical statements, write instructions that would enable the printing company to create the enlarged design.

ISBN: 9780170416016

Instructions:

Cellphone cover

Step 1:

Step 2:

Step 3:

Step 4:

Step 5:

Other relevant observations (symmetries, invariant points, inverse transformations, etc.):

 ISBN: 9780170416016

Tablet cover

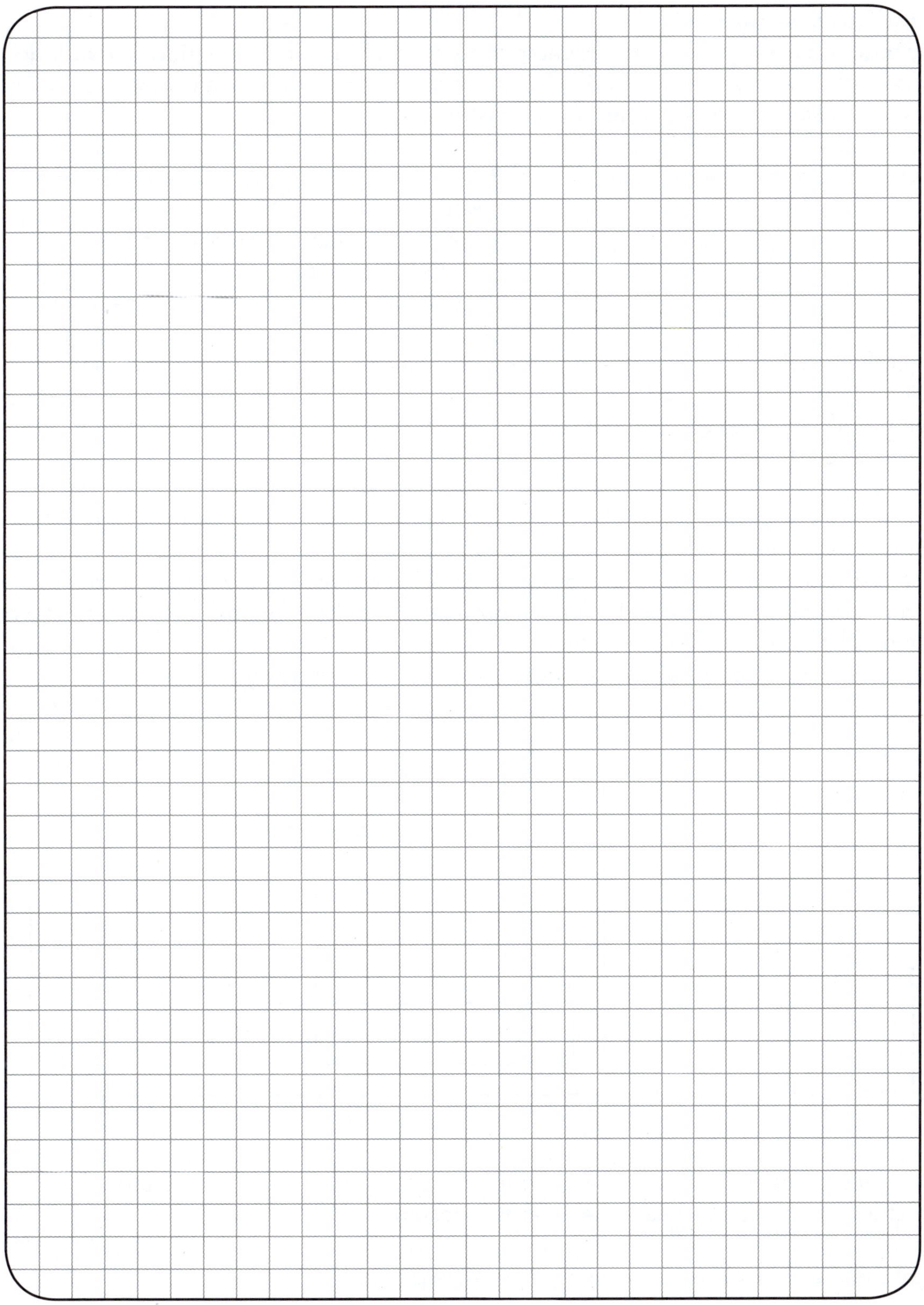

ISBN: 9780170416016

Practice task three

Logo and business card

You are required to create a design suitable for use on a logo, and then modify your logo design so that it can be used as a strip design for along the bottom of a business card. Both designs must use the initials of **one** of your customers.

The initials of current customers are:

PD (you may wish to use an upper case P and a lower case d)
IH (remember that in some scripts, I can be written as I)
UN (you may wish to use lower-case u and n).

- Select the initials you wish to use, and then use transformation geometry to create a design to be used on a logo.
- Then modify your design so that it can be used as the strip design for along the bottom of a business card.
- Your designs must involve at least three different transformations.
- Show the steps used to create your designs, from the beginning initials through to the completed designs.
- Write instructions for using your chosen initials to create your design. Your instructions need to include descriptions of the transformations that have been used and enable your design to be reproduced accurately.
- Describe any symmetries and invariance in your completed design.

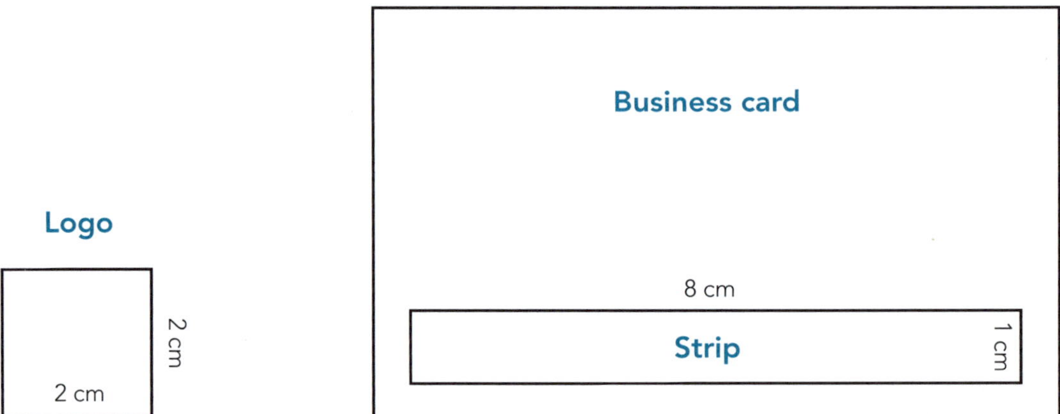

Using correct mathematical statements, write instructions that would enable the manufacturing company to create the enlarged design.

You may use the scale grids on the next page to help you.

 ISBN: 9780170416016

Business card strip

Logo

ISBN: 9780170416016

Instructions:

Step 1:

Step 2:

Step 3:

Step 4:

Step 5:

Other relevant observations (symmetries, invariant points, inverse transformations, etc.):

 ISBN: 9780170416016

Answers

Translation (pp. 7–17)

	Stays the same	Changes
Size	✓	
Shape	✓	
Orientation	✓	
Position		✓

Describing translations of points — vectors (pp. 8–11)

1 $\begin{pmatrix}3\\2\end{pmatrix}$ 2 $\begin{pmatrix}4\\-2\end{pmatrix}$

3 $\begin{pmatrix}-4\\1\end{pmatrix}$ 4 $\begin{pmatrix}-3\\-2\end{pmatrix}$

5 $\begin{pmatrix}9\\-4\end{pmatrix}$ 6 $\begin{pmatrix}-7\\-2\end{pmatrix}$

7 $\begin{pmatrix}0\\2\end{pmatrix}$ 8 $\begin{pmatrix}-6\\0\end{pmatrix}$

9 Right one and up three
10 Right four and up two
11 Up three
12 Left two and up three
13 Right two and down one
14 Left one and down two
15 Right two
16 Down one

17

$\begin{pmatrix}3\\1\end{pmatrix}$	$\begin{pmatrix}-4\\-2\end{pmatrix}$	$\begin{pmatrix}-3\\2\end{pmatrix}$	$\begin{pmatrix}-2\\0\end{pmatrix}$	$\begin{pmatrix}-3\\-1\end{pmatrix}$	$\begin{pmatrix}0\\3\end{pmatrix}$	$\begin{pmatrix}-2\\-2\end{pmatrix}$	$\begin{pmatrix}3\\-2\end{pmatrix}$	$\begin{pmatrix}3\\2\end{pmatrix}$	$\begin{pmatrix}2\\3\end{pmatrix}$
b	h	a	e	d	j	c	g	i	f

18

$\begin{pmatrix}2\\-1\end{pmatrix}$	$\begin{pmatrix}4\\3\end{pmatrix}$	$\begin{pmatrix}2\\1\end{pmatrix}$	$\begin{pmatrix}-3\\1\end{pmatrix}$	$\begin{pmatrix}1\\-1\end{pmatrix}$	$\begin{pmatrix}2\\0\end{pmatrix}$	$\begin{pmatrix}0\\-3\end{pmatrix}$	$\begin{pmatrix}5\\-1\end{pmatrix}$	$\begin{pmatrix}5\\2\end{pmatrix}$	$\begin{pmatrix}-4\\0\end{pmatrix}$
a	b	c	d	e	f	g	h	i	j

19

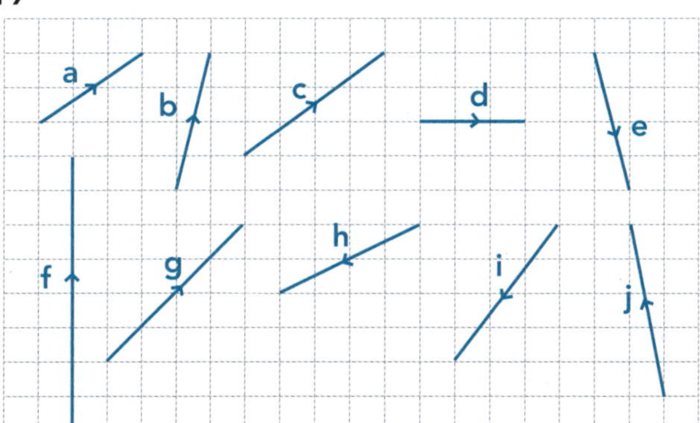

20 Accept 1mm either side of.

a $\begin{pmatrix}49\text{mm}\\37\text{mm}\end{pmatrix}$ b $\begin{pmatrix}17\text{mm}\\-41\text{mm}\end{pmatrix}$

Describing translations of figures (pp. 12–13)

1 $\begin{pmatrix}-5\\1\end{pmatrix}$ 2 $\begin{pmatrix}4\\-3\end{pmatrix}$

3 $\begin{pmatrix}-5\\-1\end{pmatrix}$ 4 $\begin{pmatrix}4\\1\end{pmatrix}$

5 $\begin{pmatrix}5\\1\end{pmatrix}$ 6 $\begin{pmatrix}4\\0\end{pmatrix}$

7 $\begin{pmatrix}5\\-2\end{pmatrix}$ 8 $\begin{pmatrix}-6\\1\end{pmatrix}$

9 $\begin{pmatrix}5\\3\end{pmatrix}$ 10 $\begin{pmatrix}-5\\1\end{pmatrix}$

Drawing translations (pp. 14–15)

1

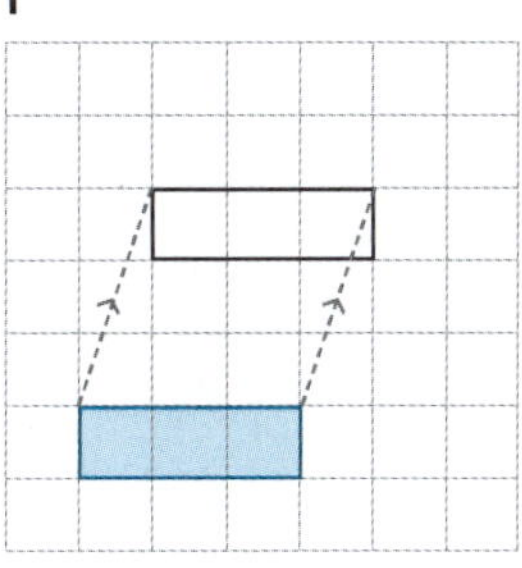

2

3

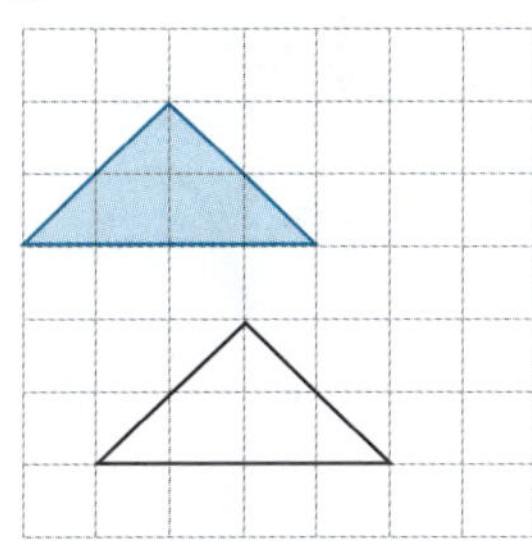

4

5

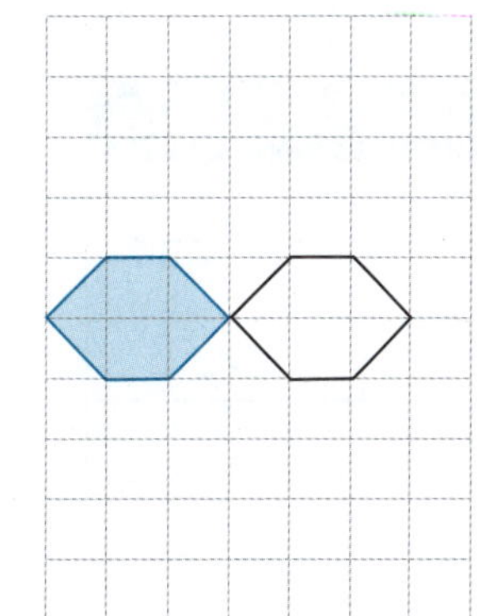

6

7

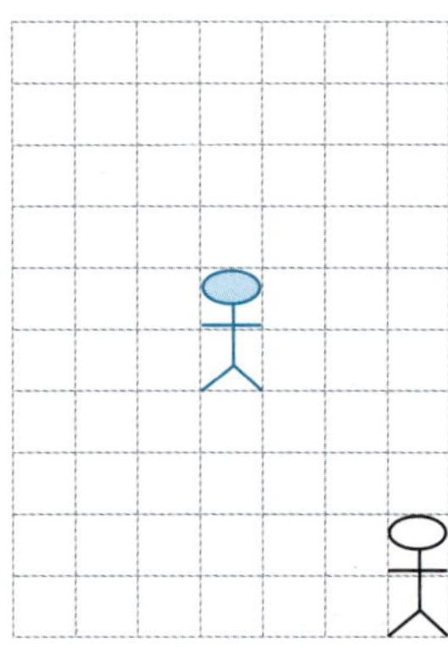

8

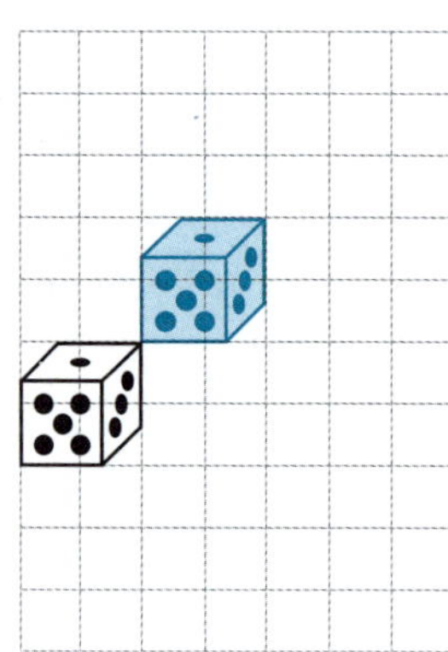

9

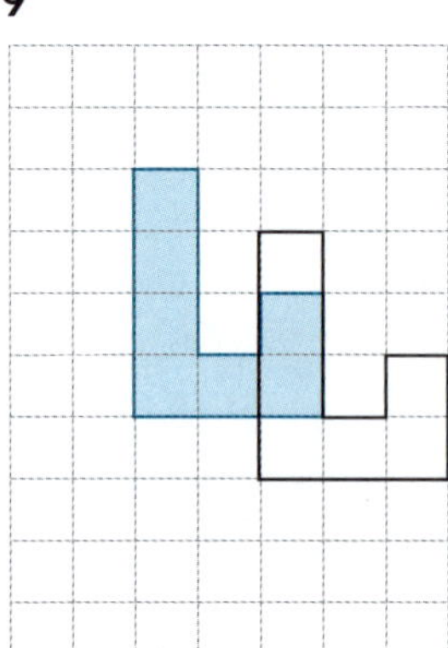

10

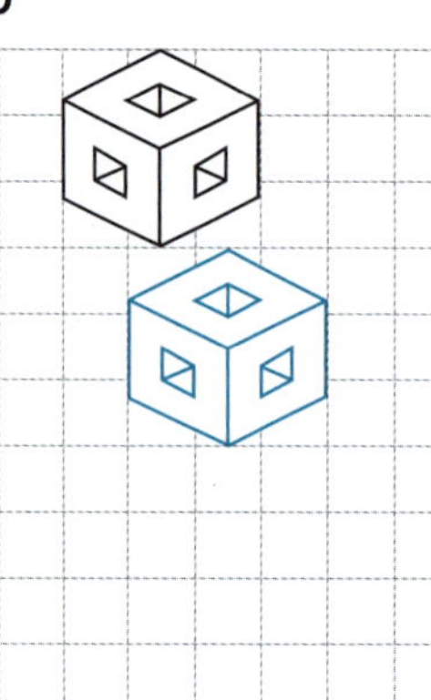

Challenges (pp. 16–17)

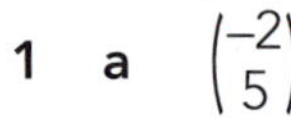

1 a $\begin{pmatrix}-2\\5\end{pmatrix}$ b $\begin{pmatrix}14\\1\end{pmatrix}$ c $\begin{pmatrix}-2\\8\end{pmatrix}$

d $\begin{pmatrix}1\\-6\end{pmatrix}$ e $\begin{pmatrix}-15\\-2\end{pmatrix}$ f $\begin{pmatrix}-5\\5\end{pmatrix}$

2

A A′

Reflection (pp. 18–33)

	Stays the same	Changes
Size	✓	
Shape	✓	
Orientation		✓
Position		✓

Describing reflections — mirror lines (pp. 19–21)

1

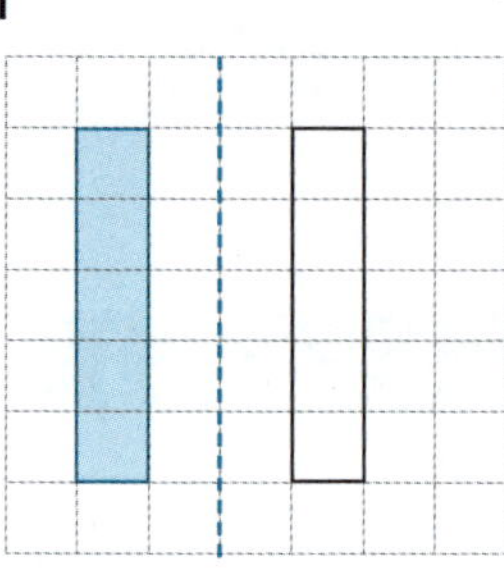

2

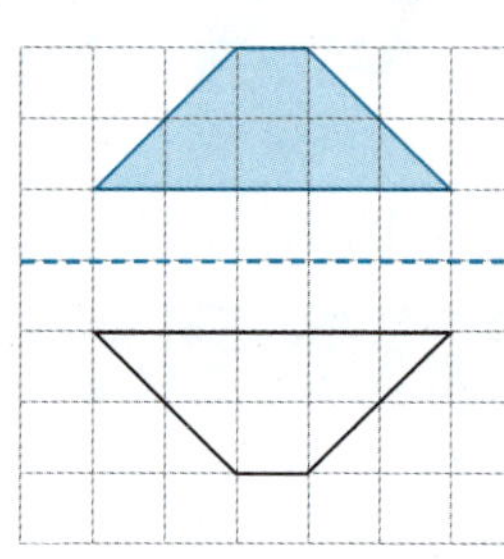

3

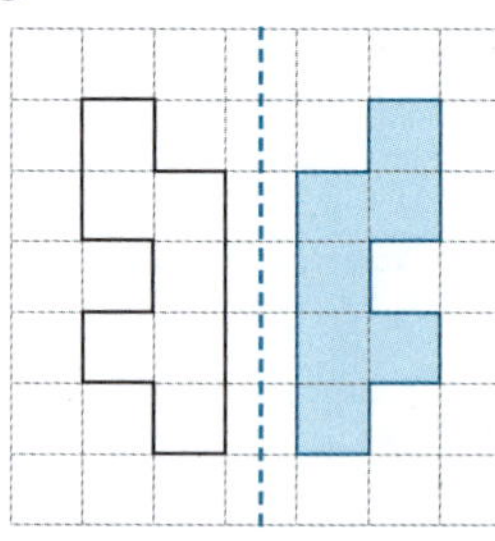

4

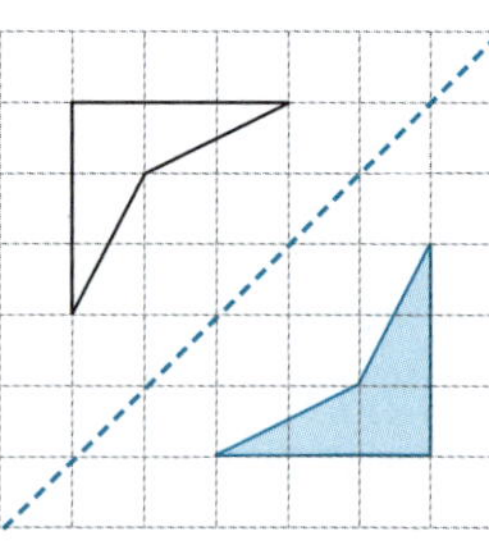

5

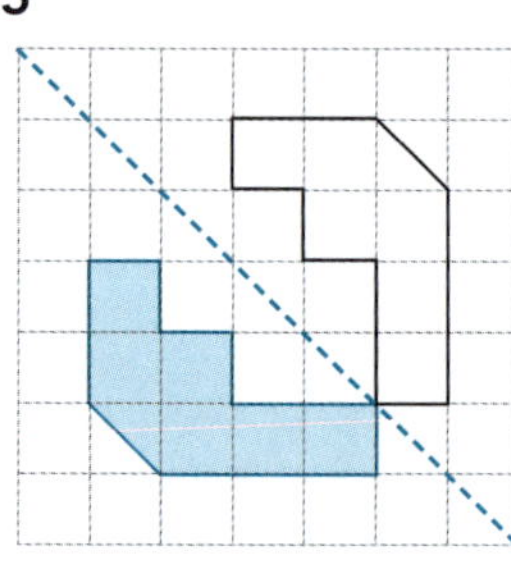

6

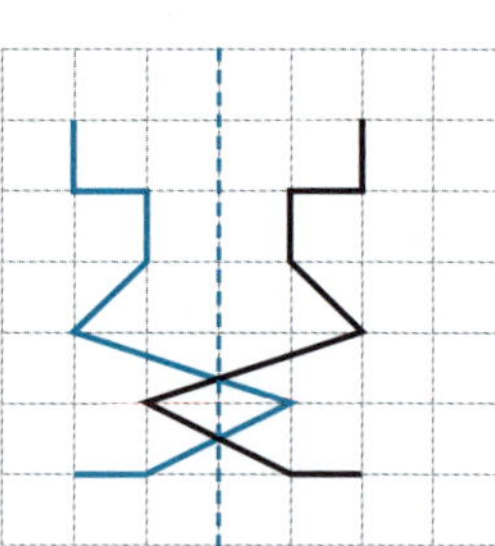

7

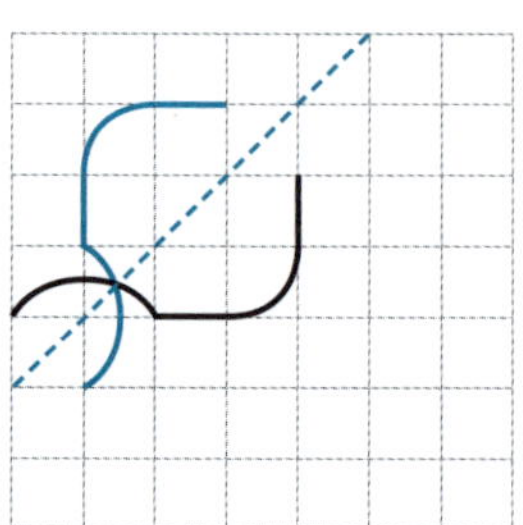

8

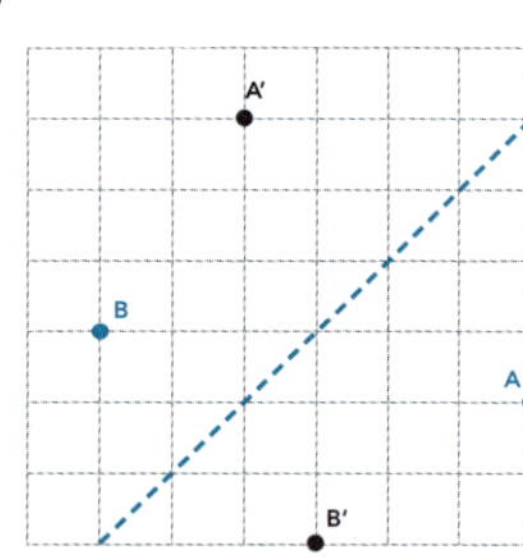

Drawing single reflections (pp. 22–25)

1

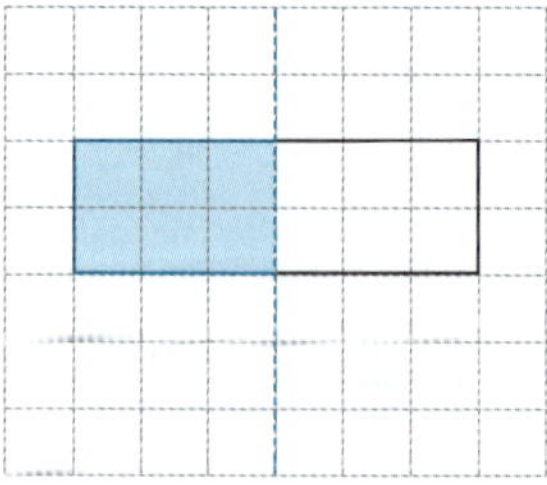

2

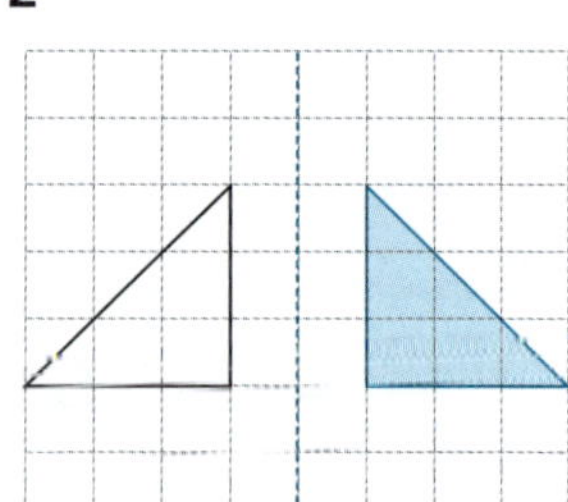

 ISBN: 9780170416016

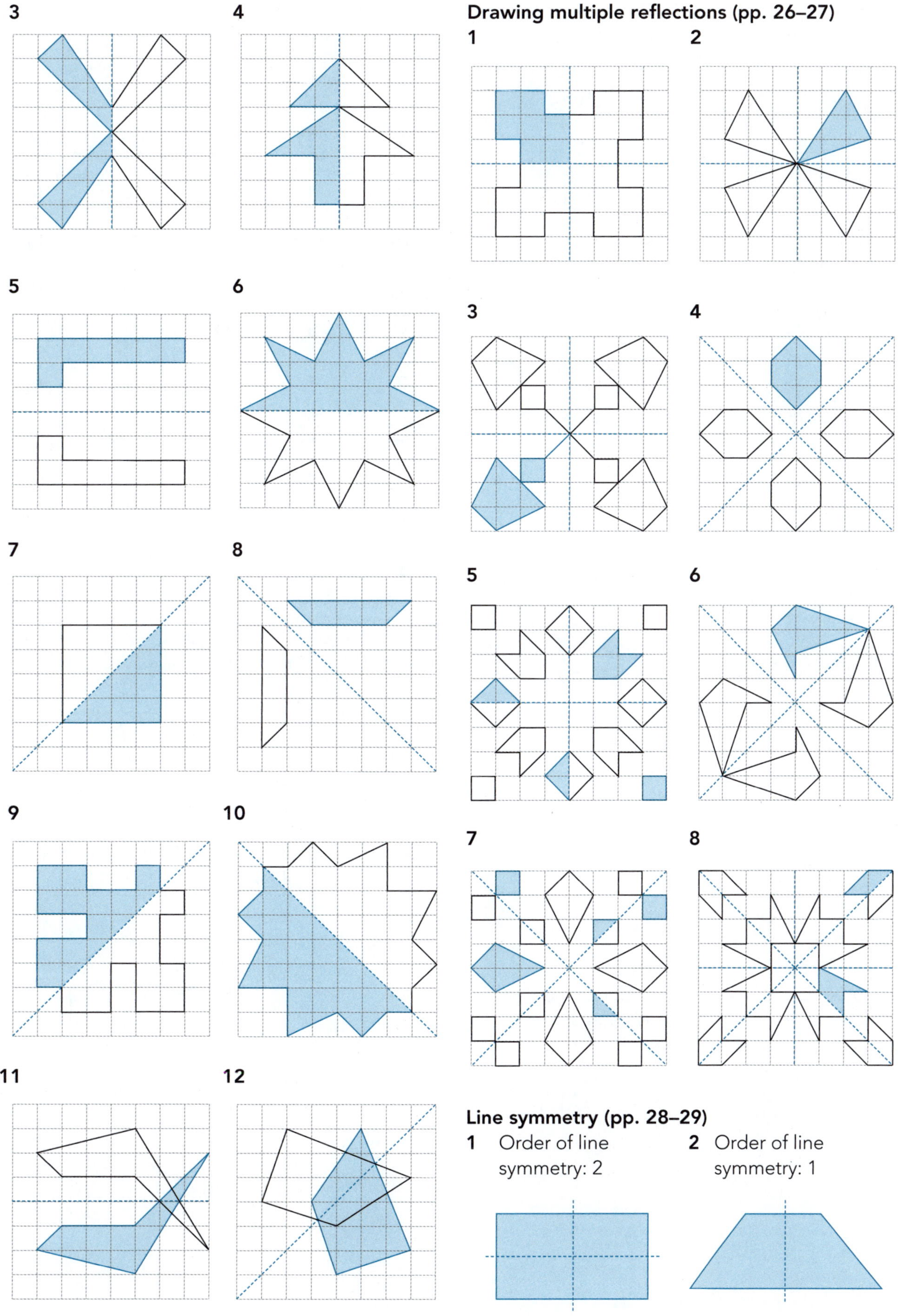

Drawing multiple reflections (pp. 26–27)

1 2 3 4 5 6 7 8

Line symmetry (pp. 28–29)

1 Order of line symmetry: 2

2 Order of line symmetry: 1

3 Order of line symmetry: 1

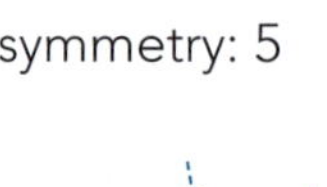

4 Order of line symmetry: 5

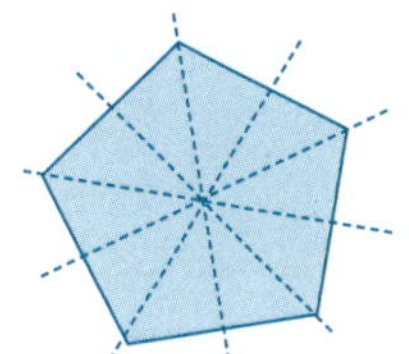

5 Order of line symmetry: 2

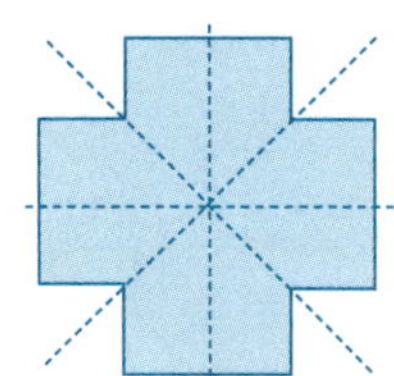

6 Order of line symmetry: 4

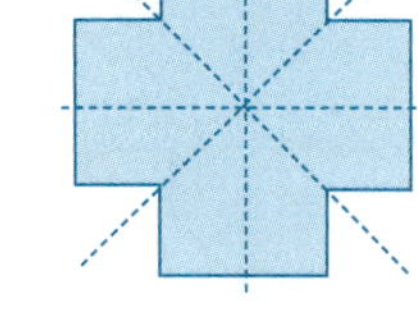

7 Order of line symmetry: 0

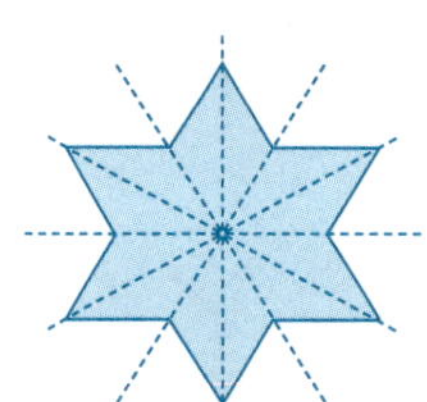

8 Order of line symmetry: 6

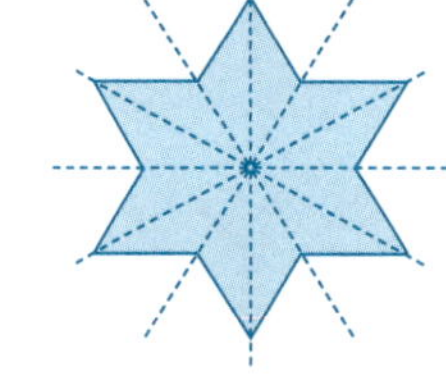

9 Order of line symmetry: 5

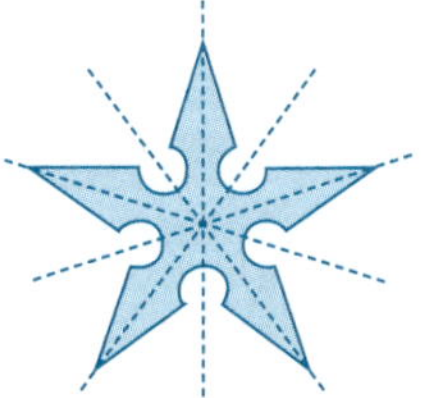

10 Order of line symmetry: 0

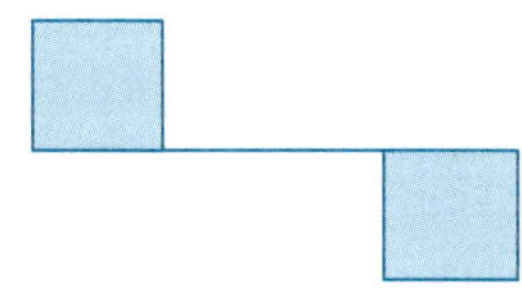

11 Order of line symmetry: 1

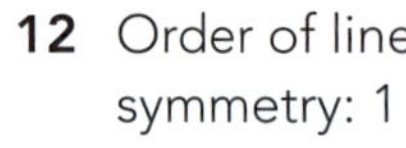

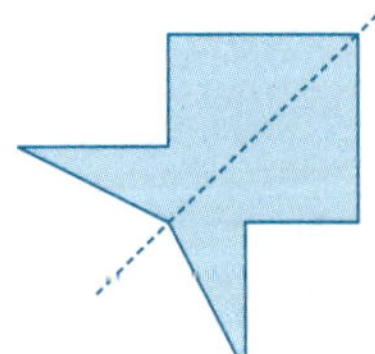

12 Order of line symmetry: 1

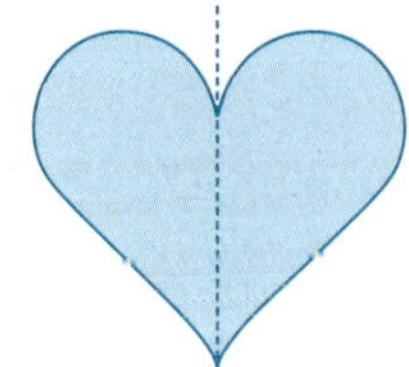

Challenges (pp. 30–31)

1 Ask your teacher to check this.

2 Ask your teacher to check this.

3

≈	☽	⇔	⓪	ϟ
0	1	2	2	0
ꝏ	✪	☢	✦	π
0	5	3	0	0
✌	♣	✶	☠	❄
0	1	6	1	6
☯	✠	☸	☺	✿
0	4	8	1	0
⌘	✡	➤	▣	✹
4	6	0	4	12

4

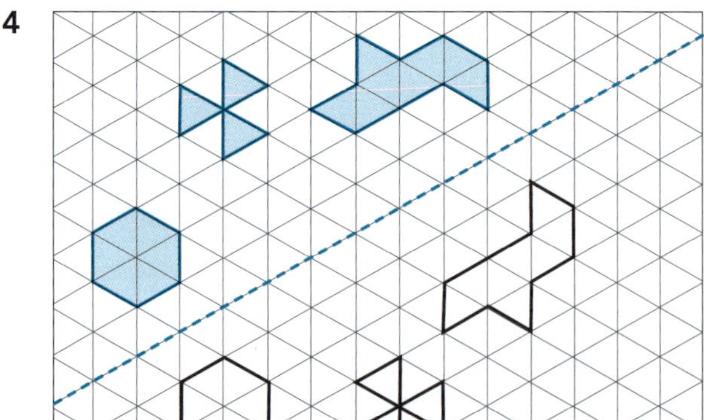

5

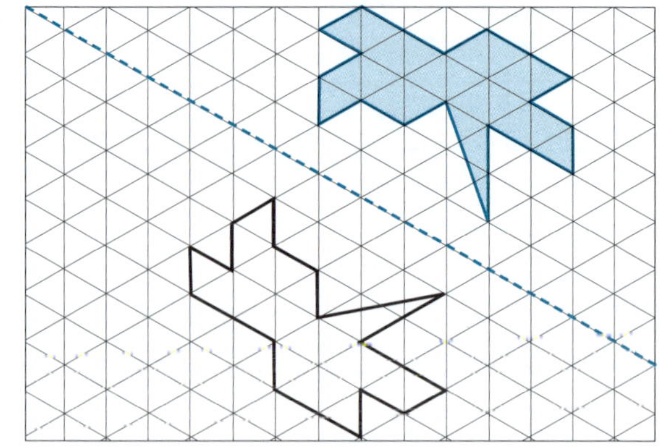

 ISBN: 9780170416016

Mixing it up (pp. 32–33)

1 Reflection

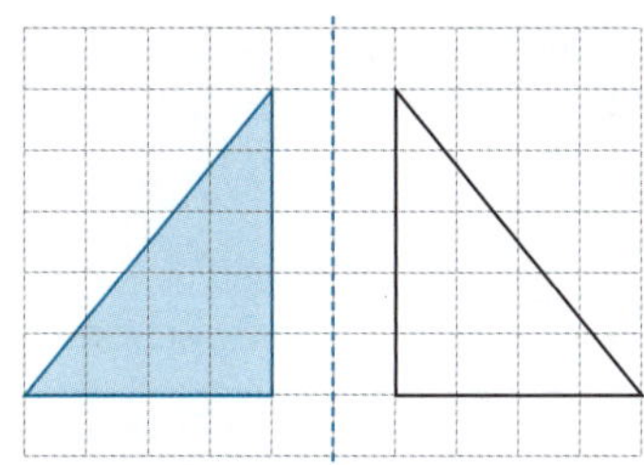

2 Translation $\begin{pmatrix} -4 \\ 2 \end{pmatrix}$

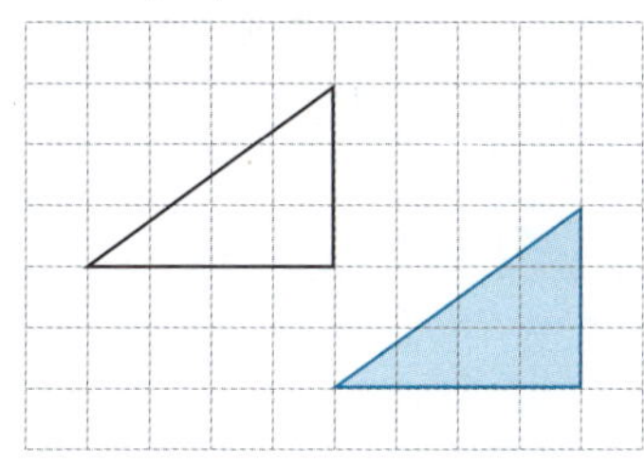

3 Reflection

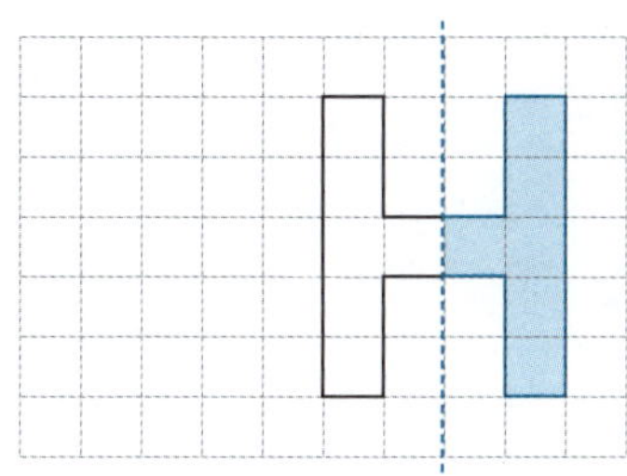

4 Both $\begin{pmatrix} 0 \\ 4 \end{pmatrix}$

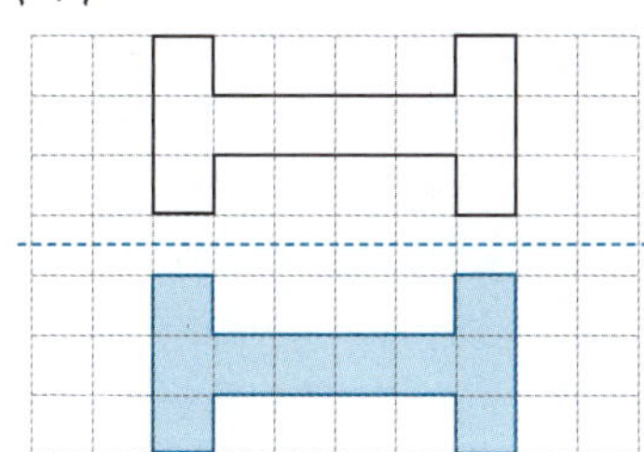

5 Both $\begin{pmatrix} -3 \\ 3 \end{pmatrix}$

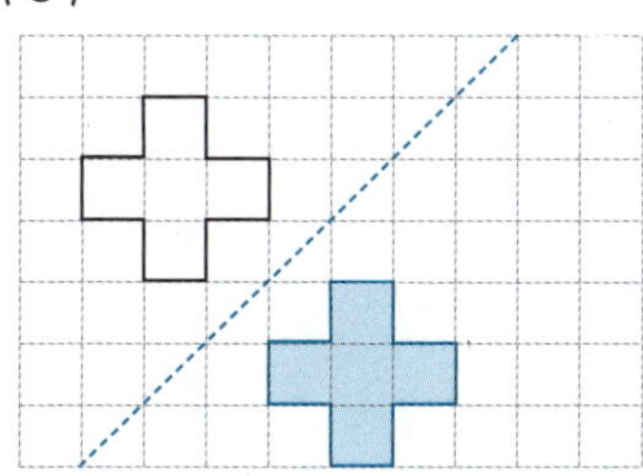

6 Both $\begin{pmatrix} -6 \\ -4 \end{pmatrix}$

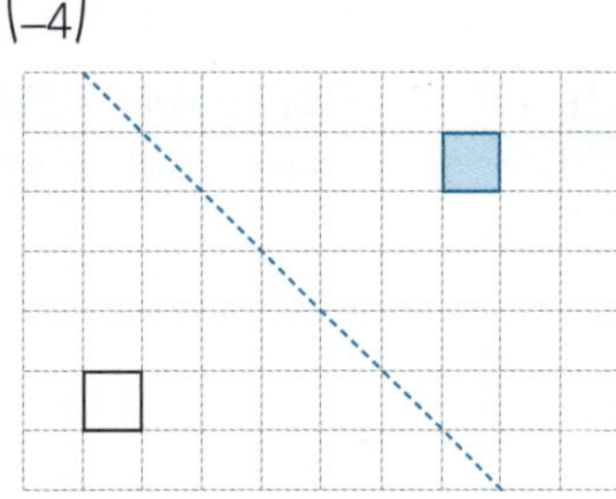

7 Reflection

8 Reflection

9 Neither (see the tail)

10 Both

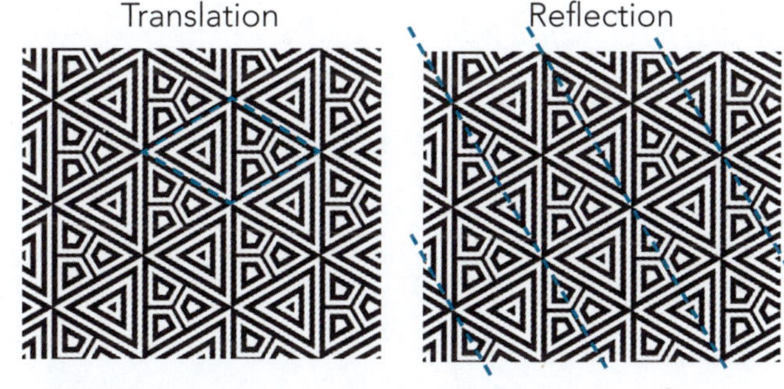

11 Translation

ISBN: 9780170416016

Rotation (pp. 34–53)

	Stays the same	Changes
Size	✓	
Shape	✓	
Orientation		✓
Position		✓

Describing rotations (pp. 35–39)

1 Finding the angle of rotation (pp. 35–39)

1 Rotations from an attached point

1	90°	**2**	180°
3	270°	**4**	45°
5	90°	**6**	135°
7	270°	**8**	45°
9	225°	**10**	270°

2 Rotations from an unattached point

1	180°	**2**	270°
3	180°	**4**	90°
5	90°	**6**	270°

2 Finding the centre of rotation (pp. 40–42)

1 **2**

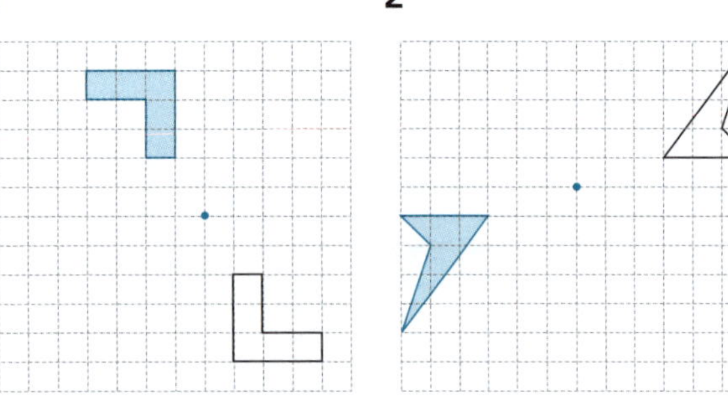

3

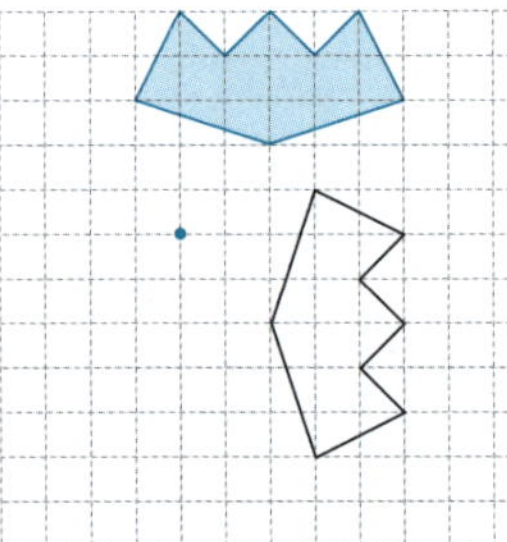

4

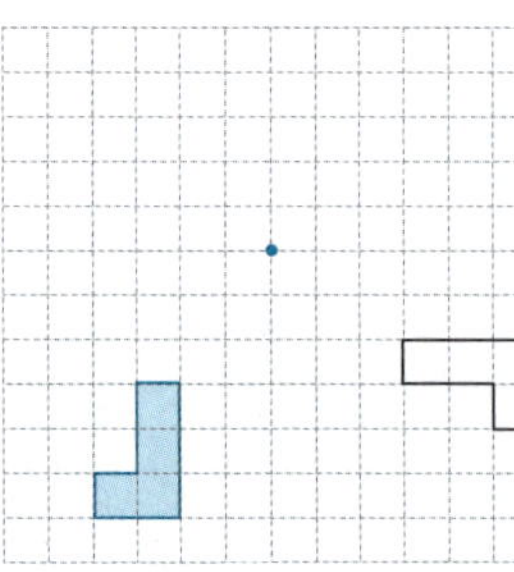

5

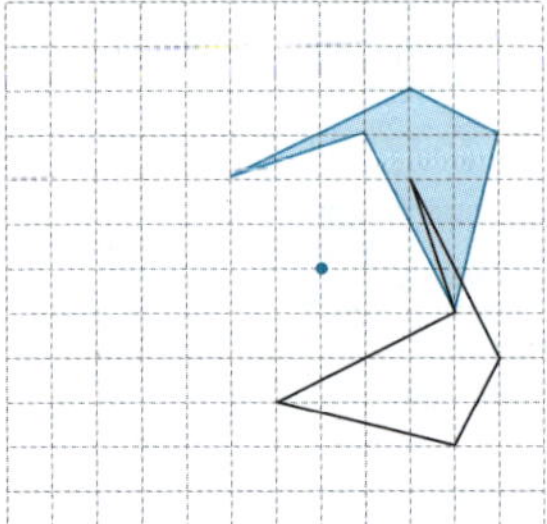

6

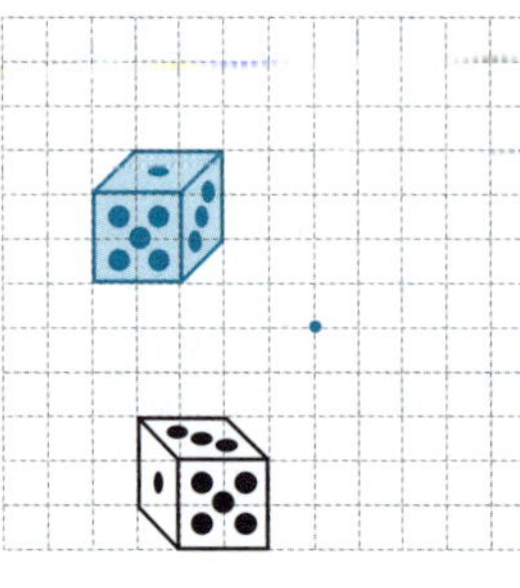

7

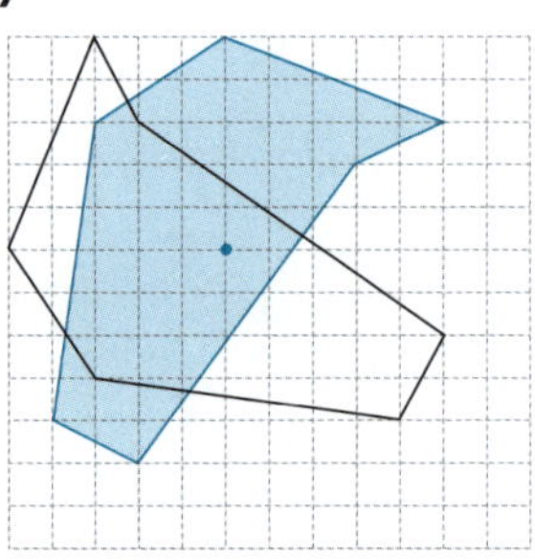

8

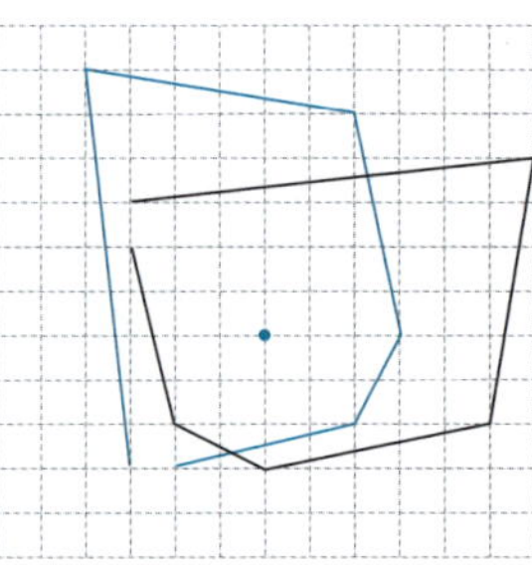

Drawing rotations (pp. 43–48)

1 Rotations from an attached point

1

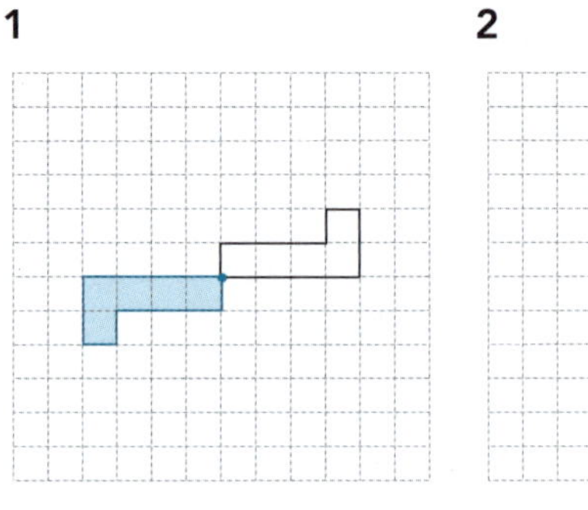

2

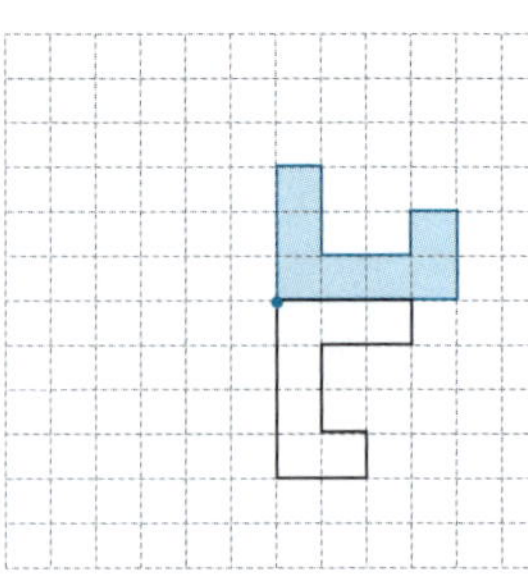

3

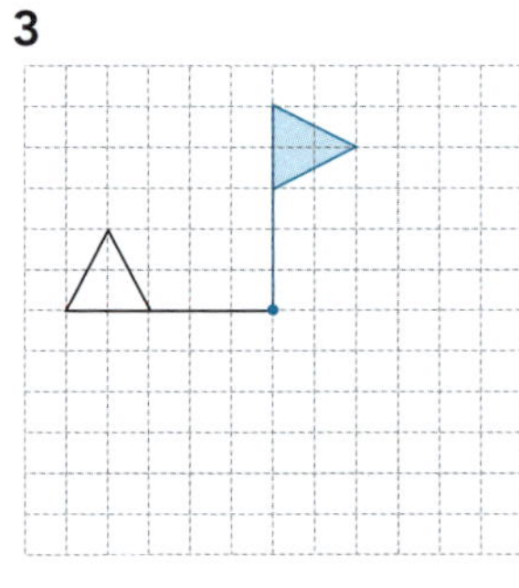

4

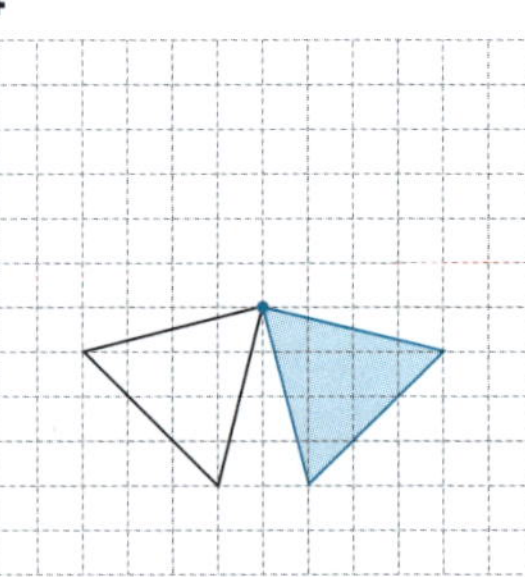

5

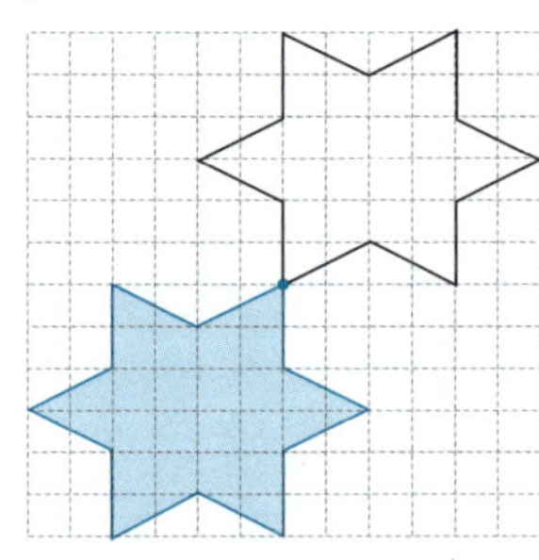

6

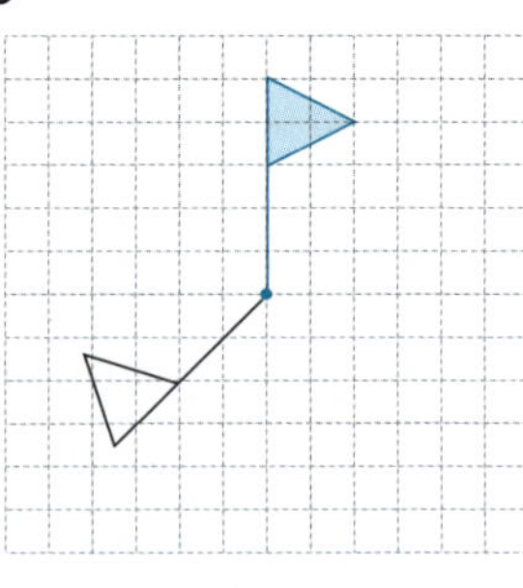

7

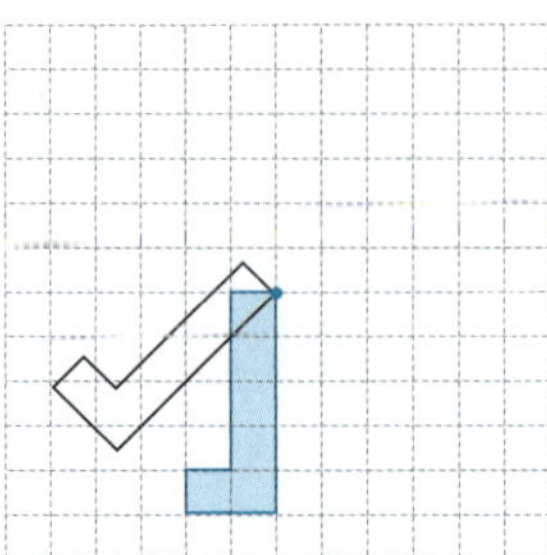

8

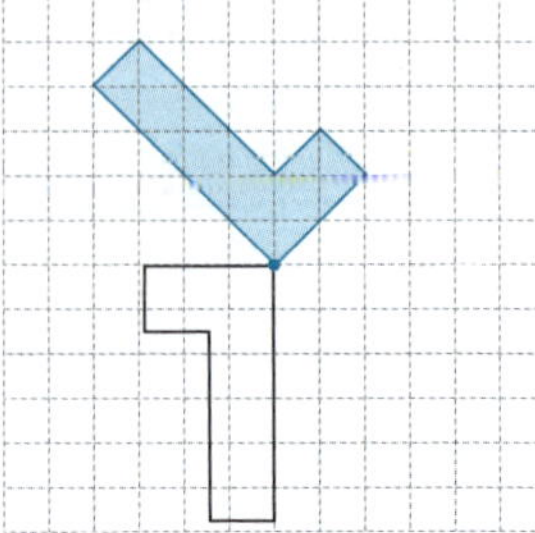

 ISBN: 9780170416016

2 Rotations from an unattached point

1

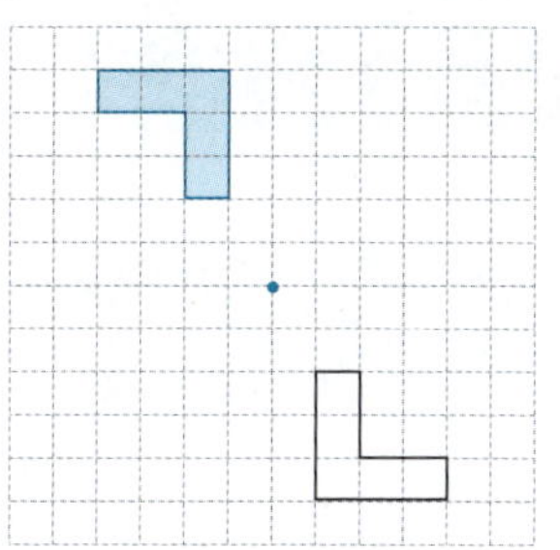

2

3

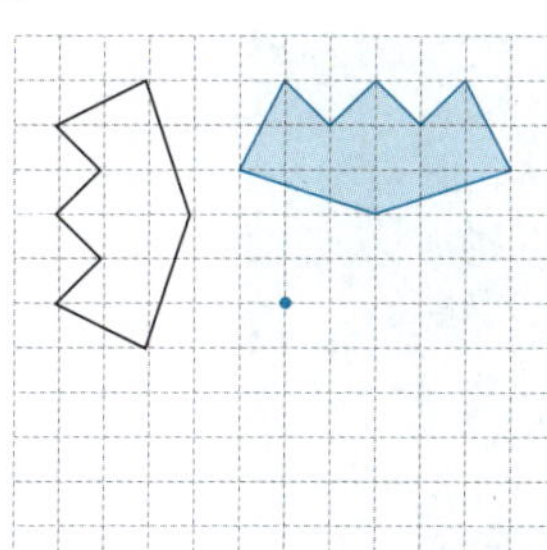

4

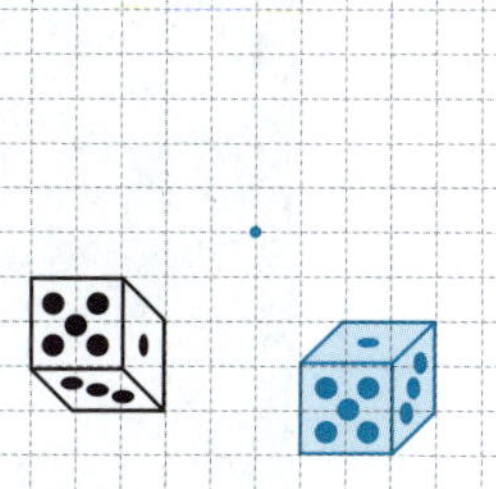

5

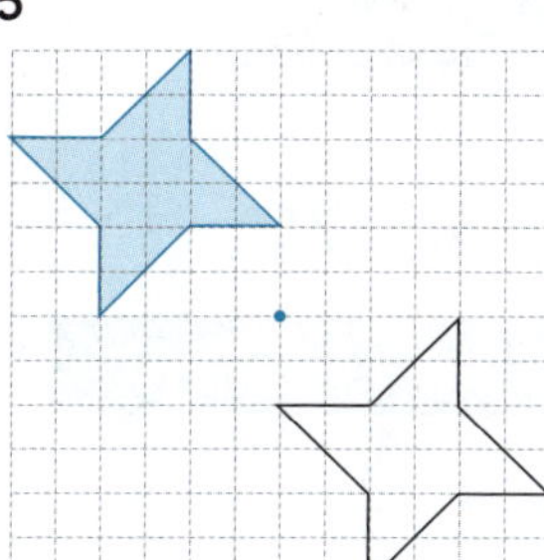

6

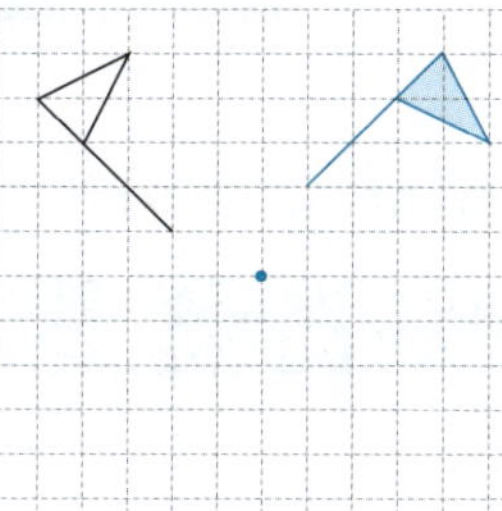

7

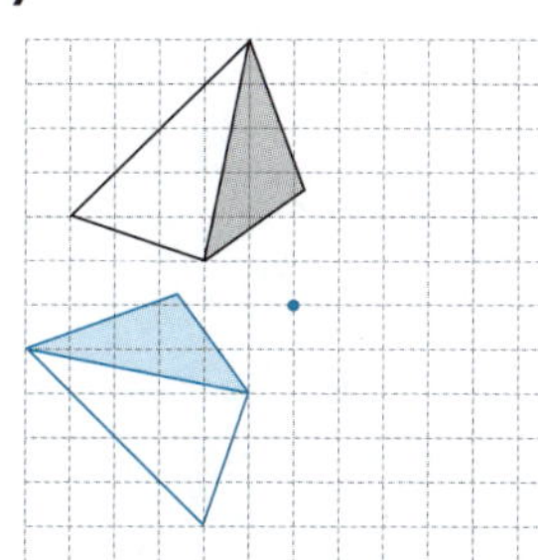

8

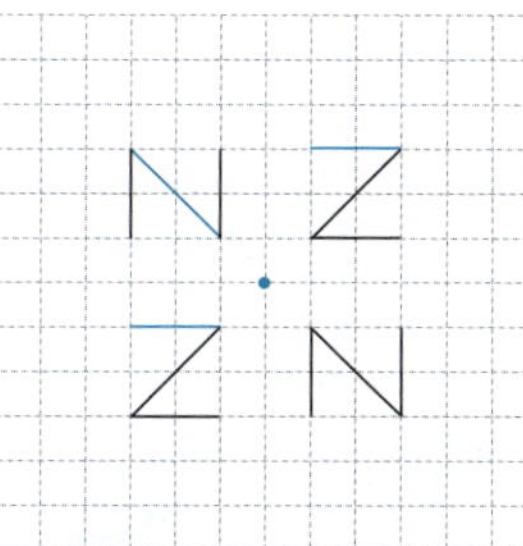

Rotational symmetry (pp. 49–50)

1 Order of rotational symmetry: 2
2 Order of rotational symmetry: 1
3 Order of rotational symmetry: 1
4 Order of rotational symmetry: 5
5 Order of rotational symmetry: 2
6 Order of rotational symmetry: 4
7 Order of rotational symmetry: 1
8 Order of rotational symmetry: 6
9 Order of rotational symmetry: 5
10 Order of rotational symmetry: 2
11 Order of rotational symmetry: 1
12 Order of rotational symmetry: 1

Challenges (p. 51)

1 Ask your teacher to check this.
2 Ask your teacher to check this.
3

≈	☽	⇔	⓪	ϟ
2	1	2	2	1
	✪		✦	π
1	5	3	4	1
✌	♣	✶	☠	❄
1	1	6	1	6
☯	✠	☸	☺	✾
1	4	8	1	4
⌘	✡	➤	▣	✹
4	6	1	4	12

Mixing it up (pp. 52–54)

1 Rotation of 270° clockwise.

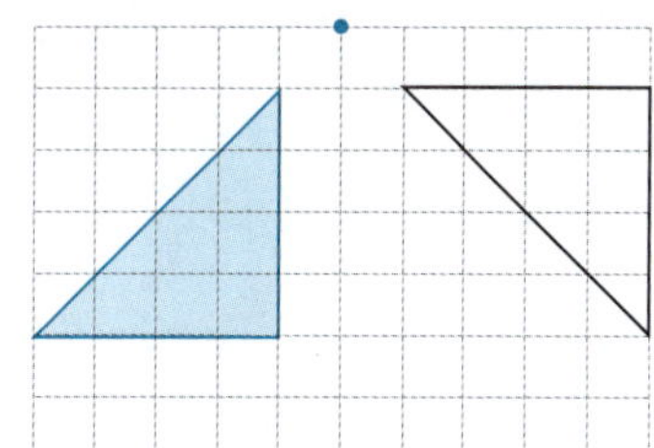

2 Reflection or rotation of 180° clockwise.

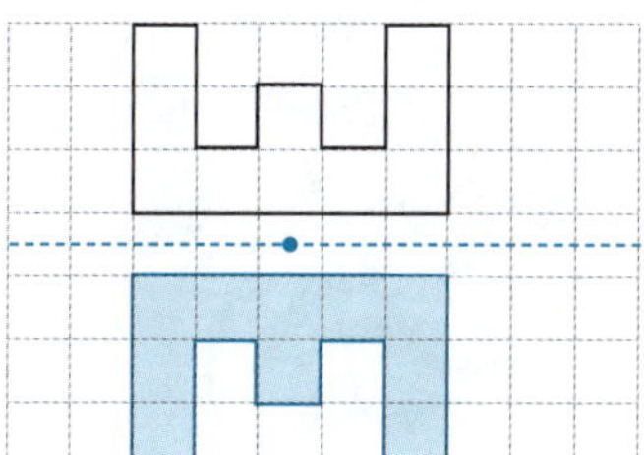

3 Reflection or translation by $\begin{pmatrix}-5\\0\end{pmatrix}$ or rotation of 180° clockwise.

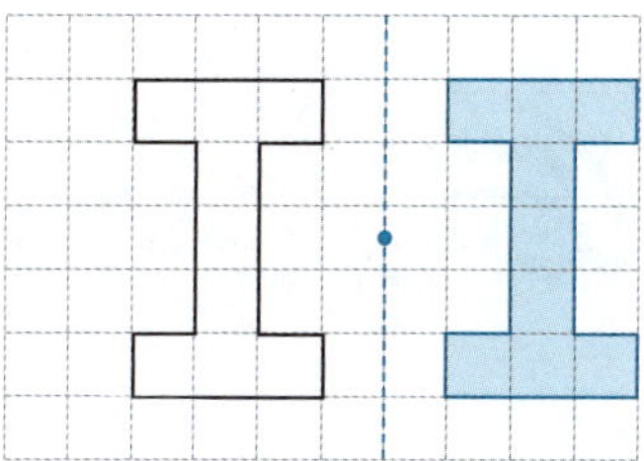

4 Reflection or rotation of 90°

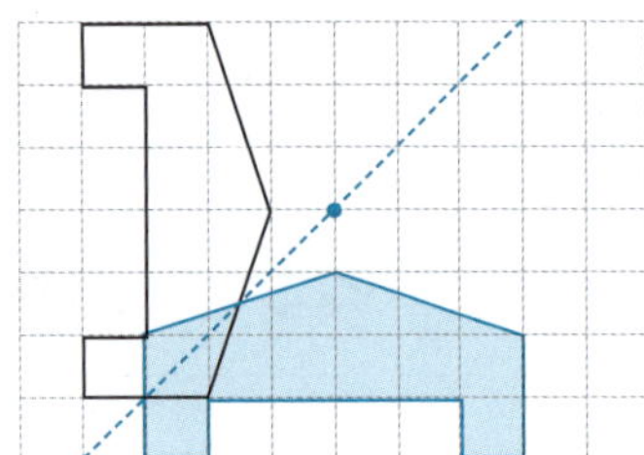

5 Reflection or translation by $\begin{pmatrix}-3\\3\end{pmatrix}$ or rotation of 270° about **B** or 90° about **A**.

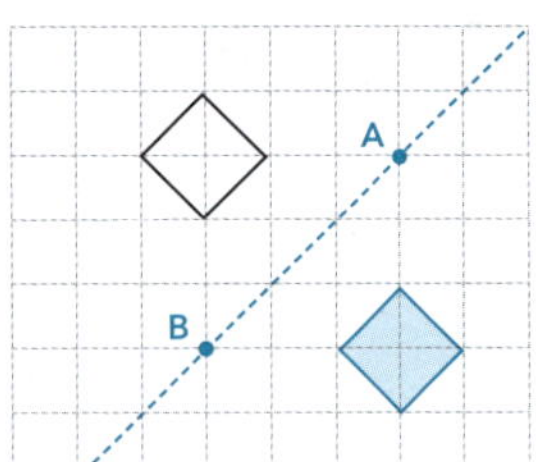

6 Translation by $\begin{pmatrix}-6\\-4\end{pmatrix}$ or rotation of 180° clockwise.

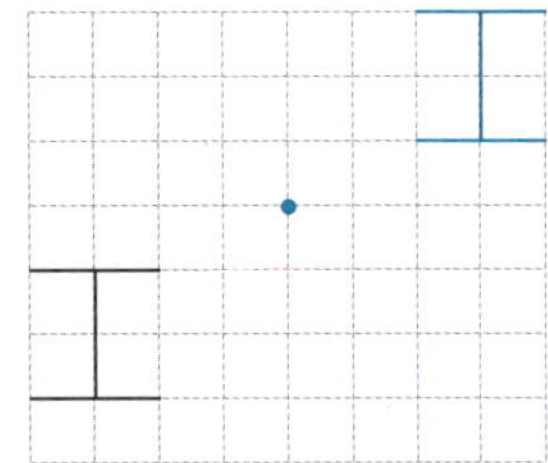

7 Rotation of 180° clockwise.

8 Reflection

9 Reflection

Translation

10 Reflection
Rotation of 180° clockwise about the centre.

Enlargement (pp. 54–72)

	Stays the same	Changes
Size		✓
Shape	✓	
Orientation	✓	
Position		✓

Describing enlargements (pp. 55–59)
1 Finding the scale factor (pp. 55–56)

1 **a** 2 **b** $\frac{3}{2}$ **c** 1 **d** $\frac{1}{2}$

2 **a** 2 **b** 1 **c** $\frac{2}{3}$ **d** $\frac{1}{3}$

3 **a** 3 **b** $\frac{1}{2}$ **c** $\frac{3}{2}$

2 Finding the centre of enlargement (pp. 57–59)

1 Scale factor = 2

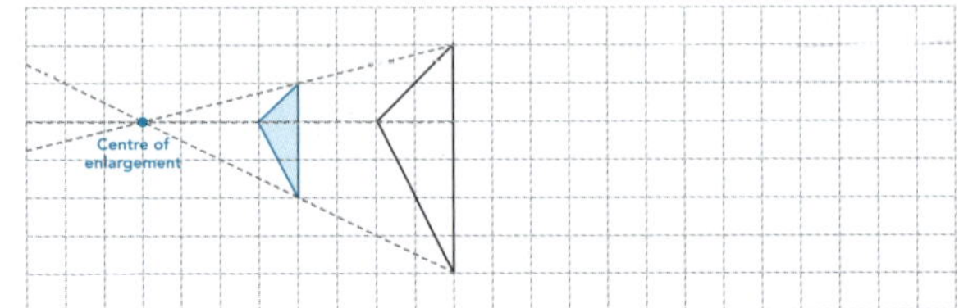

 ISBN: 9780170416016

2 Scale factor = 3

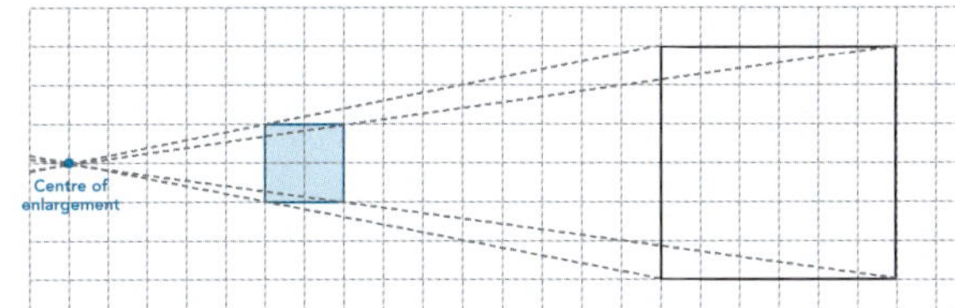

3 Scale factor = $\frac{1}{3}$

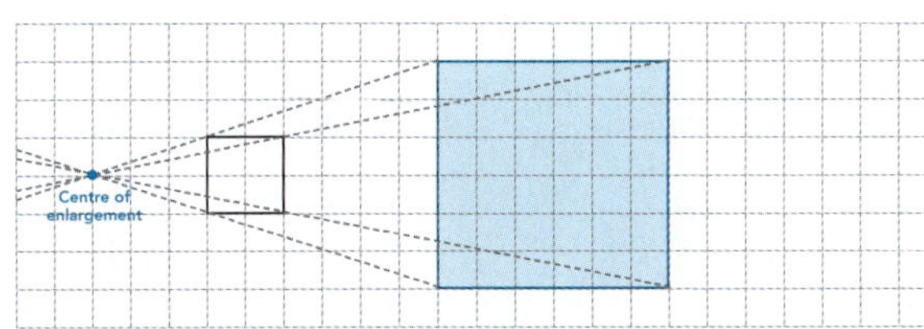

4 Scale factor = $\frac{1}{2}$

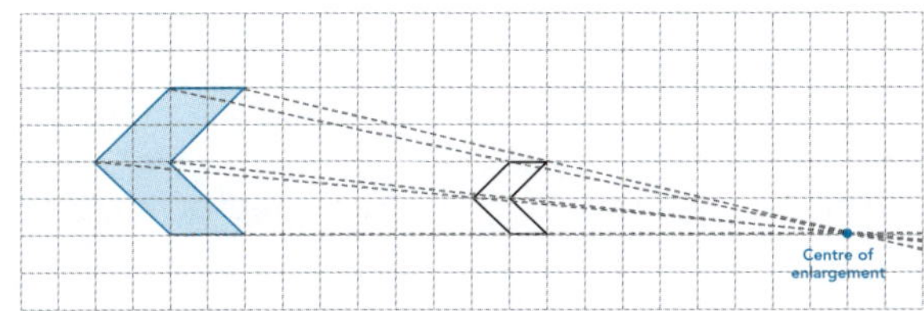

5 Scale factor = 2

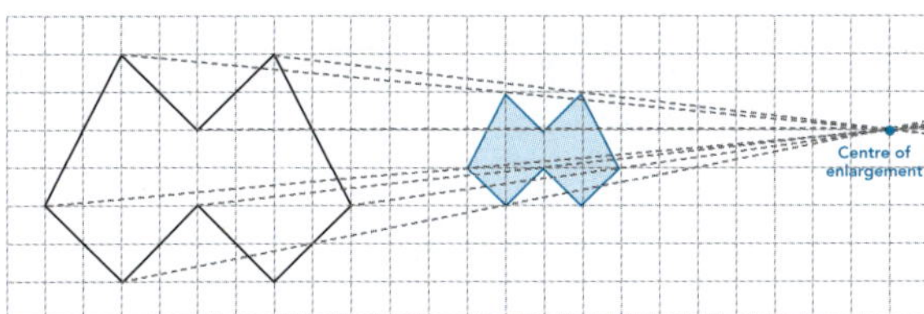

6 Scale factor = $\frac{2}{3}$

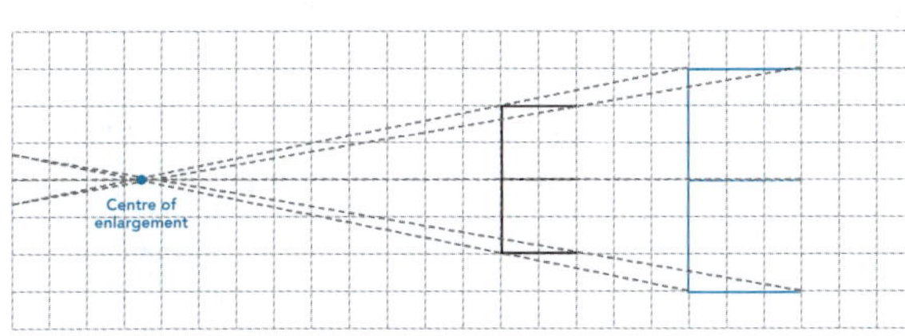

Drawing enlargements (pp. 60–63)

1 Scale factor = 3

2 Scale factor = 2

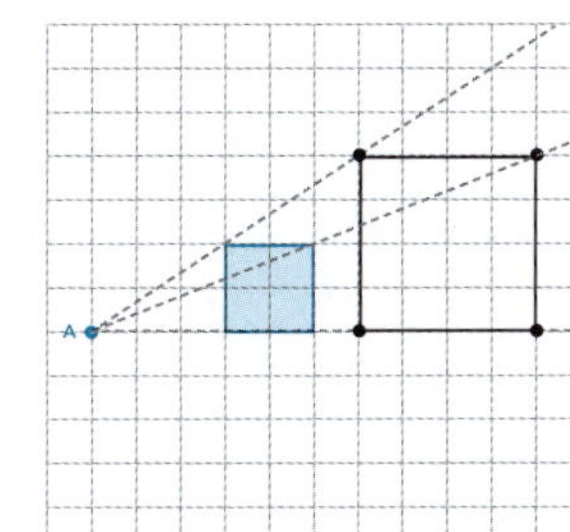

3 Scale factor = 2

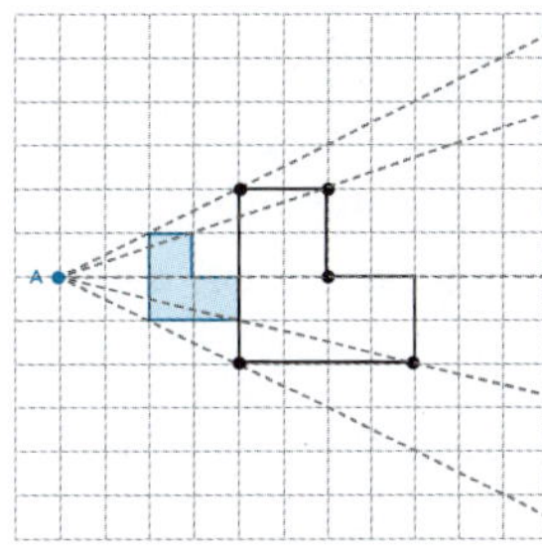

4 Scale factor = $\frac{1}{2}$

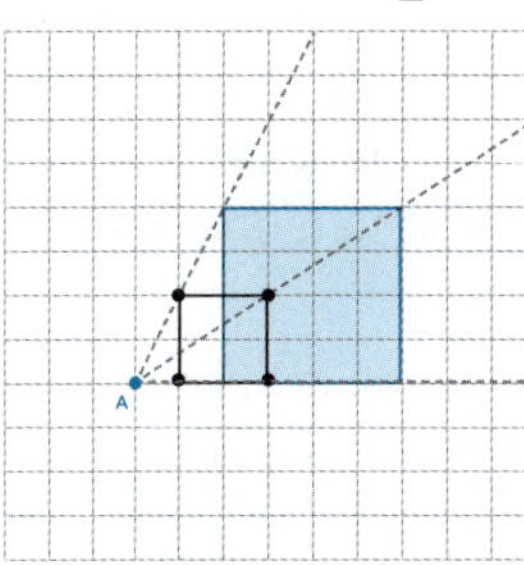
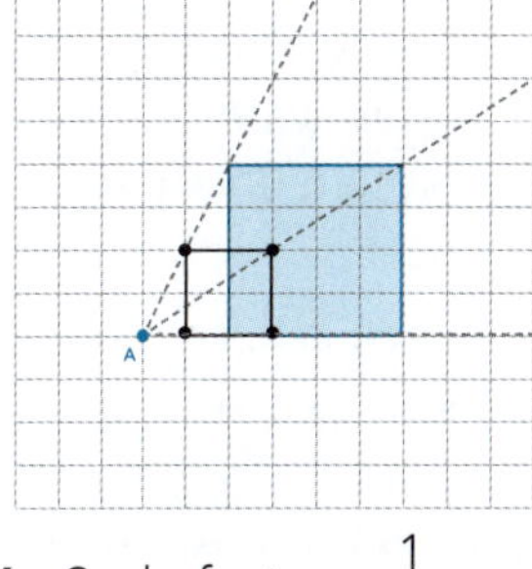

5 Scale factor = 3

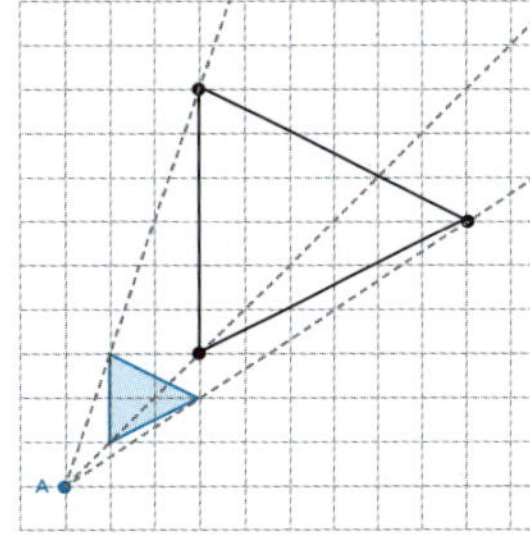

6 Scale factor = $\frac{1}{3}$

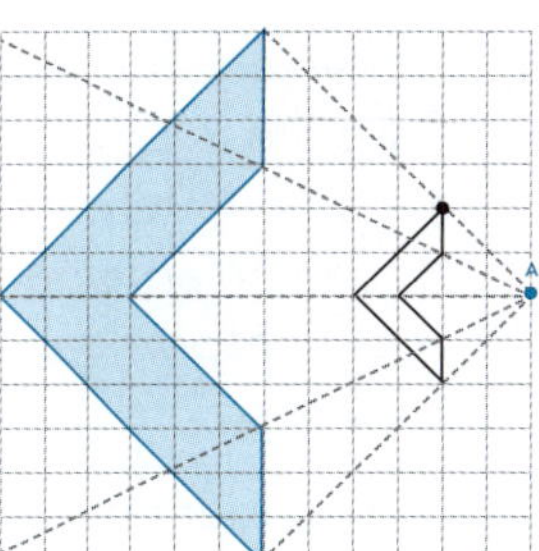

7

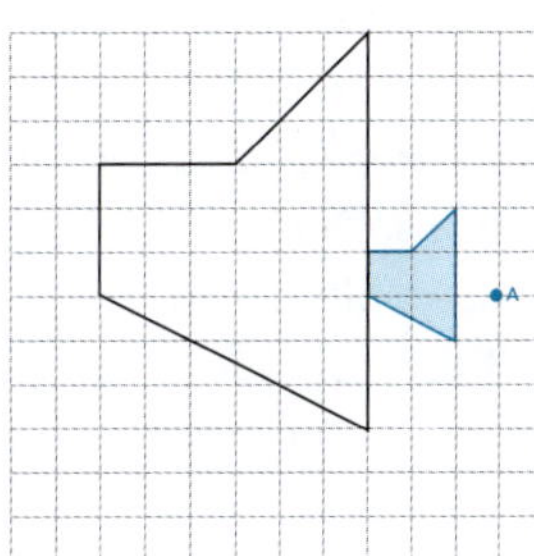

8

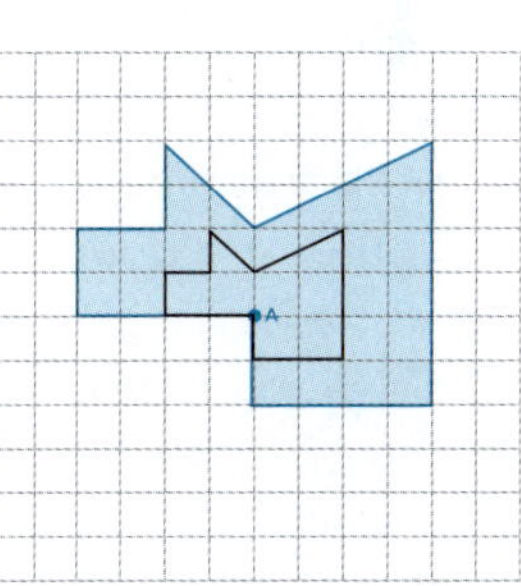

9

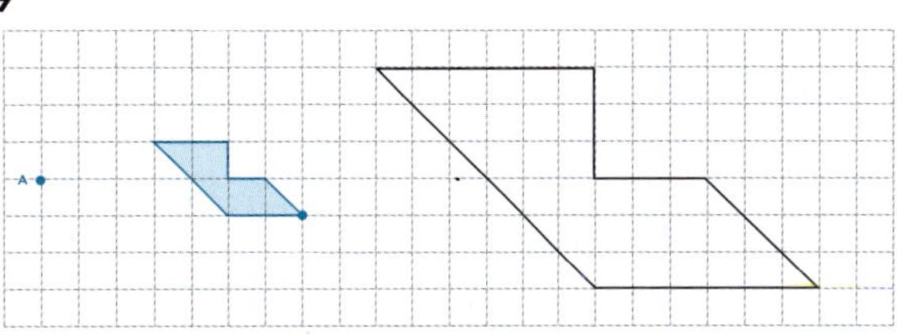

10

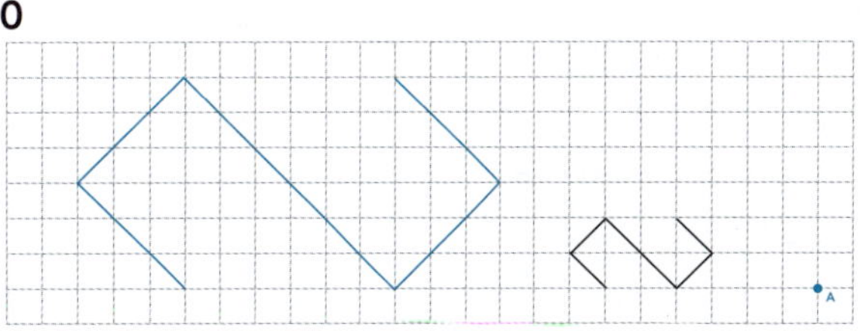

11

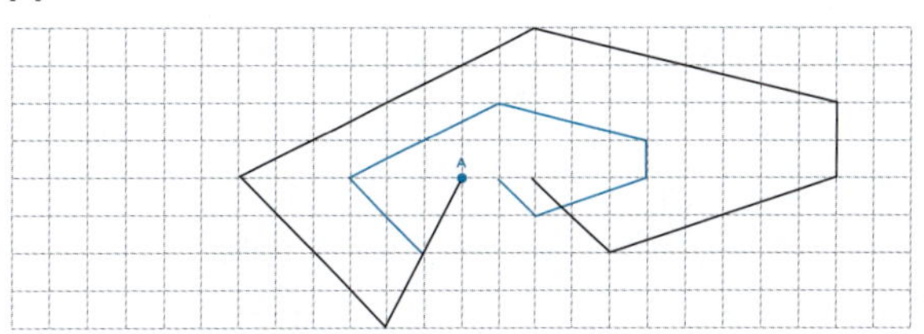

Recognising enlargements (pp. 64–67)

1 Enlargement because the sides are in proportion with a scale factor of 4, and the figures are orientated in the same way.

2 Not an enlargement because the sides are not in proportion. The scale factor for the base is 3, but that for the height is $\frac{5}{2}$.

3 Not an enlargement because the sides are not in proportion. The scale factor for the sides is 1, but that for the tops and bottoms is $\frac{4}{5}$.

4 Not an enlargement because although the sides are in proportion with a scale factor of 2, the orientation of the figures is different.

5 Not an enlargement because the sides are not in proportion. The scale factor for the right side is $\frac{3}{2}$, but that for the base is $\frac{9}{7}$.

6 Enlargement because the sides are in proportion with a scale factor of $\frac{1}{3}$, and the figures are orientated in the same way.

7 Enlargement because the sides are in proportion with a scale factor of 2, and the figures are orientated in the same way.

8 Not an enlargement because although the sides are in proportion with a scale factor of $\frac{1}{2}$, the orientation of the figures is different.

Challenges (pp. 67–70)

Drawing enlargements without a grid (p. 67)

1

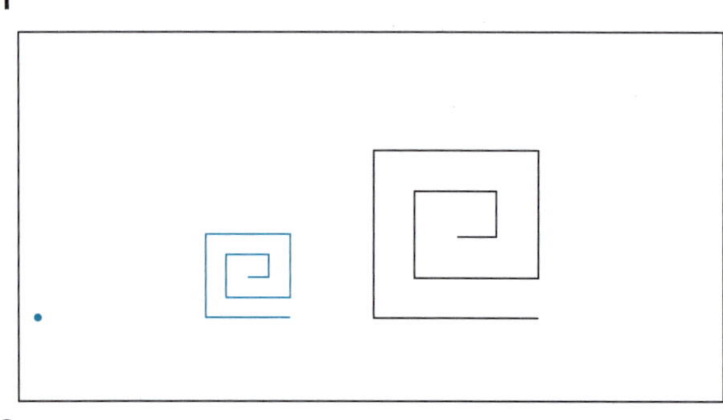

2

Negative scale factors (pp. 68–70)

1 Scale factor = –1

2 Scale factor = $-\frac{1}{3}$

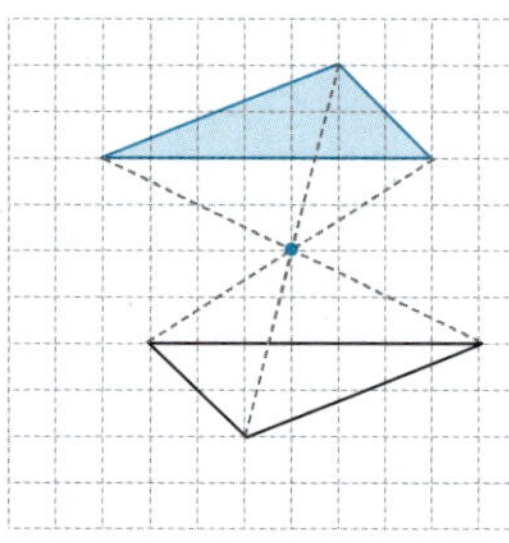

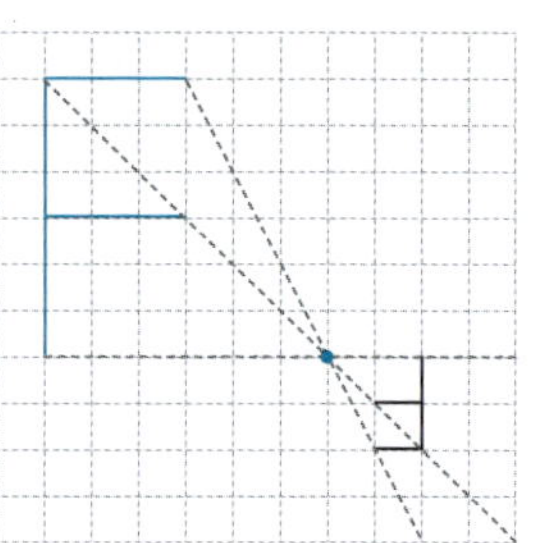

3 Scale factor = $-\frac{1}{4}$

4 Scale factor = –2

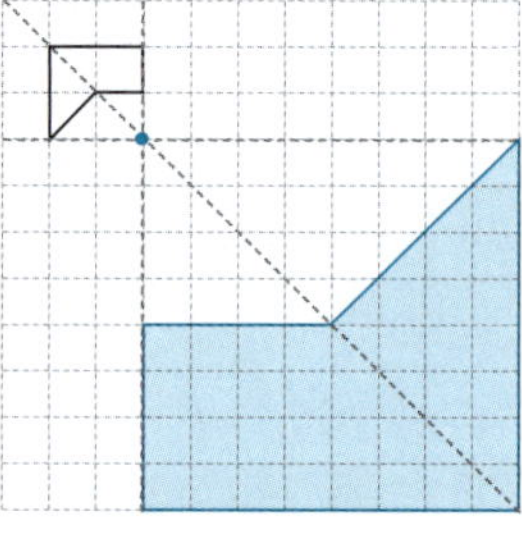

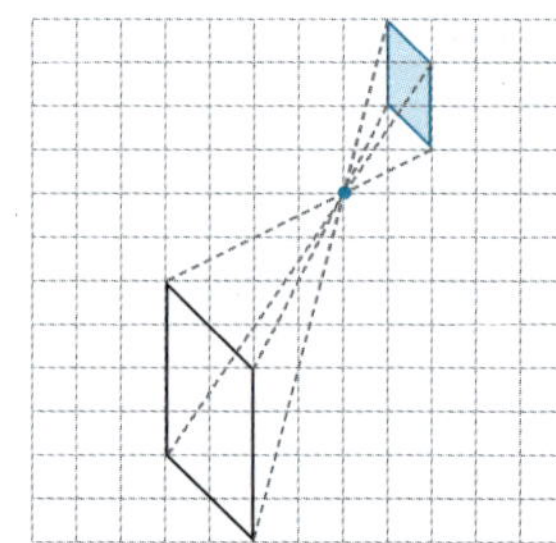

5 Scale factor = $-\frac{1}{2}$

6 Scale factor = $-\frac{1}{2}$

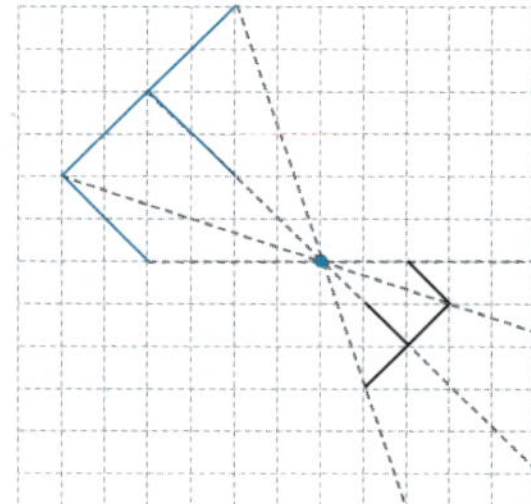

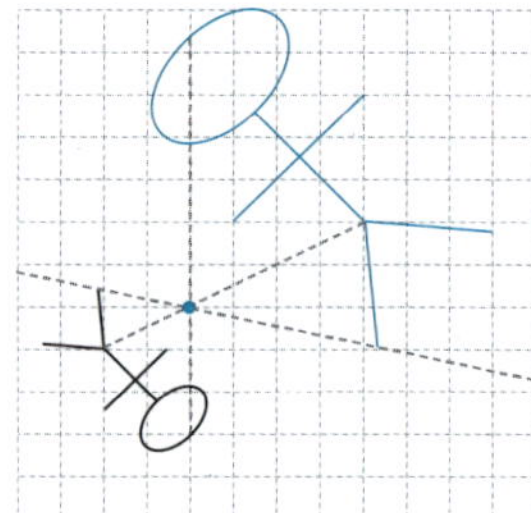

7 Scale factor = –2

8 Scale factor = $-\frac{1}{2}$

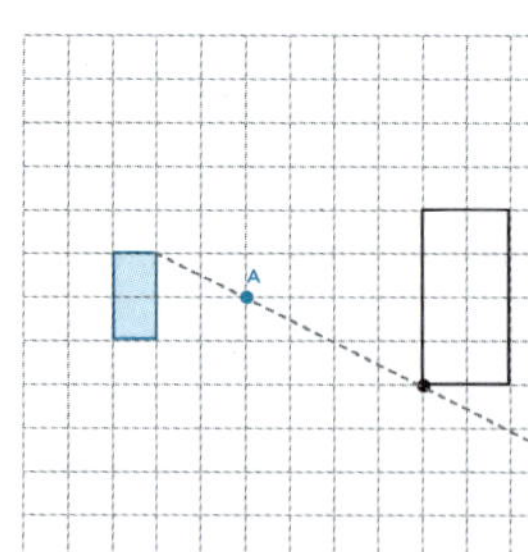

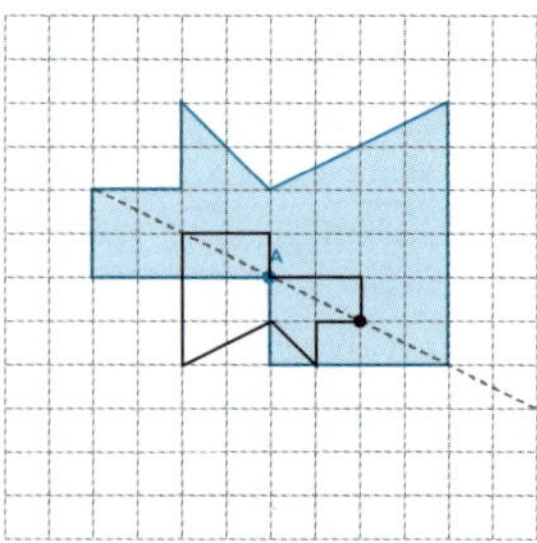

9

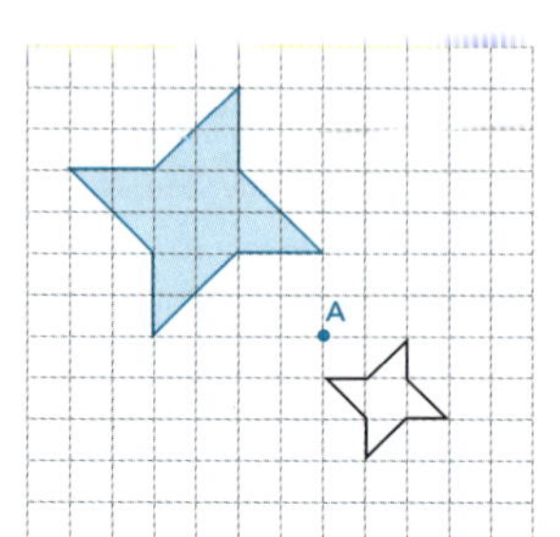

10

 ISBN: 9780170416016

11

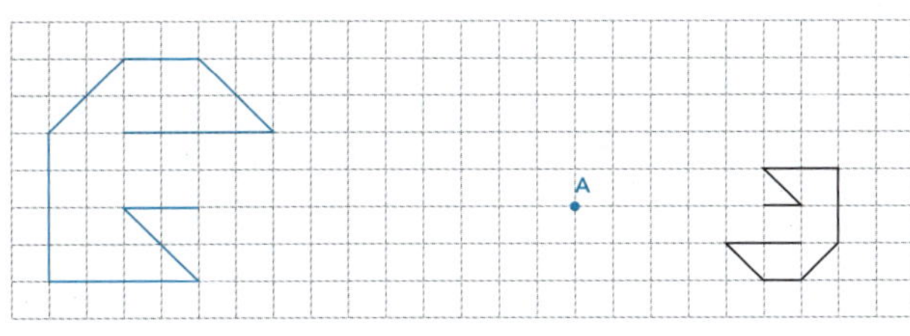

Mixing it up (pp. 71–72)

1 Reflection
Rotation of 180° clockwise.
Enlargement with scale factor of –1.

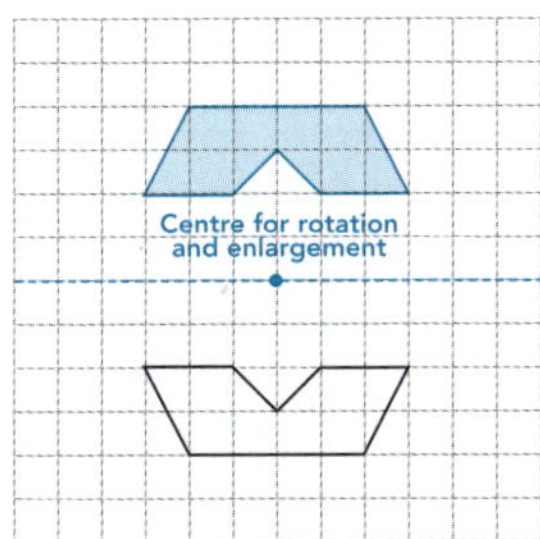

2 Translation of $\begin{pmatrix} -4 \\ -6 \end{pmatrix}$
Rotation of 180° clockwise.
Enlargement with scale factor of –1.

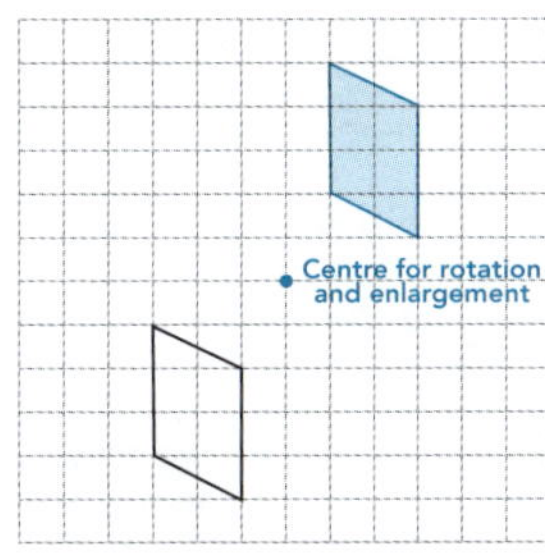

3 Enlargement with scale factor of –2.

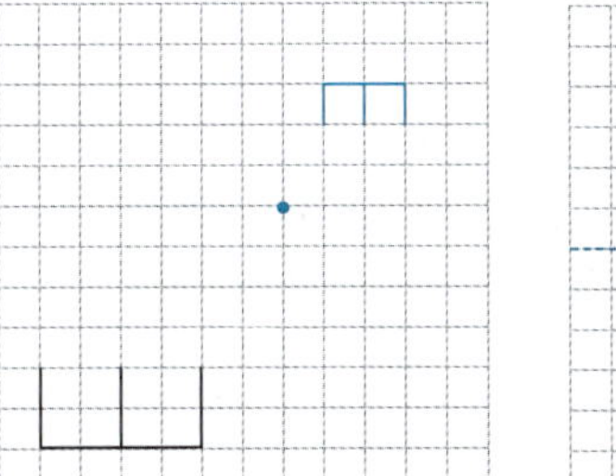

4 Reflection. Rotation of 180° clockwise. Enlargement with scale factor of –1.

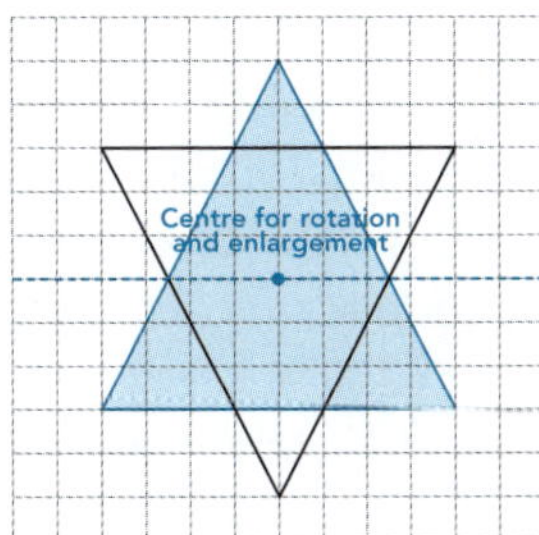

5 Rotation of 180° clockwise.
Enlargement with scale factor of –1.

6 Enlargement with scale factor of 2 or $\frac{1}{2}$.

7 Enlargement with scale factor of $-\frac{1}{2}$ or –2.

8 Reflection

9 Reflection

Rotation of 180° clockwise.

Translation

Enlargement with scale factor of –1.

Invariant points (pp. 73–74)

1 Enlargement with scale factor of 2.

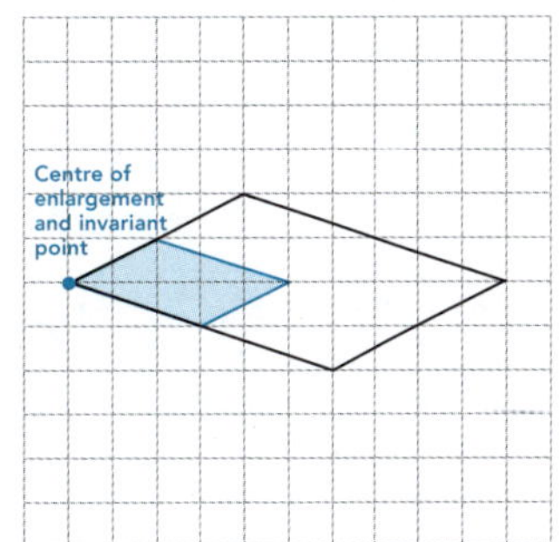

2 Reflection
Enlargement with scale factor of –1.

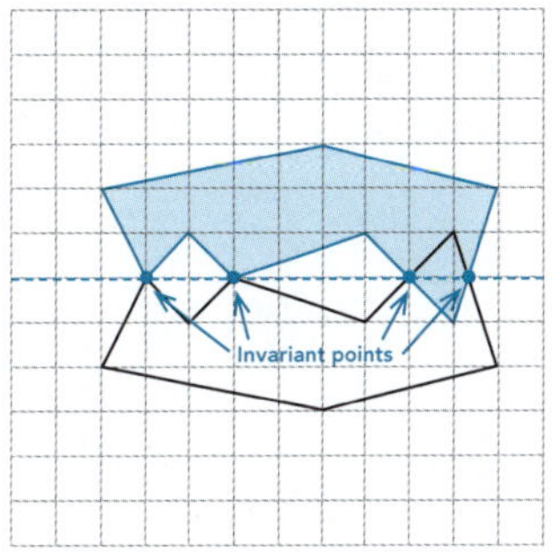

ISBN: 9780170416016

3 Rotation of 180° clockwise or enlargement with scale factor or −1.

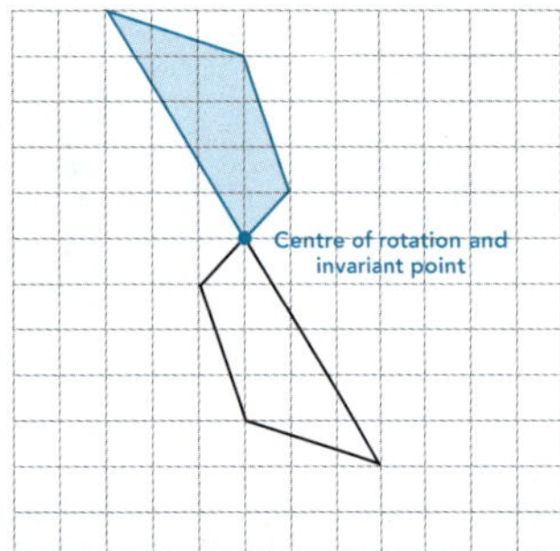

4 Reflection

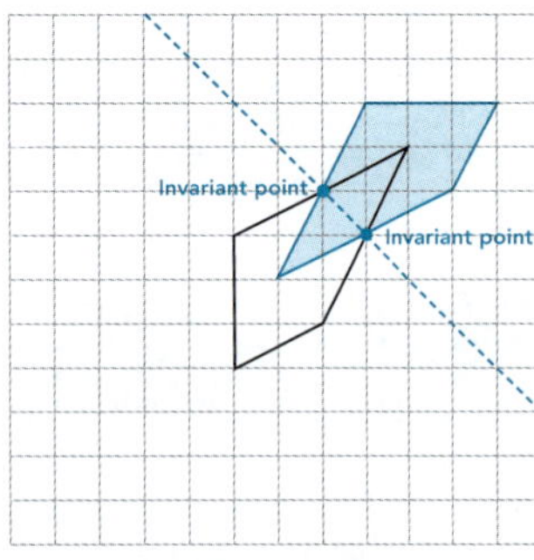

5 Rotation of 270° clockwise.

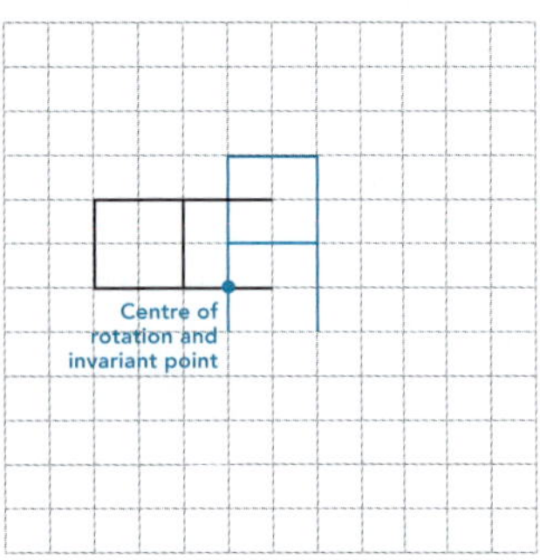

6 Enlargement with a scale factor of $\frac{1}{3}$.

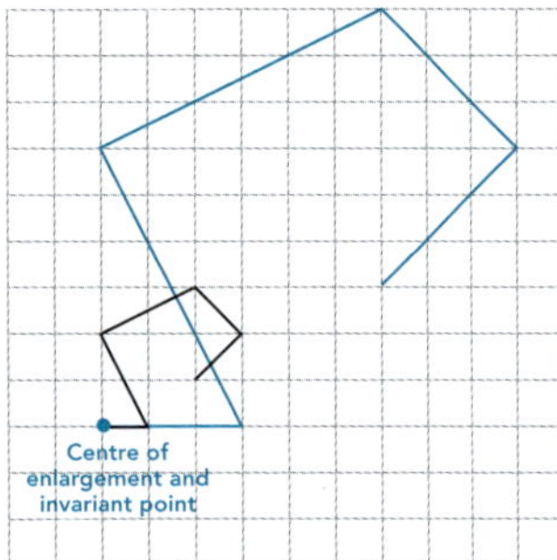

Inverse transformations (pp. 75–78)

1 Inverse transformation: A reflection in the mirror line.

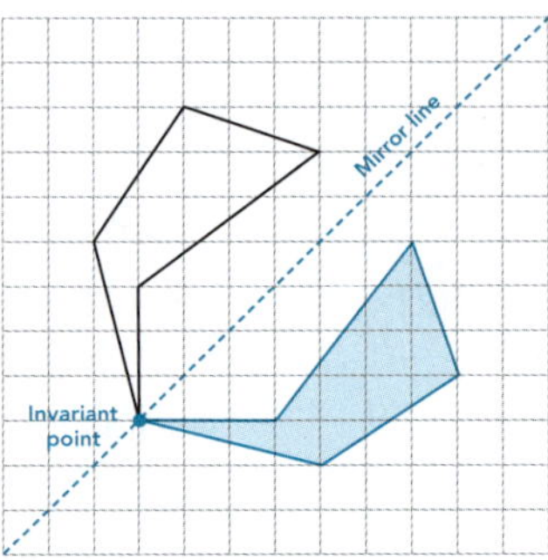

2 Inverse transformation: Enlargement with a scale factor of $\frac{1}{3}$.

No invariant points.

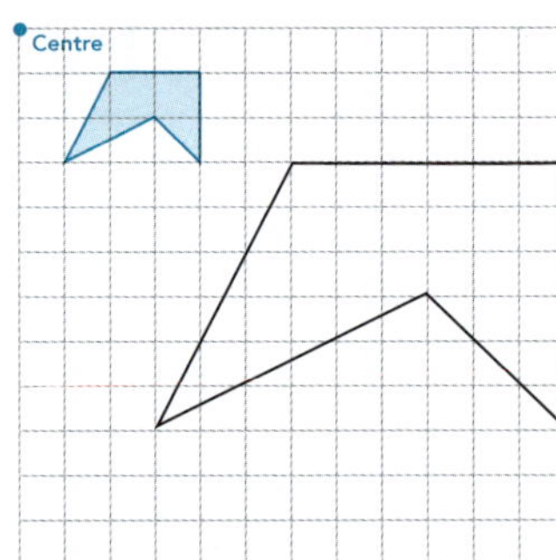

3 Inverse transformations:

Reflection in the mirror line.

Rotation clockwise around the centre of 90°, or a rotation anticlockwise around the centre of 270°.

No invariant points.

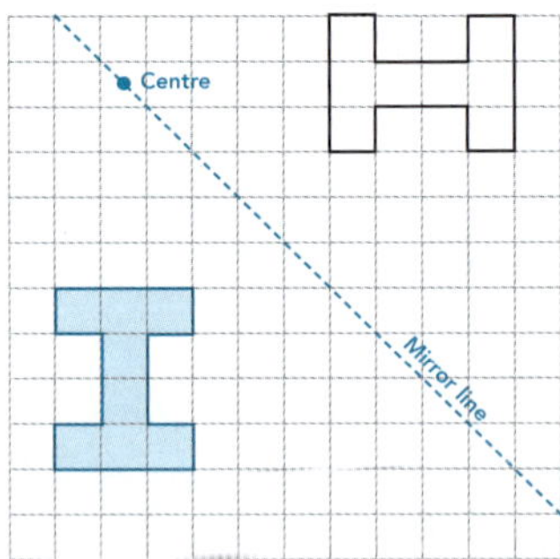

 ISBN: 9780170416016

4 Inverse transformations:
Translation of $\begin{pmatrix} 6 \\ -6 \end{pmatrix}$.
Reflection in the mirror line.
Rotation clockwise or anticlockwise around the centre of 180°.
No invariant points.

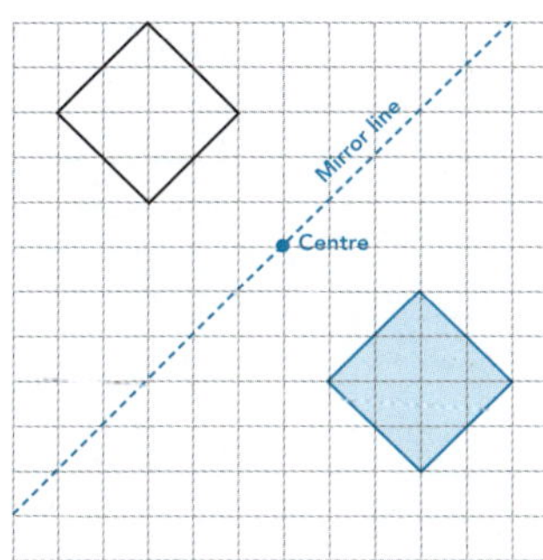

5 Inverse transformations:
Reflection in the mirror line.
Rotation clockwise or anticlockwise around the centre of 180°.
Enlargement with scale factor of –1.
Invariant points: 4 marked •.

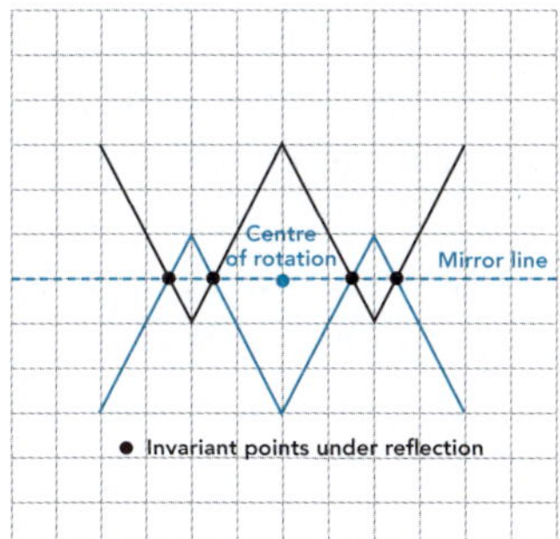

6 Inverse transformations:
Translation 22 mm to the right and 28 mm down.
Rotation clockwise of 270° around the centre A
or
Rotation clockwise of 90° around the centre B
or
Rotation clockwise of 180° around the centre C.

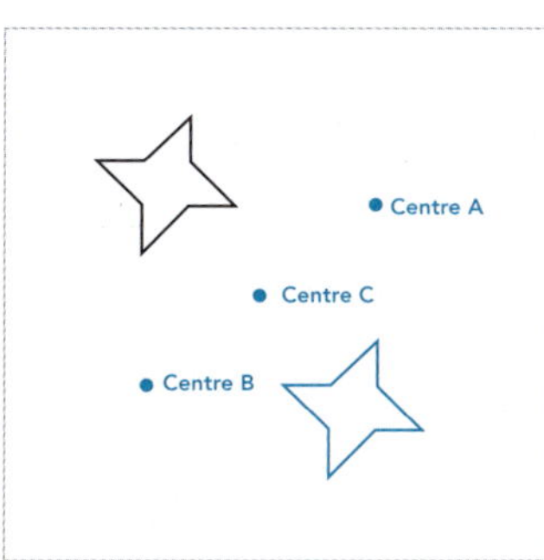

Mini tasks (pp. 79–81)

Note: These are not the only answers to some questions. If you get a different answer, check it with your teacher.

1 **Step 1**
Rotate 180° clockwise about point A.

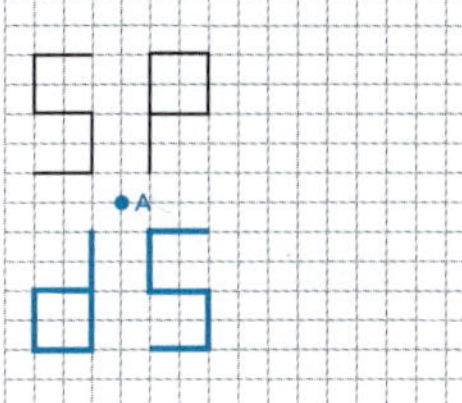

Step 2
Reflect in the dashed vertical line.

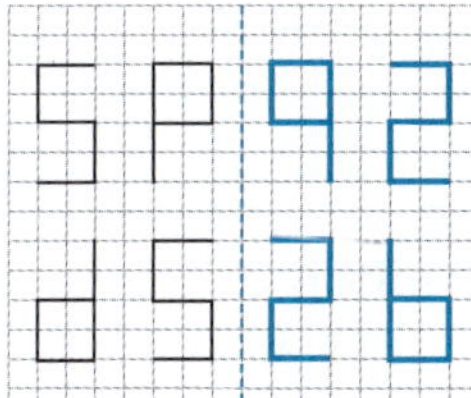

Step 3
Translate marked area by $\begin{pmatrix} 16 \\ 0 \end{pmatrix}$ and then by $\begin{pmatrix} 24 \\ 0 \end{pmatrix}$.

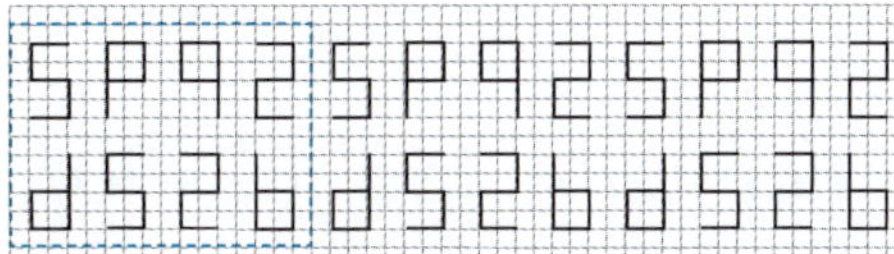

2 **Step 1**
Rotate 180° clockwise about point A.

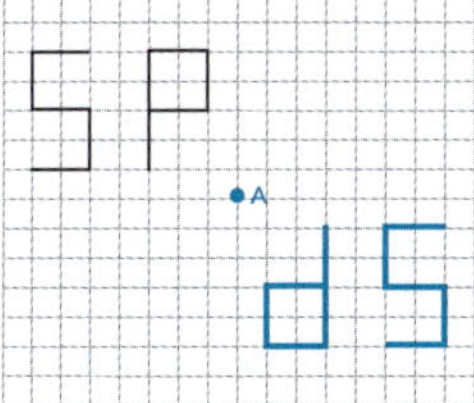

Step 2
Reflect in line A or B.

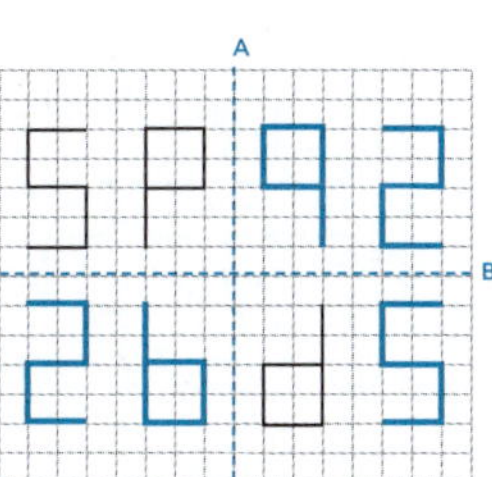

Step 3
Translate marked area:
by $\begin{pmatrix} 16 \\ 0 \end{pmatrix}$ and then by $\begin{pmatrix} 24 \\ 0 \end{pmatrix}$.

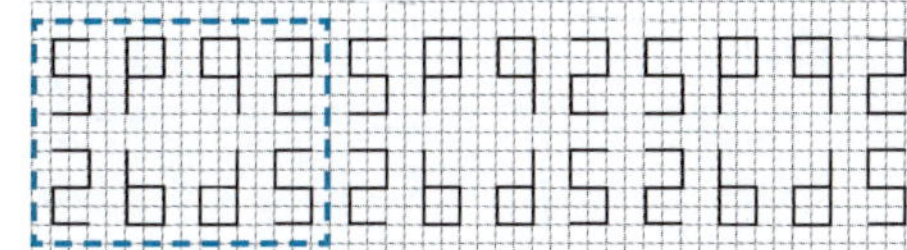

ISBN: 9780170416016

3 **Step 1**
Rotate 90° clockwise about point A.

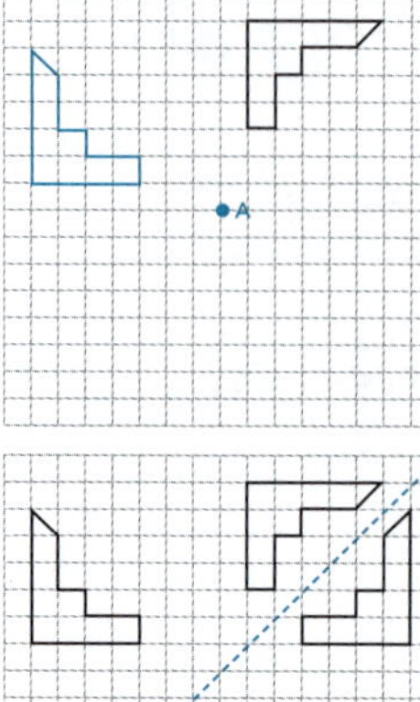

Step 2
Reflect in line A.

Step 3
Reflect in line B.

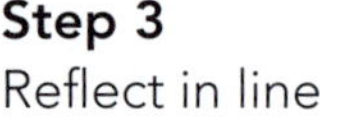

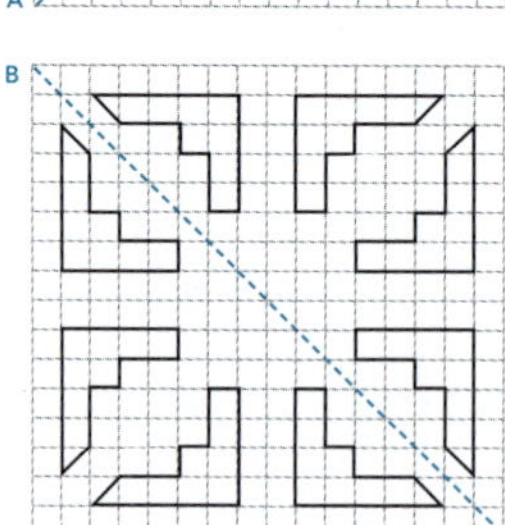

Practice tasks (pp. 82–90)

Practice task one (pp. 82–84)
Some possible patterns. (If you have other answers, check with your teacher.)

1

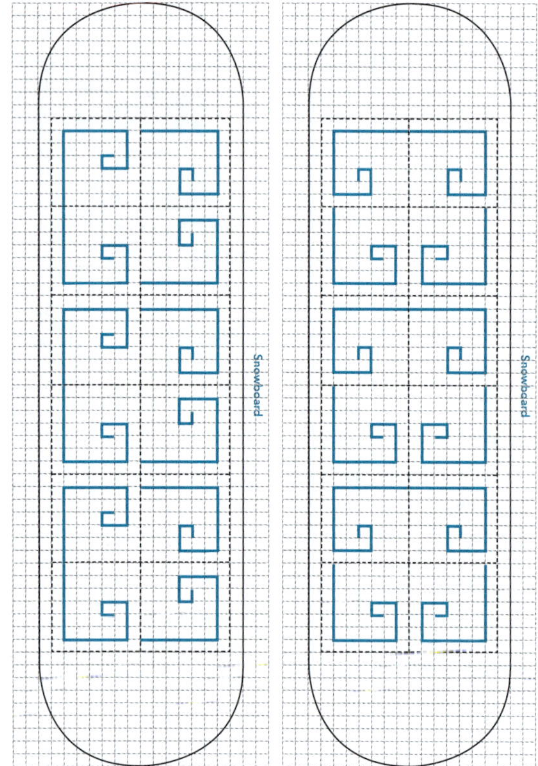

2

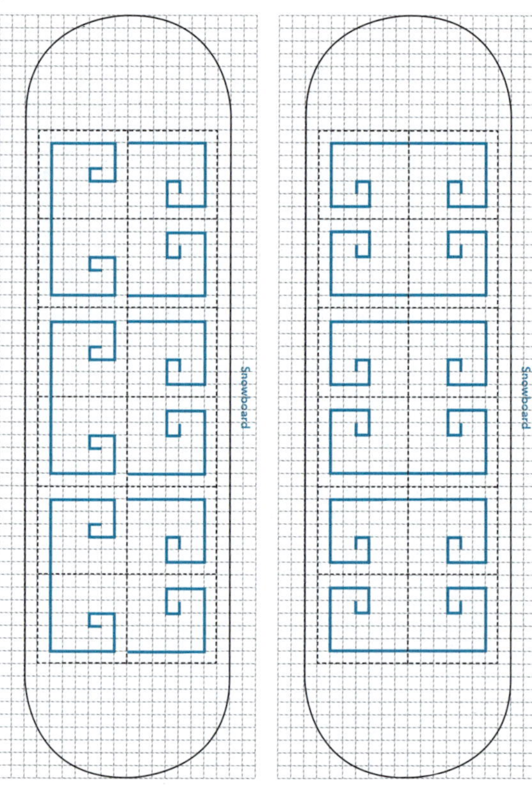

3 Ask your teacher to check these for you.
4 Ask your teacher to check these for you.

Practice tasks two and three (pp. 85–90)
Ask your teacher to check these for you.

ISBN: 9780170416016